unruly bodies

SUSANNAH B. MINTZ

unruly bodies

Life Writing by Women with Disabilities

The University *of* North Carolina Press Chapel Hill

Designed by Kimberly Bryant
Set in Quadraat and Quadraat Sans by
Keystone Typesetting, Inc.
Manufactured in the United States of America

The paper in this book meets the guidelines for permanence and durability of the Committee on Production Guidelines for Book Longevity of the Council on Library Resources.

Library of Congress Cataloging-in-Publication Data
Mintz, Susannah B., 1965–
Unruly bodies : life writing by women with disabilities / by Susannah B. Mintz.
p. cm.
Includes bibliographical references (p.) and index.
ISBN 978-0-8078-3133-5 (cloth: alk. paper)
ISBN 978-0-8078-5830-1 (pbk.: alk. paper)
1. Women with disabilities—United States—Biography.
2. Autobiography—Women authors. 3. Women's studies—Biographical methods. I. Title.
HV1569.3.W65M56 2007
362.4092′273—dc22 2007004956

Chapter 1 appeared in somewhat different form as "Transforming the Tale: The Auto/body/ographies of Nancy Mairs," *a/b: Auto/Biography Studies* 14, no. 2 (Winter 1999): 254–72. Portions of Chapter 2 appeared in somewhat different form as "Writing as Refiguration: Lucy M. Grealy's *Autobiography of a Face*," *Biography: An Interdisciplinary Quarterly* 24, no. 1 (Winter 2001): 172–84, © by the Biographical Research Center, and "Invisible Disability: Georgina Kleege's *Sight Unseen*," *NWSA Journal* 14, no. 3 (Fall 2002): 155–77, published by Indiana University Press. All are reprinted here with permission.

cloth 11 10 09 08 07 5 4 3 2 1
paper 11 10 09 08 07 5 4 3 2 1

for Beth MacKenzie

contents

acknowledgments

This book has been in the making for many years, and I've collected my share of debts along the way. To Tom Couser, an unexpected, informal mentor for at least the last decade, I am especially obliged; his early interest in my work on disability autobiography got me started, and he has been a generous source of support ever since. I owe special thanks as well to Susanna Egan, who believed in this project in the beginning, and to David Mitchell, who encouraged it toward the end. I thank Georgina Kleege and Stephen Kuusisto, for reading and responding, and the many editors and scholars who introduced me to the conversations that matter, including Jim Ferris, Kim Q. Hall, Craig Howes, Cynthia Huff, Robert McRuer, Russell Shuttleworth, Gerry Hendershot, Nancy Eiesland, Leigh Gilmore, Kristin Lindgren, and Tobin Siebers. My thanks also to Sian Hunter at UNC Press, for endorsing this project.

My interest in life writing and disability was fostered by discussions at the 2000 University of British Columbia conference on Autobiography and Changing Identities, sponsored sessions on disability issues at the 2004 and 2006 MLA annual conventions, and the 2006 Society for Disability Studies conference. I have had the privilege of working with many students whose enthusiasm for this topic has enlivened my thinking and have had numerous heartening conversations with colleagues past and current. Greg Fraser first told me this was a book, and Jennifer Travis read very rough drafts with sensible good cheer. I am indebted to Ashley Cross for helping me to sharpen my ideas with meticulous marginalia (I still have all her notes) and for her loyalty and warmth. Jean Lutes also provided invaluable comments on the manuscript and proved during a difficult sabbatical year to be a friend of rare understanding and kindness.

Research development funds from Skidmore College, including a major project completion grant, supported me in the final stages of writing this book during the summer of 2005. I am fortunate to be part of such a rich community at Skidmore and have benefited from the wise counsel and good humor of Linda Simon, Mason Stokes, Terry Diggory, Denise Smith, Kate Greenspan, Steven Millhauser, Martha Wiseman, Jacquie Scoones, and Beth Gershuny. Janet Casey helps me to remember, through inquiry and example, the importance of scholarship and is the liveliest of breakfast companions. Adrienne Zuerner is an unselfish advocate of her colleagues' intellectual pursuits; I appreciate her curiosity and her knack for sending the perfect e-card at just the right moment. I am deeply grateful to Susan Walzer, uncomplaining interlocutor, for devoting so many hours to the stories of our lives.

My family has sustained me in all the ways that count. I want to thank my stepfather, Steven Dubinett, a physician whose thoughtfulness in caretaking I so admire, and my sister, Leah Mintz, also a physician, whose cross-country advice always attends to the whole person. Her intelligence, unflagging patience, and love have shaped my identity, and thus also these pages, in incalculable ways. Finally, I dedicate this book to my mother, Beth MacKenzie, who was the first to listen.

unruly bodies

introduction

JANE: Would you still love me if I got burned in a fire?
BILLY: Yes.
JANE: If I ran into a tree and got paralyzed?
BILLY: Yes.
JANE: What if I were totally disfigured, if my face were all scraped away, I had no arms, no legs, no brain waves, and I was being kept alive on a heart-lung machine. Would you love me?
BILLY: No. But we could still be friends, though. (Laughter)
—*Kelly Preston & Kevin Costner, in* For Love of the Game (1999)

Linking two important but as yet disconnected fields of inquiry—disability theory and feminist autobiography studies—*Unruly Bodies* introduces readers to disability and illness narratives by eight contemporary American writers: Nancy Mairs, Lucy Grealy, Georgina Kleege, Eli Clare, Connie Panzarino, Anne Finger, Denise Sherer Jacobson, and May Sarton. These authors tell a kind of life story that has commanded scant literary attention or popular readership until recently, not simply because they attend specifically to their female bodies, but because those bodies diverge too dramatically from both the idealized human form of Western culture and the disembodied narrative self of conventional autobiography. Their overt intention is to challenge the troping of disability in able-bodied culture as deviance, helplessness, insufficiency, and loss, as well as to speak openly about a form of embodiment often excluded from the conversation in both disability and feminist discourse. I argue that these eight writers display corporeal difference to demonstrate the damaging effects not of disease or impairment but, rather, of the cultural mythologies that interpret those conditions in reductive or disparaging ways. In texts that deftly combine a disability politics with the revisionary flexibility of literary life writing, they generate a keener, more critical understanding of how gender and disability interact in the formation of a woman's identity.

To the extent that they present the anomalousness of their bodies as a discursive phenomenon resulting from narrow social expectations of beauty, fitness, health, or physical competence—rather than as a biological or structural aberration—these life writers subscribe in a broad sense to the social model of disability. Articulated in the mid-1970s by activists in Britain, the social model contested the dominance of a medical paradigm by defining disability not as an affliction of the individual body (an error to be fixed by surgical or chemical intervention or overcome by rehabilitation) but, rather, as a function of the complex social and political dynamics that, in setting standards of normalcy, marginalize some bodies as deviant.[1] By rewriting disability in terms of power and discourse rather than genes or physiology, the social model sought to demystify the apparent truth-status of disability as an indicator of "real" corporeal flaws. Fundamental to this paradigm is a conceptual distinction between physical impairment as the material condition of the body and disability as a set of attitudes and practices imposed upon that body to discipline its divergence from accepted norms. Contextualizing disability as a social and relational phenomenon challenges the prevalent response to disability as a catastrophic event "in" or of the body, implicates the able-bodied in the discussion, and exposes the boundaries of culture's idealized physical form as historically specific and ideologically produced. In this view, disability, as discrete from impairment, is socially constructed, and activism thus focuses on dismantling the barriers—architectural as much as ideological—that exclude disabled people from full participation in social life.

The disability movement, with the social model as its theoretical core, posed a vital challenge to the medical or "individualist" position that disability is reducible to physical dysfunction and sought to divorce the state of the body from negative assessments of subjectivity based on bodily particulars. As scholars have recently argued, however, one paradoxical consequence of its strict divide between impairment and disability is that the social model ends up construing the body in much the same terms as those of the medical model it hopes to resist. The separation between body and culture tends to reinstate a problematic mind/body binary and renders the body of the social model "an ahistorical, pre-social, purely natural object"—just as, to quote Bill Hughes and Kevin Paterson, "medicine would have it."[2] Hughes and Paterson describe this body as "devoid of history," "a dysfunctional, anatomical, corporeal mass obdurate in its resistance to signification and phenomenologically dead, without intentionality or agency."[3] Some have further protested that in the battle against prejudice waged by the disability movement, articulating the pains and frustrations of impairment has become unacceptable, as if that acknowledgment would play into the hands of "oppressors" apt to "seiz[e] on evidence that disability is really about physical limitation after all."[4] Much work in contemporary disability studies thus theorizes impairment itself as both a lived experience and an effect of discourse, a historically situated function of social and political relationships and an idiosyncratic physical situation that affects people in highly different ways.

Inasmuch as disability scholars attend to matters of representation and to the ideological practices that produce disability, many have also called for a return to the "visceral" in disability studies.[5] As Tobin Siebers concludes a recent essay on the politics of disability representation: "What would it mean to esteem the disabled body for what it really is?"[6] Siebers argues that current theories of the body, to the extent that they privilege empowerment, pleasure, and physical adaptability, fail to confront disability in any transformative way and cites this representational absence as one factor in the social and political neglect of the needs and perspectives of people with disabilities. To take serious account of the daily routines of a disabled body (how it moves, eats, eliminates, has or does not have sex, hurts, reproduces, and so on) is to invite a potential "sea change in social attitudes"[7] about independence, functionality, and social achievement and, in turn, about a host of controversial issues from abortion to genetic research. Siebers writes that "the political struggle of people with disabilities . . . requires a realistic conception of the disabled body," and he promotes "the rhetoric of realism"—the "new realism of the body"[8] that typifies much contemporary life writing of disability—as a significant mode toward dismantling dominant stereotypes that obstruct ideological change.

The autobiographers studied in *Unruly Bodies* are compelling precisely because they write their bodies—their gendered, disabled bodies—as textually produced but also phenomenologically alive, because they train their attention on the family dynamics, medical intrusions, media representations, and structural barriers that conspire to make impairments socially and psychologically disabling, while also frankly describing what William James might call the "really real" of their physical conditions. The various kinds of narratives crafted by these authors are not just manifestos for resisting oppression, detailed accounts of medical conditions, or sociological case histories, though they contain elements of each of those rhetorical genres. As suggested by several of their titles (Grealy's *Autobiography of a Face*, for instance, or Finger's *Past Due: A Story of Disability, Pregnancy and Birth*, or Jacobson's *The Question of David*), they are also open-ended histories of embodiment, tales about anomalous physicality that emphasize a poetics as much as a politics of disability identity. And as the serial autobiographers Mairs and Sarton imply, disability is an inconstant experience, its significance to the story of self requiring multiple retellings, repeated narrative shaping. These book-length, though not always continuous or linear, texts present disability as a kind of work-in-progress, a process of becoming rather than an immutable fact of physicality located beyond the scope of words to liberate and to define.

Given their emphasis on both the subjective experience of femaleness and disability and cultural constructions of that simultaneity, an equally significant feature of these texts is the challenge they present to feminist theory. These stories of embodiment go beyond simply critiquing the able, male body of patriarchy to confront feminism's presumption of certain types of female corporeality, thereby rewriting the myths of self-control that problematically exclude some women from feminism's theoretical and political agendas. Feminism has, historically, failed to engage critically with disability—with the physical or sexual limitations, the dependence on others, and even the pain and discomfort experienced by many women who live with disability and/or chronic illness.[9] Feminist disability activists have argued that the early disability movement "reflect[ed] the agenda of disabled men."[10] But as Jenny Morris states, the interests of women with illness or disabilities "are rarely incorporated" in or are "entirely absent"[11] even from feminist analyses—of, for example, job and economic equality, health- and community-care access, domestic violence, and reproductive rights. It is perhaps an accumulated frustration at being left out of the discourse of feminism that compels sociologist Carol Thomas to cite "the need for more detailed empirical research which starts out from what disabled women say about their own lives" and to announce that the "time has certainly come for disabled women to tell their stories."[12] Susan Wendell writes that feminism has "worked to undo men's control of women's bodies, without undermining the myth that women can control our own bodies," and quotes filmmaker Bonnie Klein on a common sense of exclusion: "I feel as if my colleagues are ashamed of me because I am no longer the image of strength, competence, and independence that feminists, including myself, are so eager to project. There is clearly a conflict between feminism's rhetoric of inclusion and failure to include disability."[13]

As elaborated perhaps most notably by Rosemarie Garland-Thomson, disability theory can contribute in a direct and stimulating way to the development of feminist inquiry.[14] The uncritical metaphor of women as "disabled" by patriarchal culture, for example, might be challenged to reconsider its use of disability as an inherently pejorative descriptor, just as the fundamental feminist critique of denigrations of women as "deformed" male bodies becomes more subtle when we examine the equation made between disability and inferiority. A disability perspective contests feminism's dismantling of the institutions of marriage and maternity on the grounds that this enterprise ignores the kinds of stereotypes disabled women confront—that they are asexual and unfit for motherhood, for example, essentially "incomplete" in the "basic expression of [their] womanhood"[15]—and that the struggle for women with disabilities may thus be entrance *into* such relationships, rather than freedom from them. Disability theory complicates a feminist discussion of genetic testing and abortion by revealing the ableist assumptions that may problematically—even dangerously—influence reproductive choices. Feminist arguments about the ethical dimensions of caring can be expanded by awareness of the shifting roles of caretaker and cared-for so pertinent to relationships in which disability is a factor; disability scholars have rejected the feminist "orthodoxy" that caretaking is mere "unpaid labour, performed out of duty, by women."[16] A disability perspective enriches feminist inquiry into the politics of cosmetic surgery by demonstrating the ideological similarities between cosmetic and reconstructive surgery: both are efforts to normalize bodies by eradicating difference. Finally, feminist theorizing about the gaze can be extended by considering the intersubjective dynamics of the "stare," the objectifying regard of the nondisabled for the spectacle and specimen of the disabled body.

If the concerns of women with disabilities have not been at the core of feminism, neither has embodied irregularity had much of a place in representations of identity that hope to escape confinement in the flesh. Disabled women have thus rarely appeared as the subjects of conventional autobiography, which tends to feature its narrator as pure consciousness, imagination, and memory. The subject that emerges from much life writing by women in recent decades, however, refuses many of the features of what we tend to think of as the typical autobiographical persona.[17] Not a singular, male, white, disembodied "I" who pretends to a kind of transparent self-awareness, she may narrate herself in the relational terms of family, romantic partnerships, or group identity without presuming that the story of self will be guaranteed by any absolute characteristics—or, equally importantly, that the text of self must abide by the standards of sworn truth that have historically influenced, and inhibited, autobiographical production from the margins. The important work of many recent feminist autobiography scholars has examined the ways in which women's life writing resists traditional patterns by returning to the body, explicitly representing the self in terms of such body markers as race, sexuality, class, motherhood, instances of physical trauma, and so on. Such texts "talk back" to dominant cultural paradigms and work to validate unrecognized categories of identity and experience.

Life writing by women with disabilities takes part in this larger pattern of storytelling that directly eschews the presumption of a fully accessible, distinct but also representative subject. But it also complicates standard ways of conceiving of the body that appear in women's as much as men's autobiography. Though women's autobiography presents a significant challenge to the entanglement of narrative convention with patriarchal and/or racist cultural ideology when it puts embodiment at the forefront of the story of life development, that strategy often coincides with the assumptions of an ableist society. Despite their ideological and textual defiance, texts by women may uncritically idealize an *able*—if also "othered"—body: a healthy body, capable of pleasure; a body whose reproductive function can be controlled by the individual but is not societally suspect; a body able to sense and to move in "normal" ways and to manage (if also to celebrate) its messier functions; in short, an independent body, able to control and care for itself. By presenting themselves in terms of bodies that do not abide by many of these characteristics of corporeal experience, female autobiographers of illness and disability thus introduce alternative possibilities into the cultural conversation about embodiment, revising not simply the long history of autobiography by men but also much newer paradigms initiated by feminist thinkers and female autobiographers.

Women's personal narratives of disability and illness, from this perspective, can fundamentally change the way we think about gender and disability, impairment, disease, and aging, as well as about the supposedly normal body that consolidates its borders against the demonized category of disability. It must be acknowledged, however, that the proliferation in recent years of personal narratives by people with disabilities has met with some skepticism by disability scholars concerned about the implications of pursuing the self-referential path of Western autobiography. As critics have noted, it is true that some life writers of disability (often though not exclusively men) follow conventional autobiographical patterns, styling themselves as unified, solitary subjects and reasserting the primacy of consciousness to assuage the sense of personal diminishment that may accompany a "failed" or "broken" body. Given autobiography's "devotion to narcissistic self-revelation,"[18] in David Mitchell's words, a disabled life writer upholds the myth of "rugged individualism" at the risk of perpetuating another problematic fiction, that disability is a purely personal and physical, rather than social and political, problem.[19] Mitchell argues cogently that when disabled writers indulge a penchant for self-narration, they may obscure (perhaps unwittingly or inadvertently) the wider network of discursive, ideological, and material factors that constructs disability as a matter of individual responsibility or blame. Lennard J. Davis has voiced a similar caution, that "by narrativizing an impairment, one tends to sentimentalize it and link it to the bourgeois sensibility of individualism and the drama of the individual story."[20]

I hope to show in the chapters that follow the ways in which life stories about disability *can* shift the terms by which we collectively understand and respond to urgent questions of gender and embodiment. My own classroom experience has demonstrated time and again the profound and mind-changing impact of reading stories such as the ones discussed in this book—a subtle but significant alteration in the texture of the way a community thinks about issues of identity and the body. Many critics have endorsed first-person narratives of disability as crucial contributions to a project of rethinking relations between bodies and selves, subjects and societies. Like Siebers, Helen Meekosha and Susan Wendell also argue that contemporary disability life writing offers a kind of corrective to the perceived split between medical and cultural models of disability by returning the reality of the lived body to examinations of social forces. Meekosha claims that "the rigid dualism of either a socially constructed disability or a disability grounded in biology is being disputed in the subjective discourse," and Wendell contends that "careful study of the lives of disabled people will reveal how artificial the line is that we draw between the biological and the social."[21] In his influential book *Recovering Bodies: Illness, Disability, and Life Writing*, G. Thomas Couser writes similarly that personal accounts of illness and disability are often motivated to "recover variously dysfunctional bodies from domination by others' authority and discourse, to convert the passive object into an active subject . . . to invalidate the dominant cultural tropes of 'invalidity'—to demystify and destigmatize various conditions."[22]

The texts I examine here are striking examples of what Couser has referred to as "robust disability narratives,"[23] first-person narrative acts that refuse cultural pressure to treat disability as an adversity to be overcome or an embarrassment requiring apology. They make clear that autobiography does not preclude, and indeed often fosters, the representation of social and political selves. Moreover, it seems important to bear in mind what such scholars as Sidonie Smith and Leigh Gilmore convincingly argue: that a woman does, in the very act of telling her own story, enter a political arena by asserting the legitimacy of her participation in a domain until quite recently dominated by the res gestae narratives of men. Couser's argument, more specific to the matter of disability, is that the autobiographer's access to the language of self-definition and claim of "personal autonomy" authorizes the self against an alienating medical establishment and the larger cultural ideologies that pejoratively encode physical difference.[24] Turning to life writing as "a medium for counterdiscourse that challenges stereotypes and misconceptions,"[25] to quote Couser again, these several writers retrieve their impaired bodies from hegemonic medical discourse and from the margins of cultural acceptance, feminist inquiry, and traditional as well as some instances of feminist autobiography.

Dominant paradigms of identity—normative gender roles, myths of femininity and motherhood, attitudes toward sex and sexual orientation, and the articulation of these in the context of class, religion, regionality, and so on—obscure the needs, shapes, motions, and sensations of anomalous bodies. The tales I study here, by contrast, are motivated to "reinvest the disabled body with a phenomenology predicated upon more than the rejection of stigmatizing assumptions."[26] In the manner of much contemporary disability art, these life stories are "told *through* the body," in Arthur W. Frank's words;[27] the specificity of each author's anomalous corporeality shapes the tale she tells, exploding both the artificial coherence of "disability" and the mind/body binary that relegates embodiment to the prediscursive margins. These texts offer especially trenchant accounts of disability as what Mairian Corker and Tom Shakespeare have called "the ultimate postmodern concept,"[28] writing disability as a dynamic, variable experience, determined both by individual expression and social, environmental factors. They are elaborated acts of defiance of medicine's habit of reducing the whole person to a set of symptoms, and they respond to recent calls for a renewed focus on the embodiment of disability. In turn, these stories insist on autobiography as a capacious form that can accommodate a range of subjects and articulations of self.

Unlocking the Autobiographical Self: Katherine Butler Hathaway

Katherine Butler Hathaway's 1942 memoir *The Little Locksmith*,[29] one of the first first-person accounts of a woman's experience of physical disfigurement, reveals certain assumptions about disabled women that more recent writers often admit to having internalized: that disabled women are asexual, barred from participation in romantic or erotic relationships; that physical failure must be compensated for by an enlarged sense of spiritual or creative fulfillment; and that disability is infantilizing, rendering women helpless, literally "invalid." At the same time, however, Hathaway also makes clear that she is aware of the impositions of cultural myth. Though she repeatedly acquiesces to the notion that a "deformed" woman is an undesirable one who must channel her "passions" into the romanticized roles of poet and "maiden aunt" (160), she also makes a steadfast attempt to liberate herself from a sense of childlike dependence and illegitimacy. Hathaway thus offers a set of interrelated points fundamental to my discussion of contemporary writers, demonstrating the tenacity of negative cultural interpretations of disabled women but also self-naming in a way that claims definitional control.

At age five, Katherine Butler contracted spinal tuberculosis (also known as tuberculosis spondylitis and Pott's or David's disease), a bacterial infection characterized by softening of the vertebrae and often resulting in curvature of the spine. As Nancy Mairs explains in her afterword to the 2000 reprint edition of *The Little Locksmith*, accepted medical practice at the time of Hathaway's illness dictated that children be immobilized as the slow-moving disease ran its course, often over many years, to prevent kyphosis. Though a modern reader may be shocked at Hathaway's description of the apparatus used to keep her back straight, it was, in Mairs's words, "the most advanced technology available" (242) in 1895. Hathaway provides a striking image, writing that she was

> strapped down very tight on a stretcher, on a very hard sloping bed, with [her] shoulders pressed against a hard pad. [Her] head was kept from sinking down on [her] chest . . . by means of a leather halter attached to a rope which went through a pulley at the head of the bed. On the end of the rope hung a five-pound iron weight. This mechanism held [her] a prisoner for twenty-four hours a day, without the freedom to turn or twist [her] body or let [her] chin move. (16)

She remained pinioned in this device, with brief reprieves, for ten years.

The memoir that begins with this vision of a child held captive—by physical restraints and by the power of medical authority—serves a liberating and redemptive purpose for its author. Hathaway makes quite explicit the connection between writing and her body, a link that results, perhaps predictably, from the absolute distinction she makes between "the fearful fact of [her] deformity" (42) and "the free fearless aristocracy of the mind" (44). Though she is pronounced healthy at fifteen and released from the straightening board, encounters first with a mirror and later with the reactions of family and friends inform her that "there was something the matter" with her still (61). Convinced that she has grown into "a little, pitiable, hideous figure" (47), Hathaway "renounce[s]" as illegitimate her "greedy longing for experience" (94)—by which she means romantic love but also, emphatically, sex—and takes up writing as her "lonelier way" of expressing herself and engaging passionately with the world (137). Though she survived serious illness and was described by at least one contemporary as "handsome," "slim and beautiful," and even a "mermaid,"[30] Hathaway persistently focuses on the catastrophic consequences of that survival to her body, and she depicts her desire to write as a compensatory act that very nearly stands in for sexual intercourse. She is one of the "grotesquely unbeautiful women" who must guard themselves against "the absurd effrontery" of imagining themselves to be desirable (55).

Hence the title of Hathaway's memoir, its driving metaphorical figure of the locksmith, based on an actual locksmith who came to her childhood home in Massachusetts. This real person, whose back rose to "an enormous sort of peak . . . between his shoulders" (14), takes on symbolic importance as a manifestation of what might have happened to Hathaway's own body. She recalls him as if he were a fairy-tale character: "not big enough to be considered a man" yet "not a child" (14) and, indeed, with his slender fingers and "bobbing" walk, "more like a gnome than a human being" (15). Yet Hathaway claims a powerful sense of affinity with this "fascinating" and singular individual:

> Somehow I knew that there was a special word that the grownups called a person shaped like the little locksmith, and I knew that to ordinary healthy grownups it was a terrible word. And the strange thing was that I, Katherine, the Butlers' darling little girl, had barely escaped that uncanny shape and that terrible word. Because I was being taken care of by a famous doctor nobody would ever guess, when I grew up, that I might have been just like the little locksmith. Staring wonderingly at him, I knew it. I knew that compared with him I was wonderfully lucky and safe. Yet deep within me I had a feeling that underneath my luck and safeness the real truth was that I really belonged with him, even if it was never going to show. (15)

The passage works hard to enforce contrast: the childish narrator is not a "grownup"; "ordinary healthy" people are not to be confused with "that terrible word"; and the "uncanny" realm of the locksmith lurks beyond the "safe" space whose perimeter is established by upright medical doctors and the edges of Hathaway's stretching board.

Yet the boundary protecting Hathaway from the "strange" and "terrible" fate of this deformed creature is precarious, attributed first to the random machinery of luck and next to the intervention of science (embodied in a male, paternal, renowned physician). And ultimately, what is uncanny is also familiar; Hathaway recognizes the locksmith, with his downturned eyes and "private world" (15), as a mirror image of her own feelings of isolation and loneliness. She writes that she looked at him "with a very strange intimate feeling" (14) and felt "a strong, childish, amorous pity and desire toward him," and she makes note of his "queer erotic charm" (15). Even more, he is "indescribably alluring" (14–15), unexpectedly—even improbably, given her young age and her own description of the man—seductive. What is at work in such language, I think, is Hathaway's retrospective ambivalence about her own sexuality, her sense that there is something provocative, compelling, but finally repellent about difference, about "deformity." She figures the locksmith as both a locus of her own desire for sexual experience and an analogue of her solitude, her sense of being irretrievably other, not quite a woman yet no longer a girl, somehow not quite human.

Locksmiths have a special talent, of course, for maintaining a different sort of device—not the one that keeps Hathaway pinned to a board throughout her childhood but, rather, the one that guards the thresholds of domestic space. The problem of broken locks, in one sense prosaically domestic, also signifies Hathaway's conviction that her body, too, is broken, its size and shape an impediment to crossing over into adult experience and sexual fulfillment. "Love laughed at me because my body was shaped like the locksmith's," she writes much later in the text (166), "but the answer I made was to unlock doors for everybody else while I myself remained a humble, submissive prisoner." Here, she refers literally to the house in Maine she buys with the intention of creating a kind of artists'/lovers' colony, a "refuge" (152) for those who, like her, want to "burst out in a great robust defiance of convention" (163). But she also speaks metaphorically, making her métier the interior thresholds of love, of the imagination, and perhaps most importantly, of the body. Hathaway thus "is" the locksmith in two senses, in the contours of her body and in the ability to unlock the kinds of barriers—the medical, social, psychosexual, and even literary mores of her day—that might combine to bar that body from artistic and erotic satisfaction.

When Hathaway writes that she "had turned out after all, like the little locksmith—oh, not so bad, nearly—but enough like the little locksmith to be called by that same word" (41), she underscores a slightly different aspect of her memoir, which is its concern to tell the story of a woman's life with disability. Significantly, Hathaway cannot name her condition, referring to it only by indirection and euphemism, self-disparaging description and wonder-inducing hints. "That word"—hunchback, presumably—the "terrible," "special" word that "grownups" know but that cannot be uttered even in the self-determined space of Hathaway's own narrative, becomes the omission the text amasses itself around. This thing that cannot be named is Hathaway herself, an open secret of abnormality that is never directly addressed or explicitly described. As she remarks in the context of her siblings' love affairs, "It was taken for granted that I was not to have what was apparently considered the most thrilling and important experience in grown-up life. . . . Nobody explained the reason why. . . . The reason was so obvious that no explanation was necessary. The reason was there in every mirror for me to see" (167). Repeated terms, words like "strange," "terrible," "queer," and "rare," must serve in the absence of unequivocal description of the shape in the mirror, filling the long dash that cannot be spoken: "I would have had to grow up into a—well . . ." (14).

But if disfigurement cannot be named, it can nevertheless be woven into a narrative that strives to redefine the impact of corporeal difference on a developing self. Hathaway does struggle to tell an alternative story, though in many instances she participates without hesitation in condemnation of "the body in which [she] was doomed to live" (55). But such was the prevailing attitude of her day. While it is for later women writers of disability to bring sex (not just sexuality but consummated sex, the act itself, with bold and gritty directness) into their life writing, Hathaway *has* nonetheless "written frankly about the body" (250), to quote Mairs once again—"and not just any body, not even just any woman's body, but a crippled woman's body"

(252). If Hathaway devotes a great deal of her memoir to recounting the process of repressing sexual desire in favor of her artistic aspirations, her body is nevertheless the central subject of that narration—and, perhaps most provocatively, the very fact of Hathaway's reiterated anguish about her "sexual starvation" (189) works paradoxically to keep the unseemly impulses of that body, its "continual hunger" (68), squarely in readers' view.

Moreover, Hathaway takes advantage of the revisionary possibilities inherent in life writing to broach, if tentatively, a critique of dominant assumptions about the kinds of social roles a disabled woman might be expected to take. For example, she protests quite vehemently against her mother's coddling treatment of her as a "cherished invalid child," a "gentle, childish little invalid" (141–42), well into Hathaway's young adulthood. Their conflict flares up over the issue of Hathaway's writing, which is both a provocative point of tension in its own right and a screen for the more treacherous subject of sexuality. Hathaway describes her fledgling writerly self as a "new creative ruthless impersonal being" powerful enough to "eclipse" the "cherished child" (142)—but only as long as she remains separate from the infantilizing influence, the "insistent yearning solicitude" (141–42) of her mother, which sends her, seething with "rage and irritation," into "heavy, unhappy, sullen silence" (143). Such a dynamic presages the way in which many later disability narratives represent mothers, women whose overprotectiveness may stem from a misguided assessment of their child's needs and threatens the process of individuation.[31] Hathaway implies that because of her lengthy illness—because she is "delicate" and "deformed" (141)—her mother persisted in handling her as if she were excessively fragile, a kind of precious, breakable doll.

Writing instigates but subsequently negotiates this difficult emotional territory. Not only is Hathaway's autobiographical persona a smart, lively, engaging, and thoroughly adult one; it is also, more than once, frankly and intensely angry. This is most often directed, as I have been describing, toward the mother who becomes the metonymy of oppressive attitudes toward gender, disability, and life choices—as when her wish that Hathaway "settle down into a docile life at home" fills her daughter with a "rage" (176) expressed only retrospectively in the text, never in the actual moment. That outrage is even more loudly voiced when the subject turns to romance. Hathaway reports that after many years of suffering "complete deprivation" (167) in the arena of sexual experience, she "broke the silence and reproached [her] mother" for failing to help her work through this "predicament"; in turn she is informed that the "famous" doctor who treated her when she was a child in fact advocated that she not be "thwart[ed]" (167) were she to fall in love. The revelation apparently produced amazement, but only here, in the memoir, does Hathaway fault her mother's behavior: "I didn't say anything more. Inside I was crying, clamoring, 'Oh, Mother! . . . You did thwart me! You did thwart me! . . . If I had only known he said that! If I had only known he didn't think it was impossible! You ought to have told me. . . . You have spoiled my life!'" (167). Hathaway thus depicts her mother as impeding rather than promoting her psychological and artistic growth and presents writing as the corrective mechanism that leads her to self-discovery, self-expression, and self-recuperation.

To say that Hathaway's writing sublimates erotic desire would be to place perhaps too psychoanalytic a word on what Hathaway herself describes as a completely conscious and deliberate act of substitution: "I was trying to kill my sense of loss in that direction," as she declares, by "beginning to be a writer" (136–37). For later authors, life writing dramatizes rather than stands in for sexual expression, and it overtly celebrates far more than it serves to compensate for a disabled, disfigured, ill, or aging body. Where Hathaway is evasive about what she looks like, deploying abstractions ("the disaster that had befallen my body" [35]), the writers I study here provide more direct descriptions, some including photographs of themselves within their texts or on their book jackets. Where Hathaway tends to be self-punitive (she is "a little oddity," a "quaint, small, crumpled figure" [68–69]) and takes as inevitable friends' "discomfiture" and "embarrassed glance[s]" (61), these contemporary life writers are forgiving and proud. And where Hathaway concentrates her anger primarily on her mother, the person responsible for her care, writers with a sharpened disability awareness widen the focus of their critique, examining larger social prejudices that underpin the actions not only of mothers but also of doctors, teachers, writers, lawyers, social workers, neighbors, and friends.[32]

The Little Locksmith is a text of its moment, anticipating but not quite articulating the politicized self-determination of contemporary feminism, feminist disability activism, and disabled women's autobiography. But it does inaugurate a certain kind of textual encounter with the self—literal scenes of confronting the image of the disabled self in the mirror as well as the overarching psychological struggle toward self-recognition and reclamation, terms that recur throughout the work of later life writers.

Unruly Bodies, Written Selves

One effect of the challenge to medical discourse as the defining instrument of disability has been a dramatic increase in published personal narratives and other autobiographical artwork in which disability is reconceptualized as a constitutive but not diminishing feature of identity. This coincides with the rise of public interest in life writing generally, an environment that has allowed many writers to enter the marketplace for the first time with memoir and which thus subverts expectations that an autobiographer be already known (as, for instance, a movie star, politician, or established writer) to an audience eager for the truth behind the persona. The proliferation of "familiar plausible (i.e., non-celebrity) scripts"[33] of disability and illness by first-time writers indicates not only an important shift in cultural representations of disability but also a notion of disability as a complex social, political, and embodied position from which an individual might legitimately narrate her life experience.

The authors studied here take up the matter of disability not simply as a material fact to be redefined but as a specifically textual question that can only begin to be adequately addressed in book-length exploration. It is not that they equate "self" with disability or physical dysfunction, nor do they, as a whole, employ the kinds of stereotypical rhetorical patterns that might make disability palatable to an ableist reader—the story of overcoming tragedy, for example, the inspirational tale of the "super-crip," or the narrative of compensatory accomplishment in some arena other than the physical. For Mairs, Grealy, Kleege, Panzarino, Clare, Finger, Jacobson, and Sarton, the knotty confluence of and contradictions between disability, gender, and sexuality at once initiate the story of life and are disentangled by inventive narrative shaping.

The authors discussed in *Unruly Bodies* cover a range of issues frequently debated, though often not with the same goals or theoretical principles at stake, by both feminist scholarship and disability studies. Taken together, they map out a kind of developmental trajectory—from coming-of-age identity issues (Mairs) to matters of visuality and self-appraisal (Grealy and Kleege), sexuality (Panzarino and Clare), motherhood (Jacobson and Finger), and aging (Sarton)—though drawing out thematic connections and juxtapositions rather than following a simplified life cycle is the primary purpose for the pairings and organization of my chapters. Nor have I chosen or grouped texts according to condition, preferring instead to set side by side two different authors' unfolding of a particularly pressing issue or a single author's multiple acts of self-representation. The book is framed by its two serial life writers, Mairs and Sarton, whose work, in addition to being the most anthologized and popularly read, asks us to consider what it means to persist in writing the embodied self; questions raised at the start of the book thus culminate in the discussion of its oldest and most prolific author.

My project begins in Chapter 1 with a discussion of Nancy Mairs. Throughout her many collections of personal essays, Mairs writes her "self" as inseparable from degenerative multiple sclerosis (MS), treating disability not as personal affliction but rather as a fact of life that becomes meaningful within a set of conflicting cultural narratives about chronic illness, female sexuality, and psychological health. Focusing primarily on *Plaintext* (1986), *Carnal Acts* (1990), and *Waist-High in the World* (1997), I argue that the disjointed and open-ended structure of essay collections textually manifests Mairs's own disrupted corporeality, while at the same time working as a corrective to the closure of traditional autobiography and the stable subject narrated therein. French feminism further provides Mairs with a vocabulary for the connection between the disruptive MS body and the disruptive form of the essay. Yet illness and a commitment to writing disability extend the "feminine" past a visionary sexuality that is fundamentally grounded in standards of corporeal normality. Through the medium of her physical condition, Mairs pushes *l'écriture féminine* to confront a reckless, "crippled" body whose excesses are not merely those of a multiply potential eroticism or vocality. Mairs's practice of serial autobiography, deferring conclusion, discovers an alternative form of diffuse pleasure and refuses to write the last words on her embodiment or her self.

My second chapter addresses two memoirs that critique the relentlessly visual orientation of Western ideology. Lucy Grealy's account of Ewing's sarcoma in *Autobiography of a Face* (1994) and Georgina Kleege's description of macular degeneration in *Sight Unseen* (1999) both situate the impaired female body within the spatial dynamics of staring and gazing, Grealy as a woman who does not look normal and Kleege as one who does not see normally. Grealy, who had jaw cancer at age ten, recounts protracted attempts to "correct" her face through reconstructive surgery. To the degree that female identity is scripted by cultural narratives that align self-worth with physical beauty, Grealy learns to equate the shape of her face with ontological inadequacy and ugliness. Ultimately, however, the inescapability of her sense of disfigurement leads Grealy to rewrite—literally to reconfigure—her face as a foundational aspect of her identity rather than a grotesque error to be overcome. Kleege, whose visual acuity categorizes her as legally blind, presents blindness not as a strictly biological condition but as a social status conferred by a sighted world. *Sight Unseen* records Kleege's gradual acceptance of a blind identity, even as she challenges sighted characterizations of using one's eyes differently from the norm. From their unique perspectives, Grealy and Kleege articulate both sides of the subject-object dynamic, complicating our understanding of what it means to be seen and to look, to be the object of derisive stares or even gratified gazes as well as the subject of a presumably masterful vision.

The third chapter explores the role of sexual identity in contemporary disability autobiography by women who participate in multiple and at times antagonistic groups. Concerned to rewrite the negative symbolic associations that attach to disability and illness but also to articulate specifically feminist, lesbian, queer, and leftist identities, Connie Panzarino's *The Me in the Mirror* (1994) and Eli Clare's *Exile and Pride* (1999) focus on forms of bodily impairment and sexual expression that do not always coincide easily with each other. For both writers, lesbian, queer, and disability communities provide a crucial counterweight to the oppressions of a patriarchal, homophobic, and ableist culture, but those groups are not without their own internal divisions. Self-representation is thus bound up for both Panzarino and Clare with a more dynamic form of identity politics in which it is possible to converse across boundaries of experience. Panzarino (who died in 1994 from spinal muscular atrophy), one of the inaugural "poster children" for muscular dystrophy and a disability rights activist who became involved with Ron Kovic in the post-Vietnam era, ultimately identifies as a lesbian but recounts the difficulty she encounters in being accepted both as a disabled person within the lesbian community and as a lesbian within a disability activist community wary of homosexuality. Clare (who has cerebral palsy) writes from a more complicated location, claiming herself a transgendered, redneck, environmentalist gimp who wants to force confrontation between the various groups to which she belongs, thereby exposing the inadequacy of models of identity based on similarity and wholeness.

Chapter 4 takes up the struggle of disabled mothers. Anne Finger's *Past Due: A Story of Disability, Pregnancy, and Birth* (1990) and Denise Sherer Jacobson's *The Question of David: A Disabled Mother's Journey through Adoption, Family, and Life* (1999) describe the challenges of parenting in a culture that simultaneously promotes motherhood as proof of a woman's success and stigmatizes women with disabilities as insufficient models for "normal" behavior or activity, incapable of providing adequate care for their children. If the authors discussed thus far write in part to dispel cultural ignorance about—or hostility toward—disabled women being actively sexual, Finger (who is post-polio) and Jacobson (who has cerebral palsy) demonstrate that the putatively "appropriate" and less threatening social role of heterosexually married motherhood is no less fraught with contradiction and misunderstanding. Indeed, disabled women are regarded with perhaps even more vehement opposition when they attempt to assume the culturally sanctioned position of mother. The question I pose here, then, is what happens when disabled mothers write about themselves, composing new stories of origin that disrupt traditional myths of motherhood, confront feminist suspicion of the pressures of normative mothering and caretaking responsibilities, and challenge the fear held by the able-bodied of the replication of disability.

Finally, in Chapter 5, I discuss May Sarton's many journalistic works (concentrating particularly on *Recovering* [1980], *After the Stroke* [1988], and *At Eighty-Two* [1996]), which contest conventional notions of physical trauma and aging as a diminishment of capability or social value. Sarton's diary format, which conveys the impression of overhearing the authentic record of a woman's mundane, domestic experience, subtly challenges the idea that the only legitimate voice of autobiography is one firmly situated in the public domains of politics or career. Sarton's diaries speak candidly of the disappointments and physical accommodations of aging. Her texts make copious references to friends recently dead, to doctor visits and new medications, and to the many things Sarton can no longer do alone or can no longer do at all. Yet the very dailiness of her diaries works against the mournful atmosphere created by Sarton's depression and anxiety, each new entry deferring not only the end of autobiography but the literal end of life that the author explicitly anticipates. Sarton embeds a kind of hopefulness into her texts, their very structure telling a story counter to the more despairing ones of sickness, physical limitation, and solitude. In two ways, then, Sarton defies reductive attitudes about elderly women—both by openly narrating the story of aging, in all its commonplace annoyances, and also by refusing to define herself entirely by the gendered or social parameters of that story.

Cultural messages about illness and dysfunction, like regulatory norms of gender, wield a fierce and tenacious hold on us. It is surprising to note how often these writers—whose disability and feminist agendas are undeniable—contravene that political purpose by seeming to capitulate to the very ideologies they mean to subvert and revise. When Jacobson refers to herself more than once as "hysterical," when Sarton describes recovery via an obviously triumphalist rhetoric, and when Mairs, Grealy, and Kleege promote their educational and writerly success, each may manage to deflect attention *away* from her controversial body by emphasizing mental or spiritual legitimacy. There is at work here a certain cultivation of admiration for whatever *else* the writer may feel herself to be or to do—deriving, of course, from a desire to show that impairment or pain is but one feature within a totality of self, but perhaps also from a worry about being taken seriously and a concern to prove self-worth apart from the body in question. These issues are integrally related to the effort to resist the various pressures and narratives that render "disabled woman" what some have called a "redundant intersection."[34] As Mairs openly admits, "Because I hate being crippled, I sometimes hate myself for being crippled. Over the years I have come to expect—even accept—attacks of violent self-loathing."[35] Given the extremity of such feelings about the self, which all the writers included here report, it is no wonder that their narratives would at times reveal ambivalence about the body or a powerful internalized shame in ways the writers themselves do not seem entirely aware of.

While such textual fluctuations may indicate an occasional acquiescence to stereotypes, they do not diminish the revisionary effect of these texts; to the contrary, they suggest simply that to write oneself out of and beyond dominant notions about embodiment is to confront the depth of one's engagement with them. Nancy Eiesland has argued that the "emancipatory transformation" of cultural conceptions of disability "must be enacted not only in history, but also in imagination and language," and she emphasizes "resymbolization" as a viable and necessary form of disability activism.[36] It is precisely by investigating the strategies with which these authors negotiate their complicated, sometimes hostile, and often ambivalent relationships to family, doctors, friends, and partners and to language, writing, and intellect—and, of course, to their own gendered bodies—that we can arrive at a fuller understanding of how autobiography might reinvent disability, for readers as much as writers, in dramatically liberatory ways.

1 auto/body/ography

The Fragmented Texts of Nancy Mairs

In the first essay of her collection *Waist-High in the World* (1997), Nancy Mairs poses the question that informs much of her autobiographical work: "Who would I be if I didn't have MS?"[1] Not at all glibly rhetorical, the question lies at the center of Mairs's writerly enterprise, which attempts to invent a phenomenological aesthetics that will illustrate the intersecting influences of gender, disability, and discourse in the formation of identity. As she declares in the title essay of *Carnal Acts* (1990), for instance, writing emphatically about the inseparability of body and mind, "I speak as a crippled woman. . . . No body, no voice; no voice, no body. That's what I know in my bones. . . . I couldn't write bodiless prose."[2] And, invoking Merleau-Ponty, she answers her own question at the start of *Waist-High in the World*, "Literally, no body. I am not 'Nancy + MS'" (8).[3] The refusal of that equation—of the notion of an a priori subject onto which the condition of multiple sclerosis has been added or grafted—sums up the kind of embodied self-consciousness Mairs repeatedly describes, one that derives from her effort to experience disabled identity as "all of a piece" (42).

Throughout her many collections of personal essays, Mairs promotes the generative friction between two models of identity, body and text, as constitutive of her narrative "I." On one hand, her repeated critique of Western culture's proscription of women's writing and of its demarcation of the "normal" body takes up the concerns of feminist autobiography theory and contemporary disability studies alike, both of which have made use of social constructionist theory to interrogate gender and disability as effects of language. Capitalizing on the fragmentary, suspended nature of personal essay, Mairs writes against two traditions: the "masculine" model of conventional autobiography, with its underlying ideology of stable, unified, and disembodied selfhood, and "the rules of polite discourse" (*Carnal Acts* 54; see also 60–61) that inhibit both female speech and the articulation of disabled experience. Mairs thus eschews the "certitudes," as Sidonie Smith describes them, that have traditionally structured life writing by men: "chronological time, individuality, developmental selfhood, myths of origins, the fixedness of identity, bodily wholeness, the transparencies of referentiality, the will to knowledge, the unified self."[4]

Mairs's essays also stress the enormous influence of cultural myth and expectation, out of and against which disabled subjectivity emerges as the performance of various "scripts." The word is used repeatedly in her first collection, *Plaintext* (1986), where Mairs argues that identity is constructed by the internalized lessons of literature, popular media, and the hegemonic discourses of religion, medicine, and psychoanalysis—in short, by "all the fictions my culture would yield up to my scrutiny."[5] Her challenge to cultural assumptions about a disabled body shows it to be not an absolute biological category but a historically specific construction, precipitating out of social relations, that enables and guarantees "normalcy." In Mairs's own words, "sickness forms only in relation to some standard of health which does not exist of itself in some fictional objective other world but which is created from the observations, responses, values, and beliefs of those 'healthy' subjects who seek to articulate it" (*Plaintext* 141), and as she reminds us in *Voice Lessons*, "I'm ever aware of my self as a cultural, not merely a personal, construct."[6] By writing about the realities of her disability, Mairs thus openly attempts to disturb the patriarchal ableism that has dominated both literary and cultural representations of identity.

But on the other hand, as her disbelief in "bodiless prose" suggests, Mairs experiences and therefore narrates herself in the highly individual terms of her corporeality. Interestingly, Mairs's work exhibits elements of both the unembarrassed, "blunt" honesty about disabled embodiment that Tobin Siebers calls for and the normalized body of theory that many disability scholars have critiqued.[7]

Indeed, Mairs has written at length of her affinity for the uncontainable female body of Hélène Cixous and of her desire to breach the coercive (if also fragile) "binary structure of . . . Logos" through the explosive erotics of *l'écriture féminine* (*Voice Lessons* 74). French feminism provides Mairs with a certain vocabulary for aligning the disruptions of MS with the disruptive form of the essay. In "The Laugh of the Medusa," for instance, which calls for a women's writing that would manifest "the ebullient, infinite woman," the woman of "luminous torrents," Cixous's imperatives are also Mairs's: that the female author "write your self. Your body must be heard," that "it's with her body that [a woman] vitally supports the 'logic' of her speech. Her flesh speaks true."[8] Mairs takes up the very word that Lennard J. Davis has made contentious in his critique of contemporary theory's ableist foundations: "*jouissance* . . . Even its pronunciation suggests the untranslatable pleasure of the word: the lips pout and then stretch, the sound slips back from the tongue's tip to be swallowed with a sigh. A word that happens to the body: writing" (*Voice Lessons* 47). "Feminine discourse," in Mairs's articulation, is "a babel of eroticism, attachment, and empathy" (42).[9]

This explicit association with the poetics of *l'écriture féminine* allows for many of the insights of Mairs's dismantling of patriarchal constructions of the disabled body, but it also opens her, inevitably, to the challenges leveled against theory generally by disability scholars and Cixous and Irigaray more specifically by other feminists: that such a politics of writing reifies an able body, relegates women to the body of patriarchy, and perpetuates the problematic and essentialized binary of masculine/feminine (even when, or especially when, those terms are abstracted beyond their application to human bodies). Yet the fact of Mairs's illness, along with her commitment to "esteeming" the disabled body on the page, potentially redefines how we might understand the notion of a feminine writing. The disabled body, in Rosemarie Garland-Thomson's words, is precisely "the body that *cannot be universalized*."[10] If Mairs's "crippled" form does not always enjoy the diffuse pleasures claimed by the Cixouvian body, and if its excesses defy not just patriarchal repression of female expression but also ableist standards of appeal, sensation, and comportment, then, as Thomson proposes, "disability, as a formal category, can pressure feminist theory to acknowledge physical diversity more thoroughly." Through the reality of her own physical condition, Mairs demonstrates the need to extend the "feminine" past a visionary sexuality of multiply potential eroticism that is fundamentally grounded in a notion of corporeal normality and essentialized femininity.

In this way, Mairs writes both with and against theoretical models of embodiment that, to quote Kristin Lindgren, "too often depend on an abstract idea of a normative body."[11] Mairs's own phenomenology demands reckoning with a degenerative condition whose specific effects—pain, altered shape, and loss of function and mobility—force a continual renegotiation of the nature of selfhood. At the same time, Mairs shares with both feminists like Cixous and other writers of disability narratives a desire to celebrate bodily uniqueness in direct opposition to the cultural denigration of that body, be it female, disabled, or both. To counteract the essentializing maneuvers of patriarchal discourse, Mairs presents a self both indeterminate and adamantly embodied, capable of becoming unhinged from cultural categories but also defined by the reality of MS. Asking that her readers acknowledge both the ordinariness and radical difference of her "crippled" female self, Mairs exposes the boundaries apparently inherent in such oppositions as masculine/feminine and able/disabled as narrative fictions; by denaturalizing cultural narratives, she examines the body as the site of conflicts of power. As Lindgren argues, then, Mairs's first-person narratives at once disrupt easy certainty about gender and disability by exploding a humanistic notion of unified selfhood and offer new "knowledges" about embodiment that are "richer, more specific, and more inclusive" of both difference and change.[12] Disability becomes, in Mairs's candid appraisal of her life as a (white, Catholic, educated, middle-class, straight) woman with MS, a new sort of postmodern trope for ambiguous selfhood, one that forces vigilance about not settling into the confinements of identity categories defined by patriarchal or ableist paradigms.

If life writing generally has the potential to redraw ideological and conceptual boundaries, the essay may be particularly well suited to the representation of disability, as G. Thomas Couser suggests, because its resistance to closure and resolution evokes the paradox of chronic conditions like Mairs's MS—the stasis of a condition from which one will never recover coupled with the constant unpredictability of the disease. Mairs has explicitly characterized her purpose in writing essays as an attempt to challenge the reductive, static categorizing of gender and disability inherent in masculinist symbolization. She writes that her " 'I' seems simply not to be the male-constructed 'I': It is more fluid, diffuse, multiplex" (*Voice Lessons* 86), and she claims to "write essays in the Montaignesque sense of the word," as "*tests*, trials, tentative rather than contentious, opposed to nothing, conciliatory, reconciliatory . . . their informing movement associative and suggestive, not analytic and declarative" (*Voice Lessons* 75). "I do not wish," she continues, ". . . to produce an autobiography bound by the narrative conventions of temporal linearity" (*Voice Lessons* 115). Essay collections allow Mairs to create heterogeneous "bodies" of writing that range through memory, experience, and location in a way that simultaneously suspends the progress-narrative of classic autobiographical prose and evokes the open-ended corporeal reality of living with multiple sclerosis.[13]

As I explain in the introduction, not all disability scholars are persuaded of the viability of life writing as a mode of resistance to social oppression; some have objected that the focus on the personal obscures larger political issues that mediate disabled experience. David Mitchell and Sharon Snyder, for instance, concede that the social merit of work such as Mairs's lies in "provid[ing] readers with an alternative perspective on what it means to live with a disability," but they also worry that "first person narratives of disability have historically fed a public appetite for confessional writing" and "cannot singularly provide the interpretive paradigms needed to revise cultural understandings of disability."[14] When Mitchell and Snyder write that Mairs's work "shifts attention away from institutional pathology and social attitudes toward the individual's experience of disability" and therefore "remains *cloistered*" in the realm of personal affliction,[15] they imply that the first-person strategy inherently fails to engage or negotiate the complex cultural forces that constrain the disabled and nondisabled alike.

Yet as I argue in the introduction and elsewhere,[16] life writing as a genre necessitates neither that an author construct a singular, individualistic narrating consciousness nor that he or she retreat from conceiving of identity in political and/or communal terms. I hope to show in what follows that Mairs is important as an autobiographer of disability precisely because her work insists on the intricate connections between subjective experience and cultural narrative, examining both gender and disability as a "cultural text," in Thomson's words, "that is interpreted, inscribed with meaning—indeed *made*—within social relations."[17] Indeed, Mairs's personal essays may be least "personal" when describing her life with MS—bound up in her narratives with an immersion in and then defiance of patriarchal stereotypes of feminine behavior—because the representation of that life entails so thorough a challenge to the medical model of disability and to bourgeois claims of individuality or immunity to social conditioning. Lindgren is careful to point out that while first-person narratives such as Mairs's do not offer "unmediated access to the body's truths," they do nonetheless generate "knowledge . . . critical to the development of theories of identity, subjectivity, and the body."[18]

"Like all negative terms," Mairs writes in *Waist-High in the World*, " 'disability' is part of a binary, existing in relation to a privileged opposite: that is, one is 'disabled' only from the point of view of another defined by common social values as 'able.' . . . Whoever gets to define ability puts everyone else in place, which . . . then becomes other, outside" (13–14). This kind of assertion encapsulates the position Mairs takes throughout her essays, one that emphasizes the social and linguistic locations of disability and gender while also hoping to "*normalize*" her female, disabled body (*Carnal Acts* 125; emphasis in original), to render its characteristics unremarkable, commonplace. Mairs's essays proceed as a series of dislocations, inviting but also refusing identification with her audience, striving to convince readers of the ordinariness of her daily embodied life even as they call attention to the ways in which it is marked as tragic, deviant, or strange. In this, Mairs's work accords with Davis's contention that "we are all nonstandard"; in her more colloquially articulated concern to "stir" the able-bodied "to recognition of the similarities that underlie their experiences and mine, to illuminate and delight in and laugh over the commonalities of human life" (*Voice Lessons* 109), we can hear Davis's concept of disability subjectivity as "a commonality of bodies within the notion of difference."[19] Indeed, that goal of stimulating recognition and acceptance across boundaries is one of the defining features of Mairs's life writing.

The imbrication of semiotic readings of self with essays that posit the body as the locus of meaning is particularly evident in *Plaintext*. Here Mairs deploys the essay as an act of resistance to the power exerted on the body and, at the same time, attempts to rewrite the cultural myths that coerce women into positions of subservience and self-hatred. The preface baldly sets the terms of the relationship between authorship of self and text: "A few years ago I almost died by my own hand, and when I woke from that disagreeable event, I recognized for the first time that I was fully and solely responsible for my existence. . . . These essays enact that responsibility . . . in the terms in which I can understand it: as a writer of my life" (*Plaintext* xi). To "write a life," then, means not simply to record the stuff of its continuity but to understand textuality as a literal, and more literally life-affirming, body/self: "I have to write. If I avoid that mandate, I wind up trying to kill myself. It's as simple as that" (104).

The predominant texture in *Plaintext* is one of interwoven narrative, where the present moment of an essay, for example, will be interrupted by excerpts from Mairs's own youthful diaries, or where the insights of contemporary feminist theory are pitted against such cultural "myths" as fairy tale or medical discourse. The corrective to the force of patriarchal discourse, revealed by Mairs's analysis of her own implication within its oppressions, is her tactically polyvocal style, heteroglossic within essays (conversing with different "selves" through diaries, old essays, photographs of herself, and so on) and destabilizing across essays (the book's temporal looping, its refusal to collate individual pieces into a single life trajectory). In this sense she disproves what Couser has claimed about disability narratives generally—that they tend to be formally conservative, "rooted in [the] familiar solid world" of "premodernist narrative conventions."[20] In part, Couser implies, the restraint imposed on the formal may result from the very danger of the content, which is "transgressive" simply by giving voice to disabled experience. *Plaintext* proves its own initiating claim, that writing can be a threshold to radical self-renewal, specifically by contesting expectations of narrative continuity.

The widely anthologized "On Being a Cripple," from the first section of *Plaintext*, illustrates through juxtaposition the way in which subjectivity can be conceived as precipitating out of the friction—and the gap—between discourse and corporeality. The essay, which includes a gentle refusal of the obfuscations of more "politically correct" terminology such as "handicapped" or "differently abled," is in part Mairs's defense of "cripple" as the word she uses to identify herself (an Orwellian argument writ small);[21] she then goes on to provide a condensed history of her experience with MS. Despite the author's protest that "I am not a disease," "On Being a Cripple" does in fact explore the complicated ways in which cultural assumptions, which assign meaning to bodies according to narrowly conceived parameters of normalcy and beauty, enforce a sense of identity for the crippled, other body for whom the ideal is unavailable (17). While the essay remains for the most part in the present tense, being primarily a richly detailed account of the impact of MS on a current "I," it does allude to past and future "Nancys" whose needs and suffering are not those of the speaking self: "At the beginning, I thought about having MS almost incessantly. . . . Gradually I came to understand that the Nancy who might one day lie inert under a bed-sheet . . . was not the Nancy I was at present" (18). A single, unified "Nancy Mairs" disappears in the narrator's refusal of the norm that would marginalize her and in this multiplicity of selves, between whom likeness can be no more fully guaranteed by bodily continuity (since her physical state is ever-changing) than by consciousness, desire, or memory.

Being diagnosed with MS, Mairs suggests, literalized early on a "sense of self-alienation" that she already had as a young woman "well off the ideal" of femininity (17). As Mairs describes her, that ideal woman "seems to be between the ages of eighteen and twenty-five; her hair has body, her teeth flash white. . . . She is trim and deeply tanned; she jogs, swims, plays tennis, rides a bicycle, sails. . . . Though usually white and often blonde she may be black, Hispanic, Asian, or Native American, so long as she is unusually sleek. . . . But she is never a cripple" (16). Mairs contrasts her own form: "My shoulders droop and my pelvis thrusts forward as I try to balance myself upright, throwing my frame into a bony S. . . . One shoulder is higher than the other and I carry one arm bent in front of me, the fingers curled into a claw. My left arm and leg have wasted into pipestems, and I try always to keep them covered" (17). What the cultural expectation makes metaphorical, then—that a woman who deviates from the standard is "monstrous" and unworthy of sexual attention—Mairs feels herself to embody in a far more actual and psychically damaging way: "When I think about how my body must look to others, especially to men, to whom I have been trained to display myself, I feel . . . loathsome" (17). Hers is a doubly other body, marginalized not simply from the hale and coherent body of masculinist culture but from the normatively beautiful body of conventionalized femininity as well.

On one level, Mairs presents the body with MS as a freakish cultural other. Her self-description, in its repetition of images of unevenness, rigidity, and collapse, signals her distance from the perfect graceful solidity of the woman who engages in sports or has both the energy and the strength to "trave[l] widely" or to prepare "meals that take less than twenty minutes."[22] Against her depiction of an exuberant, autonomous, outward, and unquestioned motion, Mairs renders her own corporeal state as grotesquely witchlike, a form that sinks and twists into itself and juts in awkward angles as if unable to abide by some metaphysical, even moral, straight and narrow. To the degree that this self-presentation seems startling—for its raw, uncomfortable physicality and the way it makes visible the body's paradoxes (lithic, spongy interiority and the capacity to self-devour)—but also luridly exposing, Mairs plays on both the historical legacy of the freak show and a literary tradition of the grotesque, according to both of which the extraordinary body is a spectacle that confirms—and confers—normality.[23] As Thomson posits, "The disabled figure operates as the vividly embodied, stigmatized other whose social role is to symbolically free the privileged, idealized figure of the American self from the vagaries and vulnerabilities of embodiment."[24]

Initially, then, Mairs's description may validate some readers' sense of able-bodiedness through her difference. She then surprises her audience into a double recognition—of their desire for the feminine ideal whose characteristics she has just detailed as well as their own (unconscious) acquiescence to the ugliness of her otherized body—and thus underlines the cultural code that defines beauty and success by a single set of near-impossible criteria. But the power of that narrative is fierce, and when Mairs admits to succumbing to its rhetorical force ("I have always had an uneasy relationship with my body"), she invites a new sort of powerful identification ("like many women I know") that brings her body back from the margins (16).

At the same time, though, the physical experience of MS has other, more salutary psychological effects, and in the amassing of different examples, the essay presents a counternarrative, this time not of idealized perfection but, rather, of a more realistically ambivalent effort to occupy a body that offers both pleasure and despair:

> I lead, on the whole, an ordinary life, probably rather like the one I would have led had I not had MS. . . . In addition to studying, I teach writing courses. . . . I have raised a foster son . . . and I am still escorting my daughter and son through adolescence. I go to Mass every Saturday. I am a superb, if messy, cook. I am also an enthusiastic laundress. . . . I play a fiendish game of Scrabble. When I have the time and the money, I like to sit on my front steps with my husband, drinking Amaretto and smoking a cigar. . . .
>
> This lively plenty has its bleak complement, of course, in all the things I can no longer do. I will never run again, except in dreams, and one day I may have to write that I will never walk again. . . . I have to select my clothing with care not so much for style as for ease of ingress and egress. . . . I can no longer do fine stitchery, pick up babies, play the piano, braid my hair. I am immobilized by acute attacks of depression. (12–13)

The listing of apparently mundane activity in an essay is typical of Mairs—she means thereby to insist on the similarities between her daily life and that of the "nondisabled"—but her speaking "I" seems always to emerge from the interaction between what she deems "the plenty and the privation" (13). Just as the woman of fashion magazines derives her mythic status through an always-implied contrast to "ordinary" women (the supermarket checkout line is a kind of obligatory litmus test that reconfirms the average woman's inadequacy),[25] Mairs sets up another contrast here, which renders similarly visible the discursive fiction underlying cultural categories of meaning. In her first list, the details are organized to emphasize unthreatening regularity and a principled committedness to profession, parenting, and faith; but the speaker is also contradictory in a "normal" way, someone whose overtly feminized activities are punctuated by good liqueur and cigars.

"Domesticity," in this passage, is no longer solely the domain of a constrained femininity (since women who do laundry can also drink and smoke a stogie), nor is it to be associated with mere drudgery (since its tasks can be enjoyed "enthusiastically" or even "messily"). Mairs questions, too, the legitimization of only those physical activities demonstrated by the magazine model as constituting "capability" and even "pleasure"; her own enjoyment of more quotidian action—specifically, the language with which the quotidian is celebrated—raises it to a level of achievement that requires a radical shift in perspective (as in the subject of *Plaintext*'s first essay, "On Having Adventures," which remarks that "the minutiae of my life have had to assume dramatic proportions" [6]). The first part of the passage challenges easy acceptance of physical health as synonymous with an obvious and visible athleticism and proposes an alternate vision of how one might experience embodied pleasure; what follows, however, unsettles even that perhaps straightforward dichotomy. All that Mairs *can't* do reminds her readers again of the fact of a body in failure, so that, retroactively, the small undertakings of her life are made to seem exquisitely vulnerable and therefore precious; a prior bravado seems to modulate into something that is not at all self-pity but rather a matter-of-fact awareness of inevitable decline. What emerges from this sequence seems far from a question of chiding others to appreciate the quaint simplicity of domestic rituals. Mairs "want[s people] to wince" (9); the force of difference sets even her own investment in the ordinary against the unpredictability of MS. Describing an "exacerbation"—a sudden, severe experience of symptoms that signals further neurological damage—suffered during a trip to California, Mairs writes that "the incident spoiled my self-satisfaction" and "renewed my grief and fury and terror, and I learned that one never finishes adjusting to MS" (19).

At the same time, Mairs credits MS with a different sort of subjective change: "I have always tried to be gentle with my doctors. . . . I incarnate the limitation of their powers. The least I can do is refuse to press on their tenderest spots. This gentleness is part of the reason that I'm not sorry to be a cripple" (20). Mairs's acceptance of always potential displacement—the way MS makes her other to herself in frightening but also gratifying ways—is embedded into the essay's structural reluctance to proclaim a single self and prohibits readers as well from the appropriating moves of identification or sympathy. As Janet Varner Gunn has argued of the autobiographical situation, the reader is "[put] to work" in such a way that "the *otherness* of the text" is experienced, "keep[ing] the appropriative activity of interpretation from becoming expropriative." "New understanding," she continues, "allows neither assimilation (the reader's takeover of the text) nor accommodation (the text's takeover of the reader). Autobiographical response requires, instead, an integration."[26] Presenting herself always as both ordinary and extraordinary, Mairs asks readers to consider the ideological perimeters of those adjectives, the power investments that motivate any such characterization.

This strategy of definitional duality is made explicit in a similar passage from *Carnal Acts*. Mairs states first, "I'm not . . . MS. MS, a walking, talking embodiment of a chronic incurable degenerative disease. In most ways I'm just like every other woman of my age, nationality, and socioeconomic background" (32). Here she reaches outward in a way designed both to include herself as a part of "normal" society and to assuage the anxiety of the onlooker; despite surface appearances, she is "just like" anyone else and thus knowable, readable. But in talking about also being at the literal margins of that society, made *un*readable by its constructions of health and beauty, Mairs reiterates her "refus[al] to pretend that the only differences between you and me are the various ordinary ones that distinguish any one person from another," as she proclaims in "On Being a Cripple" (*Plaintext* 10). While "advertisers . . . deny the existence of me and my kind" so that "the viewer won't feel threatened by her or his own physical vulnerability" (*Carnal Acts* 33), the reader of Mairs's essay is never allowed to participate in that kind of complacent "effac[ing]" of the disabled body. As David Hevey asks, "When did you last see a picture of a disabled person? It almost certainly wasn't in commercial advertising since disabled people are not thought to constitute a body of consumers and therefore do not generally warrant inclusion."[27]

It is to this broad cultural absence, of course, that Mairs's self-representations most urgently respond. "Imagine a life in which feasible others—others you can hope to be like—don't exist," she continues. "At the least, you might conclude that there is something queer about you, something ugly or foolish or shameful. In the extreme, you might feel as though you don't exist" (*Carnal Acts* 33–34). But though the fundamental message of these paragraphs is an inclusive one—that there should be accurate cultural models for *all* forms of human experience—their effect is to recall an equally fundamental difference, "the specificity that bodily existence confers" (*Voice Lessons* 49). Mairs may not resemble the cover model of fashion magazines, but the majority of her readers, she implies, will not look like the model *or* Mairs. To become aware of the layers of disjunction is to begin to recognize the insufficiency of normative myths of beauty, female sexuality, and embodiedness.

In a "sociolinguistic system over which [women] have had relatively little power," a "crippled" woman experiences what Mairs calls "a kind of double jeopardy. How can she construct a world that will accommodate her realities . . . ?" (*Waist-High* 58). The answer, fittingly, is both physical and linguistic. "If I want people to grow accustomed to my presence, and to view mine as an ordinary life . . . then I must routinely roll out among them" (104). Such "roll[ing] out" is, of course, enacted by every instance of self-representation Mairs has composed. And just as Mairs "prefer[s] the self-defined 'cripple' " (14) because it operates beyond the system of naming and meaning-making, so too does she rename "people who lack [disabilities as] . . . 'the nondisabled,' since in relation to me, they are the deficient ones. Already, in this way, I begin to reconstruct the world" (14). The subtlety of Mairs's language is precise: "lack" is relocated in the bodies of the "normals," transforming disability from its place of deviation or loss to something the absence of which might actually be mourned as a liability. At the same time disability is retrieved from the margins of threatening excess by being figured as "non"-deficient, successful corporeality.

The four essays in the final section of *Plaintext* amplify these kinds of juxtapositions. Mairs uses the controlling metaphor of "script" or "tale" to expose and then circumvent cultural demands for closure and unity as well as claims to knowledge and authority. Each essay locates itself at a series of provocative thresholds, between self and culture, between older and current selves, between women and men, and between the allegedly separate "self" and "body." Moving back and forth across these discursive boundaries where women, particularly women writers, are tenuously poised, Mairs becomes a *bricoleur* of self, allowing the interplay of voices and explanatory systems to create a kinetic energy of disruption. The essays are thematically linked, each focused on Mairs's experiences as a newly married woman struggling with depression and agoraphobia, her rape by a high school boyfriend, her determination to keep writing, her worsening condition with MS, and the impact of text (scripture, fairy tales, diaries, literature and literary criticism, sociology, and psychoanalysis) on the construction of identity—but they excavate those issues from slightly shifted perspectives and illustrate them with different anecdotes and examples.

Together the four essays fashion what Mairs refers to, in another context, as a "patchwork" version of a life, which functions subversively to forestall expectations of wholeness or unified subjectivity. Such reiterations and overlappings exemplify Mairs's use of a *mise-en-abyme* method to suggest that the "truth" of the body or the self is endlessly interpretable and illustrate what Sidonie Smith has suggested about feminist autobiography—that it rejects the teleological model of a unified and universal speaker locating "proof" of itself in the past and speaks instead "to the future" with hope about the potential for change.[28] "The stuttering adventure of the essay," as Mairs characterizes it (*Voice Lessons* 87), challenges entrenched cultural standards for both writing and identity because its mode is "contemplative, exploratory, even equivocal, not definitive. If there are absolute answers to the kinds of questions I can ask, I don't know them" (*Waist-High* 17).

This commitment to "not knowing" works strenuously to undermine the claims to authority of able-bodied, patriarchal culture. Mairs's adolescent diaries, for instance, become a kind of anti-authority, proving the enormity of cultural expectation on identity formation but also subverting the expectation of a continuous self- or body-trajectory. By exposing the naïveté of the diaries' trust in the marriage plot of romantic fiction, Mairs willingly bares her own immersion in fantasies about a stereotypical form of love, "shamelessly" presenting herself *not* as the individualist of men's self-writing who bucks the system with scrappy ingenuity (one thinks, for instance, of the narrator of Tobias Wolff's *This Boy's Life*) but as a poignant figure desperate for a sense of physical well-being that would match a fairy-tale ideal. Her style of confession is thus less truth-telling than a form of self-parody that allows her to observe that younger self as other, a self to whose unthinking acceptance of cultural myth Mairs is no longer subject.

Smith writes that women's autobiographies "confron[t] the process of repetition whereby fixed identifications ('woman,' 'black,' 'lesbian,' etc.) authorize only certain performances of identity at the exclusion of others."[29] Mairs performs a different sort of "iteration" here, one designed to weave and refract, break down and rebuild. In a sense, it is by making the self seem "incoherent" that Mairs represents her female/disabled subjectivity according to new rules of coherence.[30] If there is no single story of the embodied self, or no single way to tell it, then the autobiographical mode loosens and slips into what Smith describes as works that embrace the "polyphonic possibilities of selfhood."[31] Mairs's essay collections reveal what Felicity Nussbaum and Shari Benstock refer to as "fissures of female discontinuity," which challenge an autobiographical model based on a metaphysics of self-wholeness and narrative seamlessness.[32] Mairs suggests instead that the tale of the disabled female life cannot be unbrokenly narrated, that indeed that "self" is constantly shifting to the side—into the next essay, into a new paradigm of meaning or understanding, into a new phase of MS.

In *Waist-High in the World*, Mairs writes that marginality "means something altogether different to me from what it means to social theorists. It is not a metaphor for the power relations between one group of human beings and another but a literal description of where I stand (figuratively speaking): over here, on the edge, out of bounds, beneath your notice. I embody the metaphors" (59). Her physical position becomes a way of *re-vising* a world that she views from "the slant of a wheelchair" (106). In this sense she counters narrative patterns common in men's accounts of physical paralysis, which typically perpetuate a gendered dichotomy between the continued activity of the mind or spirit and the immobility of the body. In Reynolds Price's memoir *A Whole New Life*, for example, the shame of impairment is redeemed by an ecstatic vision in which the author is assured by Jesus that he will be "cured"; Price's challenge to stereotyped denigrations of disability depends more on the assertion of his own spiritual election than on any broad, more direct confrontation with ableist myths or standards. Andre Dubus's account of paralysis in both *Broken Vessels* and *Meditations from a Movable Chair* trades similarly on the ecstatic experience of spiritual reception as the antidote to no longer feeling "whole."[33] As Madonne Miner has argued, Dubus, in contrast to Mairs, "repeatedly returns to stereotypically masculinized questions of agency, responsibility, and guilt" and "reaffirms [his] manliness and heroism."[34]

Mairs's self-representational project, far from denying the condition of the body, *insists* on it, lowering the "nondisabled" to her waist-high level in order to transvaluate the way the world is ordered and experienced. Mairs wants to assure her potentially reluctant audience that the prospect of seeing the world from her vantage point—which is in itself a kind of metaphor for widening one's vision to include the broadest range of embodied uniqueness—is a positive one, that the initially destabilizing effects of acknowledging difference are ultimately rewarding. "The more perspectives that can be brought to bear on human experience," Mairs insists, ". . . the richer that experience becomes. If it is both possible and pleasant for me and my kind to enter, the world will become a livelier place. You'll see" (*Waist-High* 106). *Waist-High in the World* is thus composed as a record of the "consequences" (16) of difference on an individual's ability to determine, represent, and experience herself.

In a culture that privileges only the white, male, "able" body as the "neutral" and normative self, disability is both an emphatically particular embodied reality and a trope for disenfranchisement: "Disability is at once a metaphorical and a material state, evocative of other conditions in time and space—childhood and imprisonment come to mind—yet 'like' nothing but itself. I can't live it or write about it except by conflating the figurative and the substantial, the 'as if' with the relentlessly 'what is' " (58). At the "what is" level, Mairs writes of the practical matters of living with MS in a world constructed according to a single conception of normal physical mobility and of the psychological damage such enforced, literal marginality produces. The ideological "success" of this aspect of representation is, in turn, whether or not it allows Mairs to transform the "as if" from a culturally enforced conception of disability as the unpoliceable, uncontrolled body that threatens the nondisabled with both the promise of their own future failure and the exposure of their privileged position as fictional. The disabled body, Mairs suggests, is simply one more form of human corporeality, but at the same time it might also serve as a liberating metaphor—for multiple perspectives, for resistance to oppression, and for a way of making difference radically visible, not merely to reinscribe the "normal" body, but as and in itself.

Mairs balks at language that reinforces the notion that "I myself—my thinking self—[am] no body, as though this disembodied self could speak not only for the body that it is not but for bodies in general," and she refuses "to divorce the speaking subject from her own corporal existence while permitting her to make free, in the chastest of senses, with the bodies of others" (*Waist-High* 40). Describing her own and her husband's necessary efforts to "come to terms with" (41) increasingly ill bodies (Mairs's husband, George, underwent radical treatment for melanoma), Mairs remarks that "the physical processes of a perfectly healthy person may impinge so little on her sense of well-being that she may believe herself separate from and even in control of them" (41). By representing *her* self as inextricably enmeshed with her "troubled" body, Mairs recalls intellect to the body. Such language also seems designed to make one become aware of one's own physical interiority, to probe it experientially, to literally test one's *sense* of *self*. The effect of her language is that one suddenly comes to inhabit a perhaps utterly unfamiliar corporeal self.

Waist-High in the World frequently marshals such uncanniness. Again searching for language with which to render her body, Mairs writes, "Here is my troubled body, dreaming myself into life: a guttering candle in a mound of melted wax, or a bruised pear, ripe beyond palatability, ready for the compost heap. The images, though they vary, always bear the whiff of spoliation" (44). The attention to diffusion and loss of shape here, the sensation of a body rotting from within and easily indented from without, the sense of losing structure and solidity and even purpose (the candle that can no longer be lit, the pear destined for the garbage)—and, moreover, the implication that such instances of self-punitive naming might proliferate without end—all appear staged to evoke a flash of shock and pity, allowing readers to pull out of their bodies (if momentarily) so that the specter of Mairs's failure, a failure both of the body and of the will (illness as deserved punishment for sin; low self-esteem as undignified self-absorption) can be safely contained at the farthest possible distance from the reading self. The move is deft and strategic, because no sooner has Mairs encouraged that sort of differentiating move than she reels her audience in again, surely and inescapably: "Mostly I was, *as I was trained to be*, disappointed in myself. . . . I could not imagine a body that didn't require at least minor structural modification. I still can't, *and neither can any other woman I know*" (44; my emphasis). One is caught gawking at, disdaining, the shadow of the self.[35]

Mairs repeats this strategy of a layered (un)familiarity throughout her work because it militates against the alienating moves inherent in oppressive social configurations. Sex is one human activity she is particularly concerned to show the disabled body having and enjoying, and her discussion of this stands in obvious opposition to dominant cultural assumptions about the disabled and women alike: "Most people . . . deal with the discomfort and even distaste that a misshapen body arouses by dissociating that body from sexuality in reverie and practice. 'They' can't possibly do it, the thinking goes; therefore, 'they' mustn't even want it. . . . I really do like sex. A lot. Especially now that the issues of power and privacy that vexed me then have resolved themselves with time" (*Waist-High* 51–52). Mairs protests here the mind-bending contradiction of inhabiting two mutually exclusive, and multiply oppressive, constructions: the asexualized, abnormal, sterile body of the disabled and the inescapably sexualized, shameful female body of Western culture.[36] She represents herself as mature and psychologically astute, as a woman of considerable patience and experience ("issues" have "resolved themselves with time"), as a woman no longer persuaded by culture's tale of her own objectification and thus at ease with the fact of her body, eager for its pleasures—as, in short, more self-actualized than many "normals" (103).

But once again the disabled body is both like and unlike, for Mairs's story of the enjoyment of sex, newly discovered in "coming to terms" with her body, is always necessarily open-ended, bound up as it is with the ever-deteriorating condition of multiple sclerosis. Her narrative thus shifts course, as does the course of MS; the speaker who boldly claims to "like sex. A lot" and thereby conveys the impression of an active and ongoing sexual life is a momentary incarnation. As she goes on to explain, due to her husband's impotency (a result of chemotherapy), she "will never experience [intercourse] again" (52). But while the inability to engage in the forms of sexual contact she likes "best of all" "shrouds" Mairs in "sexual sadness," it does not preclude her from experiencing a multitude of highly charged erotic intimacies with George:

> Whether for making love or not, our bodies—one twisted and nearly inert, the other scarified, both softening now with age and indulgence—instinctively seek each other out. Even our most mundane interactions bear an erotic charge. . . . He may stroke my neck when he brings me a cup of coffee. And since my wheelchair places me just at the height of his penis . . . I may nuzzle it in return. We carry on a constant, often hardly conscious, corporeal conversation regardless of our other pursuits and preoccupations. Without my disability to throw us together thus habitually, our bodies might spend their days racing separately from one activity to another, coming across each other only in time to tumble into sleep. (53–54)

It is *disability*, Mairs provocatively claims, that renders her "normally" sexual, disability that enlarges the experiential field to enable her to locate the extraordinary in the ordinary. What seems most striking about this manifesto for the eroticism of quotidian chore is that Mairs is not so much describing *actions* that are radically different from what the nondisabled would routinely perform but, rather, a mode of *perception* that allows her to view those activities differently, investing them with meaning according to a different conceptual frame. Exposing the limitations of the worldview of "able-bodiedness," with its monological definition of the erotic or the tender, Mairs offers, as Lindgren has argued, new knowledge about the relationships between self, body, and sexuality. If Nancy's and George's respective impairments instigate various adaptations to bodily reality in response to erotic need, it is writing, Mairs suggests, that effects the theoretical or imaginative significance of that adaptive strategy: the "hardly conscious, corporeal conversation" *becomes* conscious and overt in the pages of the text, where readers, in turn, are introduced to a way of thinking about actively desirous, disabled bodies.

This layering of perceptual shift—first in the "personal" sphere of

Mairs's lived experience and next in the public exchange between her text and her audience—recalls Siebers's claim "that physical barriers are each and every one of them psychic barriers as well. . . . When we come to a barrier, we realize that our perception of the world does not conform" to that of the able-bodied.[37] While Siebers is referring here to actual architectural obstacles like staircases and curbs, I would argue that conventionally imagined, heterosexual intercourse similarly constitutes a kind of physical barrier that Mairs and her husband, given their bodily realities, must maneuver around, and that, in turn and more critically, Mairs's depiction of her erotic behavior reveals less the limitations of her or George's body parts than of a perception of sex as exclusively genital, male-directed, missionary, or even orgasmic. Importantly, by reorganizing the relationship between bodies *that* desire—emphatically, a female body—and concepts *of* desire, Mairs's first-person narrative rethinks the parameters of how a woman might want, have, and talk about sex. "Women with every kind of disability must learn to speak forthrightly about their needs and appetites," Mairs writes elsewhere, "even when society appears to ignore or repudiate their feelings."[38]

It is this commitment to soliciting the perspectives of women with disabilities that impels the *Waist-High* essay "Young and Disabled," for instance, a compilation of excerpts taken from a survey Mairs conducted. The piece reads as an exhilarating cacophony of idioms, condensing the kind of message that Mairs's life writing has consistently tried to enact: against master narratives that reduce subjectivity to the coercive and inaccurate attribute "disabled"—itself already the product of cultural narrative—there is the possibility of shared experience, "elements common to the human condition" that may take on a "particular significance in terms of disability" (*Waist-High* 11–12). This is made provocatively clear as Mairs, herself one of the "disabled," struggles to distill the self-representations of her respondents. "Their disabilities varied so widely that it was difficult—even deceptive—to generalize about such women," she states, "who may have less in common with each other than they do with some nondisabled women and who may even be made uneasy by women with disabilities different from their own" (127–28). Rosemarie Garland-

Thomson agrees, writing that "disabled people seldom consider themselves a group. . . . Only the shared experience of stigmatization creates commonality. Having been acculturated similarly to everyone else, disabled people also often avoid and stereotype one another in an attempt to normalize their own social identities."[39]

Mairs has a difficult task, then, in bringing together so many tales of disabled life without blurring their important differences. She navigates that problem by taking the position of facilitator rather than master-interpreter, quoting her respondents amply so that they speak for themselves and intertwining her own voice with theirs as simply one other, and not the dominant, perspective. As Mairs says of this project, "I hope that, as these women speak, 'disability' will emerge as one element of their complicated personalities and not as a confining category" (128). The result is that the essay not only demonstrates the multeity of disabled experience but also defocuses attention on Mairs as the "author" of and authority on the disabled. In a sense she relinquishes control even of the writing act, giving over the space of the essay to others' voices, and by thus refusing to monopolize, she insists that the varieties of experience, which should and do proliferate, must be represented as such.[40]

In turn, what one understands of disability, femaleness, and identity is continually being unraveled and rewoven. The reading process mirrors, in this way, that necessarily continual revision of self that chronic illness causes: "After I learned that I had multiple sclerosis, the transitions I had to make, involving the development of a new sense of who I was and what I was good for, required mourning the loss of the 'old me' as I confronted a new one who seemed like a stranger. . . . With degenerative conditions like mine, self-definition may have to be revised in this way again and again as new limitations develop" (133). Here is evidence of what Lindgren describes as Mairs's "uneasy identification with her crippled body," a process of reconciliation with the consistent alterations of embodied experience and understanding that is both "conscious" and "developed over time."[41] Lindgren's point is that by constructing a "new corporeal schema" as part of a deliberate relationship with the progression of MS, Mairs resists the sense of dissociation that can happen when physical changes make the embodied self seem strangely unfamiliar. "Young and Disabled" is not, then, a piteous narrative of diminishment and loss. Rather it reinforces what Mairs has consistently argued about disability, that it is both private and communal, physical and ideological, an ongoing and crucially self-conscious act of *being* (and not just being "in") a transformed and transforming body.

In the final essay of *Waist-High*, "Writing West: A Reclamation Project," Mairs describes a request to compose a piece on being a Western writer: "They want me to write a story essentially like other women's stories with the trifling but possibly intriguing difference that I happen to experience whatever befalls me at the height of those women's belt buckles. But that's not how disability works. . . . It does not merely alter a few, or even a great many, details in a life story that otherwise conforms to basic narrative conventions: the adventure, the romance, the quest. Instead, it transforms the tale utterly" (182). Transforming the tale, of course, has been Mairs's fundamental "reclamation project" since her first collection of essays. But the key distinction here may be not simply that disability wholly reshapes one's life trajectory but more specifically that a disability like MS requires a multiplicity of stories: telling the story of "being" MS requires repeated acts of representation because that self is never what it once was. Leigh Gilmore refers to "this pattern of returning to the autobiographical scene" as "serial autobiography" and argues that recurring textual engagements with "becoming a person" or "working through personae toward personhood" may be especially helpful to, even inevitable for, the writer working through traumatic experience.[42]

This is precisely what Mairs seems to be getting at when she writes, "We can't decide . . . whether or not someone gets MS. MS just *happens*. But—and this is the exciting part—we can choose how we will respond to that happening, what kind of role we will give it in the story we're making up as we go along" (*Carnal Acts* 124). Two important points surface in this encapsulation of Mairs's defining writerly tactics. First, Mairs stresses again her belief that MS—or any other condition, whether physically impairing or culturally disabling —occurs randomly, without design, motive, or fault. Second, she foregrounds the possibility of narrative reframing in the subjective experience of that condition, whatever its corporeal realities. The psychical and political utility of Mairs's life writing lies in the conjunction of these attitudes toward the body, in the concept of an arbitrarily configured physical form paired with the assertion that disease is simply one element of the continually revisable relation of a life. Mairs conveys a kind of pedagogical aim to her writing in the upbeat emphasis she gives here to the shared enterprise of rethinking how physical impairment matters: with MS or not, "we" have the "exciting" opportunity, and implicitly the responsibility, to think carefully about the kind of meanings we attach to disease and disability.[43] Most importantly, perhaps, there is a hopeful continuity at work in the present tense of this passage: whatever our bodily particulars, whatever state of impairment or aging or change we may find ourselves in as we read Nancy Mairs, she grants us the authorship of our own going along.

2 tyranny of the visual

Lucy Grealy & Georgina Kleege

The textual display of a disabled female body places in especially high relief the role of the visual in subject making, at once disclosing and disobeying what is nearly an axiomatic relationship between female identity, sexuality, and the gaze. From psychoanalytic theories of mirroring to the regulatory mechanism of Foucauldian surveillance, from feminist critiques about the specularity of cinema to the erotic watching of sexual encounters, and from the theatrics of autobiography to the importance granted visibility in identity politics, the dynamics of vision tend to hold primacy of place in contemporary theorizing about selfhood. The texts to be considered in this chapter both accord with and complicate that privileged cultural status of sight. *Autobiography of a Face* (1994), Lucy Grealy's account of numerous attempts to surgically restore a jaw lost to cancer, and *Sight Unseen* (1999), Georgina Kleege's collection of personal essays about partial blindness, are at once trained on looks and looking as barometers of self-worth and are concerned to devise alternate modes of self-knowledge and intersubjective communication. Because neither Grealy nor Kleege "looks like" anyone else, their stories expose the fallacy of a presumably universal visual dynamic, not only to claim the possibility of a reciprocal or female-authored exchange of looks but, more crucially, to disrupt the relationship between seeing and selfhood altogether.

Looking as an instrument of power that guarantees both an able-bodied and masculine subject position is a staple feature of psychoanalytically informed feminist film theory as well as histories of the freak show. In the well-rehearsed formulation of Laura Mulvey, the scopophilic encounter of film empowers an active male gaze that objectifies and controls a passive female surface. Male viewers' looking coincides with that of the camera and of male heroes, while women must take the position of either the men in the audience (thus contorting their subjective position) or the women on-screen (thus colluding in their own objectification). The pleasures of looking are wholly enjoyed by the man, who participates with the idealized male protagonist of the narrative in gazing at the eroticized female image and who thus determines both the course and the meaning of the narrative.[1] The female figure, in contrast, is a troubling and even stalling presence, soothing through erotic fantasy the terrible threat of castration that her own displayed body provokes. The scene of looking has thus come to be understood as marked by inequities of power: by the male subject's desire to penetrate, know, and dominate and by the silencing of the female object.

Critics since Mulvey have protested against the apparent impossibility of a legitimate female gaze, a look-back from the woman that neither dissolves in narcissistic self-appraisal nor serves to dismember a now-immobilized male—or, for that matter, that even involves men at all. Jackie Stacey contends that psychoanalytic readings of film operate within a binary model of sexual difference according to which the structure of desire is always heterosexual; the "rigid distinction between *either* desire *or* identification," Stacey writes, requires that the complex exchange of gazes between women in the audience and women on-screen must either "be collapsed into simple identification" or mapped onto masculine heterosexual desire.[2] Stacey argues for a more complex understanding of female looking, one that exceeds the limitations of the "three rather frustrating options of masculinisation, masochism or marginality" while maintaining the space of difference between women. Critics have also reexamined texts in which women are the main characters and whose perspective thus directs the narrative. Lorraine Gamman, for example, has suggested that female characters who control point of view "don't invert power relations, claiming total mastery for themselves, but instead subtly displace such relations."[3]

A similar reclaiming of representational perspective characterizes contemporary disability theater, performance art, and photography.

Rosemarie Garland-Thomson writes that in an "ocularcentric era," "the stare sculpts the disabled subject into a grotesque spectacle."[4] Freak shows literally commodified human "oddities" or "nature's mistakes," displaying physical anomalies in carefully packaged exhibits that conferred transparent normalcy upon viewers.[5] In a modern scientific age, the medical gaze isolates and pathologizes deviant or deformed body parts. Charity posters sentimentalize disabled children whose infirmity cries out for rescuing from benevolent "normates." And everyday encounters enforce the categorical separation between disabled and nondisabled through what Thomson calls a "stare-and-tell ritual" in which the disabled are called upon to explain "what happened."[6] Such objectifying scenes of looking may be counteracted, however, by visual art by people with disabilities that stares back at an ableist audience, challenging its assumptions about corporeal difference.[7] The photographs in Alexa Wright's series *I*, for example, in which different forms of congenital disability are digitally superimposed onto images of the artist, pry apart the correspondence between body trait and character inherent in acts of stigmatizing, problematize conventional notions of beauty and artistic value, and challenge viewers to question what they think they know based on what they see. Performance artists such as Mary Duffy and Cheryl Marie Wade similarly confront spectators with unabashed displays of female, disabled bodies that invite only to invalidate the power of the ableist stare, the look that constructs disability as oddity, medical abnormality, or pitiable misfortune. And in a theater piece called *Go Figure*, Katie Rodriguez Banister negotiates changes in her experience of sexuality after becoming quadriplegic, not simply to affirm a disabled sexual identity but, more critically, to prod viewers to reconsider normative presumptions about sexual behavior. In these various media, being looked at is dramatized as part of what materializes both gender and disability but then reorganized as an intersubjective dynamic, one in which autobiographical storytelling asks nondisabled viewers to interrogate their biases and fears about anomalous bodies.

In life writing about disability, looking can serve to transform an author who, staging herself being seen both by those who people her remembered past and by readers who encounter her in the narrated present, courts potentially objectifying stares to refute their condemnatory impact. Autobiographical writers necessarily put themselves on display, establishing a textual hall of mirrors in which the narrated object is also a gazing subject. As recent critics of self-writing agree, the self who writes never fully coordinates with the narrated self; rather, the autobiographical "I" is a gazed-upon production who not only watches him- or herself being looked at (by others during narrated scenes as well as by readers of the text itself) but who also looks back. From a post-structuralist standpoint, the visually theatrical aspect of self-writing is part of its literally re-*visionary* potential, enabling the (potentially endless) performance of new identities.[8] Making her anomalous corporeality available to be witnessed, but also controlling the parameters of that looking, the female autobiographer exploits a cultural tension between gawking at the spectacle of physical difference and unabashed gazing at women's sexualized bodies. Crafting a renewed mirroring, she forces viewers to reappraise the meaning of what they see and commands her own liberatory visibility.

It is possible, clearly, to conceptualize a scene of looking in which a woman is both subject of an active, outwardly directed gaze and the recipient of looks that are not construed as coercive or objectifying. Looking can also link up with an organizing, authorial presence in fluid, speculative ways that create a narrative space for open-endedness rather than reductive or monological closure. But in the case of women's autobiography, writing oneself onto the stage of one's own narrated life has also entailed danger; historically, the desire to expose oneself to others' eyes has been considered proof of vanity, loss of chastity, and a usurpation of male prerogative. The female life writer, like a willful Venus, holds a mirror to herself and seems to revel in the constellation of gazes that manifests her as a worthy subject: she looks at herself, she sees others looking at her, she gazes back, and she watches herself being seen. Is she, then, to be read as a blank but also anxiety-provoking surface, held in place by the scopophilic drive of her male (or masculinized) readers? Grealy and Kleege suggest otherwise. If in some ways their texts exhibit efforts to deflect certain kinds of attention—the gawking stares of the nondisabled—from themselves, they tend nonetheless to maximize the specular effects of the autobiographical situation, making transgressively apparent the very bodies that patriarchal and ableist discourse has sought to control.[9]

One question that arises here is how Grealy and Kleege maneuver through the treacherous terrain of self-representation when looking at a disabled, female self and thinking about one's looks have been so deeply inflected by shame, a longing to appear "normal," and a stultifying sense of self-loathing. Unlike Nancy Mairs, Grealy and Kleege were already designated as "freakish" by the time they were teenagers and entering the psychologically and sexually turbulent years of adolescence. *Autobiography of a Face* and *Sight Unseen* each manifests (though in unique ways) the defining impact of illness and disability on a young woman's feelings about her own sexuality, as well as on her idea of herself as a woman in a patriarchal culture in which the parameters of normative sexual identity are circulated largely through visual imagery. Grealy's narrative demonstrates that the female subject who cannot be seen—or who sees in the mirror of others' looks not affirmation but shock—internalizes the horror of difference and learns to assess her own desire as insignificant, even a form of "weakness."[10] Kleege suggests that the woman who cannot see herself, or see herself being appraised, lurks at the periphery of full engagement with the world, minimized as a helpless shadow figure or construed and then contained as a manipulative vamp. In turn, both texts also explore the issue of authentic self-representation. As Sidonie Smith and Julia Watson ask of postcolonial autobiography, "When people have encountered representations of themselves as the objects of the surveyor's gaze . . . how do they begin to assert cultural agency"?[11]

I will argue that while Grealy and Kleege articulate opposing, perhaps at times even contradictory, positions on the importance of seeing oneself being seen to a woman's identity, both ultimately challenge the primacy of specular dynamics by orienting themselves, their narratives, and their readers toward new ways of being bodies. They do court a renewed gaze—looking without dominating, looking at themselves without objectifying, and looking back without capitulating to the master's gaze. But there is more at work in these texts than reappropriation of an empowered look. They also shatter the tyranny of the visual by unveiling the fiction of seeing as a stable mode of access to identity and reality. *Autobiography of a Face* and *Sight Unseen* are (perhaps paradoxically, given their emphasis on faces, eyes, and sight) what Arthur W. Frank might call body stories: stories "grounded in some form of [the] narrative wreckage" wrought by illness or impairment, which are also "act[s] of reclaiming" the self through touching, talking, healing, and writing.[12]

Writing as Refiguration: Lucy Grealy's *Autobiography of a Face*

In this narrative of disfiguring surgery to her jaw following cancer, Lucy Grealy does more than rewrite the "script" of female or disabled identity, as if the body were simply inert, "raw material" inscribed with cultural assumptions. While she does foreground the idea that selfhood is in part narrated by such forms of storytelling as movies, TV shows, and medical discourse, she also insists that the body exerts its own force, emphasizing the combination of language and body in the formation of self. Indeed, Grealy suggests that thinking in terms of "twoness" at all—of "body" and "mind" as discrete, if connected, entities—falsely separates what are interpenetrating and constitutive aspects of self. Instead, she demonstrates that her sense of self is inseparable from the condition of her face, even if, or especially because, that face is also subject to patriarchal attitudes toward female beauty and sexuality. Grealy writes not as a passive body onto which otherness, in the form of gender or deformity, has simply been pasted, but rather as a uniquely lived body enmeshed in social practice, family circumstance, and private desire.

To the degree that we cannot detach her narrative from her disease, Grealy suggests that there is also no way to disentangle the physical from the thinking mind or writerly consciousness we discover in *Autobiography of a Face*. She *is* her body, so far as we come to know her through her text—or as she declares, echoing Mairs's phenomenology, "my face, my 'self'" (170). At one level, Grealy risks enforcing the idea that women are bound to the flesh or that the "true" nature of the disabled is condensed in their afflicted body parts. In a similar way, the fact that she records the process of accepting herself after painful encounters with prejudice may seem to heroize the experience of disease. Yet I would argue that by openly displaying her "freakishness," on one hand, and by ultimately coming to terms, on the other, with a face that does not abide by societal norms, Grealy enlists corporeal difference to force a confrontation with cultural mythology—exposing the deleterious effects *not* of disease but, rather, of normative attitudes about beauty and identity. Far from solipsistically "confessing" her physical pain and hurt pride or sentimentalizing her triumph over adversity, Grealy provokes us to reconsider the notion of the disabled figure as a "normal" body gone wrong, an inversion or perversion of the ideal.

First diagnosed with Ewing's sarcoma at age ten, Grealy underwent extensive surgery that removed part of her jaw. More than thirty subsequent reconstructive procedures—a series of largely ineffective surgeries—attest to her own, as well as her parents' and her physicians', literally invasive need to normalize her even after the malignancy had been fully removed. Long after her condition has ceased to be life-threatening in what we might pretend is a strictly "physical" sense, Grealy's reshapen jaw lives on as a badge of sickness, a frightening indication of the body's mysterious interiority, a sign of the mind's failure to remain in control—in short, what Erving Goffman calls the "deeply discrediting" mark of stigma.[13] While Grealy may be said to return to a state of health, the condition of her face continues to signify that something is "wrong" with her, to mark her as abnormal, even perpetuating a kind of unhealthiness even after she no longer has cancer.

Undergoing her last round of operations to "correct" the mistake of her face, she reveals how embedded corporeal difference is in social relations: "Since physically I was capable of taking care of myself, and medically there was no need for me to be an inpatient, it did not escape my attention that I was being treated like a sick person simply because I did not look like other people" (216). In a culture that "tells us again and again that we can most be ourselves by acting and looking like someone else" (222), Grealy's face denies her the sense of legitimate individuality that is guaranteed by identification with the dominant culture's codes of female beauty, and she internalizes the message that physical difference is the outward manifestation of an "ugliness" of character or self. Unable to subdue her unruly body or to suppress the signs of her difference, she describes floundering attempts to adhere to the only available, and ultimately deeply alienating, social narratives of female subjectivity.

Yet far from suggesting that identity is merely a pageant of superficial tableaux, Grealy's life story coalesces around the persistent presence of her face. No quantity of operations suffices to assimilate her face into a universal model of normalcy, and in this it serves to underscore the power of discourse to construct disabilities out of bodily difference. As Susan Wendell points out, facial scarring "is a disability of appearance only, a disability constructed totally by stigma and cultural meanings."[14] But the futility of Grealy's willingness to transform her "self" in accordance with cultural demand reveals another important component of the meaning of bodies in culture: to quote Elizabeth Grosz, the body is not simply "a neutral screen, a biological *tabula rasa*" onto which cultural meanings are projected, nor does it exist only through representation.[15] Grealy's experience of her face is a specific and lived reality; it is mediated by social attitudes toward difference but not fully reducible to them.

In this sense, Grealy's "autobiography" reinterprets both the mind/body binary and the notion that bodies are purely discursive by repeatedly juxtaposing depictions of self-as-performative and self-as-corporeal, suggesting that neither alone is a fully adequate point of origin for subjectivity. By foregrounding the scripting of identity as well as the transformative properties of language, Grealy indicates that new stories of identity can be fashioned, creating new ways of conceptualizing and experiencing one's body. But the enduring presence of her face—the fact that it is her face, finally, from which all stories are told and to which those stories pertain—reminds us that bodies are neither superseded by nor wholly subsumed into discourse. Mark Jeffreys has made this point strongly, arguing that "the body's surprisingly stubborn resistance to reinvention," and not just its availability to narrative revision, must be acknowledged if we are to "mak[e] our culture accommodate physical difference."[16] The very title of Grealy's text speaks to the fact that bodies are stories (they are constituted in language) *and* that they have stories to tell (they have a reality or "perspective" of their own).

Autobiography of a Face begins with a discussion of Grealy's job as a teenager working pony parties, where she locates an early awareness of who she is "supposed" to be in the responses of others—especially the "open, uncensored stares" (7) of children—to the "strange triangular shape" (3) of her face. In the exclusive neighborhoods of suburban New York, where "house after house looked exactly like the one next to it" (2), inclusion is guaranteed by "carbon-copy" sameness, so that Grealy's appearance marks her not simply as one other body among many but as extra-ordinary, at once insufficient and excessive in her divergence from a physical norm. In the specific social context of "those back yards" (7), Grealy learns to occupy multiple positions of otherness: she is the working-class outsider, an Irish immigrant, a little girl whose home life lacks the coherence of an idealized nuclear family. But it is her face—"pale and misshapen" (6), "an uneasy reminder of what might be" (11)—that serves as the most salient ground of her difference. "I *was* my face," she writes, "I *was* ugliness. . . . Everything led to it, everything receded from it" (7). Utilizing not the adjective but the noun, Grealy represents herself as embodying the very condition of ugliness. Ugliness is not just one attribute of a whole person; rather *she* is ugliness itself. In the unabashed stares of children and the averted eyes of adults, Grealy reads her own form as "dangerous" (11), grotesque, unworthy of love. The social stigma against corporeal difference, ultimately derived from arbitrary categories of meaning, subsumes her identity in the visible sign of her disease.

Autobiography of a Face thus represents illness as more than a function of brute physiological process or even the very real battle of being "authentically sick" (20). The text begins not with a transparent account of Grealy's physical condition but, rather, with a description of the complex web of power relations that makes that condition legible; her "physical oddness" as a "disfigured child" (4) induces feelings of guilt and embarrassment not because her face is somehow essentially shameful but, rather, because it can be discursively interpreted as subordinate to other, "perfectly formed," children (10). In the protracted struggle to coordinate her appearance with a developing subjectivity, Grealy repudiates the structural reality of her face as having anything to do with her "true" self, dissociating the effects of surgery from her sense of who she "is." "Maybe this wasn't my actual face at all," she writes, "but the face of some interloper, some ugly intruder. . . . I began to imagine my 'original' face, the one free from all deviation, all error" (157). Her language makes explicit the cultural demonization of atypical bodily forms: Grealy herself perceives her own "misshapen" face as evidence of her incapacity to conform, a kind of moralized straying off course that signals a failure of self-mastery. In response, she compartmentalizes her sense of self, trying to contain "ugliness" in her chin and jaw; but when she attempts to integrate the two sections of her face, "the lower half canceled out the beauty of the upper half" (157), defeating any sense of identity apart from the belief that her face is a monstrous anomaly. As Thomson explains, within the totalizing narratives of cultural expectation, "the deviant characteristic overwhelms all of a person's other, unmarked aspects" (34). Persuaded that her "missing jaw" (154) represents an essential lack, Grealy feels "completely alone and without any chance of ever being loved" (155).

Thomson contends that "disability" is "an overarching and in some ways artificial category" that encompasses many more forms of embodied difference than simply the "prototypical disabled person" who "never leaves a wheelchair, is totally blind, or profoundly deaf" (13). By using the term to refer to a shifting range of traits—including progressive disease, acute illness, temporary injury, birthmarks, obesity, amputations, and the effects of so-called normal aging—Thomson emphasizes the point that disablement and dysfunction cannot be neatly confined to a subset of bodies marked by obvious loss or impairment; disability might be said to apply to any physical type other than the white, male, heterosexual, and able-bodied norm of Western culture. A "facial disfigurement" like Grealy's, Thomson would argue, is psychologically and socially disabling though not accompanied by "physical dysfunction" (14). The perceived abnormality of Grealy's facial shape, then—what Thomson would call a "formal" rather than a "functional" disability (14)—defines her whole self: she sees herself (and is seen) as weak, in need of tending, pity, or compensation.

Indeed, it is as if cancer is replaced by a form of "illness" that Patricia Hampl has named "the beauty disease": "the stark neediness and extravagance of wanting to be beautiful" in a culture in which "simply . . . [having] a physical existence" causes many women to see themselves as "freak[s]," their bodies a fleshly encumbrance they "dra[g] repulsively through the world."[17] If such self-punition is common among women whose bodies are deemed normal by cultural standards, it is particularly pointed (as Mairs also suggests) for those whose bodies defy the normative female form as well. For Grealy, the loss of "self-esteem" (200) associated with physical abnormality is inflected in an especially charged way by the fact that her difference is contained in her face—that part of the body that most resolutely signifies individual identity and that most immediately determines whether a woman meets cultural standards of beauty. So deeply connected is the face with both beauty and identity, in fact, that it is often not even thought of as part of "the body" at all—a distinction Grealy herself initially makes, referring to her "body" as "something I had control over" (208) and writing that, after hours spent working out at a gym, "even I had to admit I had a sexy body" (207). That Grealy's conviction of her ugliness is contained in the part of the body most often looked at—the part that, in turn, does the looking—produces a psychologically debilitating overlay of ontology and disfigurement. In a visually oriented world, a world that identifies looking and looks as the very ground of subjectivity, Grealy is swiftly and absolutely persuaded that her facial abnormality reduces her to something less than fully human, that the anguish of an anomalous face surpasses all other forms of injury or difference.

For instance, in a scene describing her first reconstructive surgery, Grealy mentions the woman in the neighboring bed, who is in the hospital for breast reconstruction:

> She insisted on telling me all about her scars and her feelings of ugliness. I had no patience with her lament: her face was beautiful, and she had a husband who brought her a dozen red roses. It was true she was missing a breast, but I didn't see how that mattered as long as she had these other things. No one could see her missing breast when she walked down the street, no one would make fun of her or think she was ugly, and someone loved her. (168)

Given the fact that talking "all about her scars and her feelings of ugliness" is precisely what *Autobiography of a Face* itself engages in, and considering the possibility that the loss of a breast might also, particularly in a patriarchal context, feel like an annihilation of self, this passage reveals how thoroughly the equation between identity and an idealized definition of beauty can be internalized. The scene demonstrates in an especially compressed way Grealy's teenaged complicity (she is sixteen at the time) in subsuming her whole self into what has already been constructed as a deviant face, so that when her hospital compatriot despairs of feeling whole or desirable, Grealy can only observe the other woman's situation through the scrim of her own prior sense of ineradicable failure.

The juxtaposition of face and breast, of two forms of cancer striking women in particularly "female" places, sets in relief the way in which disease, its impact on the body, and the body itself cannot be separated from the social and ideological relations in which these occur and are experienced. Grealy explicitly deploys a ranking system that privileges the power of men to determine a woman's worth: the missing breast is directly compensated for by an attentive husband, by the romantic cliché of "a dozen red roses," by "someone who loved her," whereas the solitary Grealy, devoid of such assurance, can neither perceive the similarities between their two circumstances nor respect the other woman's characterization of her own feelings. "Her problems lay in her perception," Grealy declares somewhat recklessly. "Talking with her only strengthened my conviction of the importance in this world of having a beautiful face" (168). As if taking on the role of an insensitive doctor (or perhaps an indifferent reader), Grealy invites us to consider what it means to see oneself according to cultural paradigms that enforce heterosexual norms of appearance and lifestyle, and how the pressure to conform to those norms produces a strange form of arrogant isolation that holds women in thrall to the operations of patriarchy.

Significantly, Grealy is an active observer in scenes such as this, confidently dividing and classifying. Yet the criteria she uses to make her choices and evaluate the data are patently skewed, and as *Autobiography of a Face* makes clear, she is the most aggrieved inheritor of her own mistakes. Some eighteen years after her first series of operations, Grealy admits, she still "couldn't make what I saw in the mirror correspond to the person I thought I was" (219). Her face is an "obstacle" that can only be "compensate[d] for, but never overcome" (206); each new reconstructive surgery is an attempt to "fix my face, fix my life, my soul" (215), underscoring the way in which a body read as broken becomes a measure of both social value and strength of character or spiritual worth. After one of her surgeries, she writes, "I saw my own face reflected back at me. Was that really me? I knew it had to be, but how could it possibly relate to the person I thought I was, or wanted to be? I considered the whole operation a failure" (175). Radically discontinuous in her imagination, "self" and "body" regard each other across a seemingly irreparable chasm contoured by the ideology of beauty.[18]

One might say that both her looking and her looks are distorted—she cannot observe herself in a way that is unimpeded by the expectation of "success," so that what she sees inevitably fills her with horror. Grealy describes a scene of furtive post-chemotherapy self-evaluation:

> I went into the bathroom and shut the door, though I was alone in the house. I turned on the lights and very carefully, very seriously, assessed my face in the mirror. I was bald, but I knew that already. I also knew I had buck teeth, something I was vaguely ashamed of but hadn't given too much thought to until this moment. My teeth were ugly. . . . I rooted around in the cabinets and came up with a hand mirror and, with bit of angling,

> looked for the first time at my right profile. I knew to expect a scar, but how had my face sunk in like that? . . . I was suddenly appalled at the notion that I'd been walking around unaware of something that was apparent to everyone else. A profound sense of shame consumed me. (111–12)

This experience is dominated by shame not so much because her face seems misshapen or out of proportion but, more egregiously, because looking becomes mediated by what Grealy imagines to be others' impressions of her. It is her blithe *unawareness* of her own ugliness that is so dismaying to her; in the catalog of despicable parts, what Grealy "already" knew about herself is overtaken by the discovery that what others have already seen of her is even worse. The new perspective from which she regards herself is more than a trick of mirrors; once the object of others' stares, she now repeats that objectification, regaining a form of control over her own image only by forcing her "belief" about herself "to match up with everyone else's" (111). It is a moment of definitive rupture: like Frankenstein's creature peering in at the window, the reflection in the mirror confronts Grealy with a face she cannot fit to any other tale but one of gothic horror, and shocked at the embodiment of her worst fears of alienation, she detaches from it altogether. Years later, she writes, "I hadn't taken a good long, objective look at myself since the wig fitting, but that seemed so long ago, almost two years. I remembered feeling upset by it, but I conveniently didn't remember what I'd seen in that mirror, and I hadn't allowed myself a close scrutiny since" (121–22).

It makes sense, in this context, that Grealy almost completely suppresses the fact that she has a twin sister. Sarah is mentioned only a few times in the text and always in terms of Grealy's *difference from*, rather than similarity to, her. At the start of the "adventure" (20) of her illness—when the novelty of it and the pleasurable attention bestowed on her have not yet been subsumed by physical stress and the crushing sense of ugliness—Grealy's special status is shaped by an explicit contrast to Sarah (promoted, curiously, by Grealy's mother): "She told me how brave I was and how lucky we all were that this had happened to me and not Sarah, my twin sister, an avowed scaredy-cat. Sarah would have cried horrendously, but I was courageous and didn't cry and thus was good" (20–21). The initial experience of the apparatuses of illness (hospital visits, surgeries, recuperation at home, kindly tending from nurses, time alone with her mother, and so forth) takes on a certain thrill precisely because it is Grealy's alone, something she does not share with her sister. Given the repeatedly stated desire for uniqueness (e.g., "I was vain and proud when it came to wanting to be different from everyone else" [25]), the minimal presence of her twin seems therefore more pointed than the limited mention of Grealy's siblings generally. Grealy never explains whether or not she and Sarah are identical twins, but even this omission seems telling—why would a text devoted to difficult questions of appearance and identity so studiously avoid the fact of twinship? Grealy's silence on this score would seem to argue for identical twinship, to the degree that it compromises her desire to be special, unlike others (itself a consequence of feeling marginalized, even before she is diagnosed with cancer).

It hardly needs explaining that—assuming Lucy and Sarah look a great deal alike—Sarah represents not simply the appearance of a "normal" girl but what Grealy herself *might have looked like* had she not had cancer, the face she could have had, the face she lost. But perhaps more important is Grealy's specifically authorial suppression of the complicated visual dynamic between her own face and Sarah's, the mirroring gone awry. Sarah exists as the other side of the very binary to which Grealy represents herself capitulating, making the division between beauty and ugliness excruciatingly literal. Grealy often remarks that some aspects of her face were pretty (she is complimented on her hair; she has "big blue eyes" [101]; a school friend tells her she is "beautiful" [62]; and so on). Are we then to assume that Sarah, her twin, is legitimately, wholly, pretty? By refusing to describe Sarah's face, Grealy textually refuses her own reflection—or at least, to see and to display herself as she might have been without cancer. Even before Grealy stops looking at herself in reflective surfaces completely, her narrative has already exacted a form of self-erasure, all the more paradoxical for the fact that it is so relentlessly focused on how she looks. The significant fact that Sarah "never had to worry about [her] appearance" (120) is only once (and briefly) referred to, and then only in the context of a group of girls to whom Grealy compares herself. The reasons for never describing what Sarah looks like are surely overdetermined, but in one way at least, Grealy exacts a stringent form of control over her image by deflecting her readers' gaze away from a face that must have served as a constant and painful indication of her inadequacy, and of the failure of surgery to make her whole.

At the same time, however, the erasure of Sarah's appearance enables Grealy to emerge in the narrative as an isolate individual, an autonomous self alone in an ordeal that, for all the anguished insecurity associated with it, is also depicted in terms of its dramatic and forward-thrusting urgency. The condition of her face—and the desperate hope that future surgeries will cure it—brings Grealy into being, and the portrayal of that being in terms of singularity allows her to represent herself as a self, however troubled that may be, rather than the broken half of a now-asymmetrical couple. The motion of the narrative, with its chronological linearity and thematic structure of surgery/disappointment/resignation/surgery, quests toward an ever-receding future in which Grealy's twin, as an emissary of the past, has no place; in a curious way Sarah, despite (or because of) how closely she may resemble the "old" Lucy, may be even less integral to this story of discontinuity and reconstruction than anyone else in Grealy's family.[19] It is also possible that after the first surgery that removed the right side of her jaw, Grealy simply stopped feeling like—or even being—a twin at all. For instance, she writes that the curious stares she elicits from strangers, while not always welcome, "defined" her as "special" (101). If sameness has already been denied by Grealy's bravery in the face of pain as well as by the surgery that forever alters her physical self, she can further extricate herself from the coupling of twinship by writing the *auto*-biography of the body part that differentiates her completely from everyone.

Paradoxically, then, it is precisely her illness that grants Grealy some sense, if provisional, of separate selfhood. Much of the book is concerned with descriptions of the various wards in which she spends so much time, with explaining the procedures she undergoes (more space is devoted to this, in fact, than to her own appearance). A certain cachet attaches to her intimacy with hospitals, to her fluency with medical jargon, linking her to "the cognitive and social authority of medicine," in Susan Wendell's words, to the "unblemished aura of knowledge and power" that tends to surround doctors.[20] But perhaps less obviously, the story line of illness itself grants Grealy a way of understanding herself: it is the very "role of patient" (25) that helps to consolidate an uncertain ego. Calling herself an "alien" (7) adrift in a welter of conflicting pressures, she ventriloquizes a sequence of roles aimed at diminishing, even while they depend on, the singularity of her face. Grealy describes her childhood self as "desperate for any kind of definition" (11), a performer "dependent" on the response of her audience, even a disapproving one, to feel grounded in stable subjectivity (4).

The disfigurement of her face, freighted as it is with cultural significance, provides her with what she calls "macabre status" (11), and she transforms her life as a hospitalized patient into a TV "drama" in which she is "the principal player" (20). Wanting "nothing more than to be special" (25) and to "prove her love" (100), she takes on the role of good patient, enduring chemotherapy without crying, but she also "allowed myself a condescending tone" (21) when talking to fellow patients "new at this hospital stuff" (168). Like the "protagonist of pathography" described by Anne Hunsaker Hawkins as a "denize[n] of a strange land," Grealy becomes the "hero who ventures into the perilous underworld of illness and death and returns to the realm of the ordinary with some prize or knowledge."[21] So thoroughly does Grealy begin to see herself through the lens of illness that when she nears the end of her chemo treatments, she fears a dissolution of identity: "I was afraid of it ending, of everything changing. I wouldn't be special anymore; no one would love me. Without the arena of chemotherapy in which to prove myself, how would anyone know I was worthy of love?" (136).

If disease affords Grealy a vantage point to which she would not otherwise have had access—a perspective against which she chafes but which she also represents as bringing her into being—it also, again paradoxically, conducts her toward reconciliation with her corporeal self. *Autobiography of a Face* sustains an important tension between the insights garnered through illness and Grealy's urgent desire to eschew the face she has for the fantasy face of idealized beauty. Obsessed with ugliness, convinced that "only another's love could prove my worth absolutely" (211) even as being "lovable" is synonymous with being beautiful, Grealy "blamed my face for everything," the "tangible element of what was wrong with my life and with me" (127). She represents herself time and again as an interloper in a world in which she feels displaced: "I was myself only in the briefest of moments" (89); "The only time I was ever completely myself was on Fridays" (90); "I possessed a strong sense of myself. . . . I had no sense of myself in relation to . . . 'normal' people" (105); "The barn became the one place where I felt like myself" (182); "The hospital was the only place on earth where I didn't feel self-conscious" (187). Recuperating from chemotherapy alone in a house typically crowded with siblings, Grealy becomes a "snoop . . . looking for clues to how other people lived their lives. . . . What was it like," she wonders, "to be somebody else?" (81). These repeated descriptions of casting herself into other identities—her intimations that "being herself" is but a fleeting experience, quickly overwhelmed by a much stronger conviction that she "was too horrible to look at," that her "ugliness was equal to a great personal failure" (185)—represent "self" as a thing deferred, held in suspension as Grealy awaits the face that will finally feel " 'real' " (157). "Beauty," she writes, "as defined by society at large, seemed to be only about who was best at looking like everyone else. . . . Each time I was wheeled down to the surgical wing . . . I'd think to myself, *Now, now I can start my life, just as soon as I wake up from this operation.* And no matter how disappointed I felt when I woke up and looked in the mirror, I'd simply postpone happiness until the next operation" (187).

But the reiterated disappointment that accompanies Grealy's hopes of finally achieving the physical ordinariness that will make her, paradoxically, "an individual" (157), is countered by the way in which her experience of disease heightens her attunement to her own body, as well as to the ideological manipulation of the body in culture. Cancer, chemotherapy, surgery, and recovery make Grealy "ever more intimate with [her] body" (57), with its "rhythms," its internal organs, its capacity for pain and for healing. Describing waking up from her fourth operation—the one that removed the tumor from her jaw—and limping across her hospital room, Grealy writes that "the body is a connected thing" (56), no one part of it fully discrete or able to be isolated from the whole. There is something irreducible, Grealy implies, about physical experience, "a meaning that [does] not extend beyond the confines of one's body" (149). In this sense, the state of being "diseased" both eludes linguistic representation and is endlessly available to the narrative constructions of social prejudice. She writes, "I was becoming aware that I was experiencing my body, and the world, differently from other people," "aware that normally I'd have no reason to 'feel' my body or know it so intimately" (90–91).[22] That slight parenthetical—"and the world"—points to the text's larger philosophical argument; not just a body in pain, Grealy is precisely a body in the world, and it is that perspective, "trapped in my own body," as she puts it, that escorts her to "occasionally even telling myself I was lucky, lucky to have this opportunity to know such things" (91). "Didn't my face open me up to perceptions I might otherwise be blind to?" she asks (150), only in part ironically, since it is her certitude that she is ugly that leads her eventually to revise her conception of "real beauty," to coordinate the face in the mirror with "the person I thought I was, or wanted to be" (175).

In this sense, the repeated display of what Grealy refers to as her "various personae" (38)—or to put it another way, Grealy's narrative emphasis on these semiotic performances—demonstrates at once both the power of cultural stereotypes to enforce conformity and the fluid possibilities of identity. If, for instance, Grealy camouflages her inability to achieve culturally approved standards of beauty by affecting the stance of androgynous poet as a college student at Bryn Mawr ("with my slight figure shrouded in baggy clothes, I was often mistaken for a boy," she writes; "I felt very far away from my own femininity" [203]), she also falls in with a crowd of "eccentrics," transvestites, and New York club-hoppers whose exaggerated versions of "woman" throw notions of natural or inherent femaleness into radical question. Later still, Grealy acts out a kind of hyperfemininity, brandishing her sexuality in spiked heels and miniskirts. "Not surprisingly, I saw sex as my salvation. If only I could get someone to have sex with me, it would mean that I was attractive, that someone could love me" (206). Here is the equation fulfilled: because she "had lost out on the world of love only because of [her] looks" (207), Grealy deploys her body as a distraction. Yet even as these efforts to fulfill her fantasies of goodness or prettiness merely reinforce Grealy's belief that she is unworthy, her face, with its intractable refusal to meet societal expectations, teaches her a different lesson. If the juxtaposition of various roles undermines our hold on any single, essential "Lucy," her ever-changing face becomes an unexpected point of reference—unexpectedly stable in that it is inescapable, always there, but also unexpectedly mobile, available to new meanings, revisable.

In a remarkable instance of the power of words to create reality, Grealy recounts her realization, after several years of living with disease, that what she suffered from was in fact cancer. "In all that time, not one person ever said the word *cancer* to me, at least not in a way that registered as pertaining to me. . . . Language supplies us with ways to express ever subtler levels of meaning, but does that imply language *gives* meaning, or robs us of it when we are at a loss to name things?" (43–44). As Grealy goes on to point out, words have histories; to know that she had "cancer" would have been to live in and through a reality of illness entirely different from the one "malignancy" and "Ewing's sarcoma" had already created. But as the autobiography itself confirms, this revelatory moment does not inevitably trap Grealy in a prison house of language. Her successive performances of culturally authorized identities anticipate a later understanding that she can redefine herself from within the frame of her face; so too does this scene of newly appreciating the density of words lead her gradually to comprehend that because the violence of cultural bias is deployed through language, it can be rewritten. The child who "save[s] herself by pretending" (115), who longs so desperately for "praise and appreciation" (123) that even being censured as a "freak" (155, 200) feels confirming, learns that the very overlap of physical difference and verbal narrative by which she feels herself barred from authentic participation in her relationships can make her "the creator of [her] own situation" (101).

By bearing witness to her own implication in myths of feminine beauty and bodily inadequacy, Grealy's story becomes a politically useful revision, a blueprint for conceiving of new ways of being. Grealy writes that "the journey back to my face was a long one" (220). She describes years spent "detaching" herself (179) from any desire other than to manufacture the face that will certify her worthiness; neither androgynous anonymity nor a spate of "highly charged sexual relationship[s]" with men serves adequately to define her or to compensate for the "obstacle of [her] face" (206).[23] Only by avoiding any reflection of her own image—not simply in mirrors but even in coffee urns, sunglasses, windows, door handles, and tabletops—does Grealy begin to separate a sense of self from her consuming preoccupation with physical beauty and to name "the person in the mirror" (220, 221) as herself. This process of recognition entails reconceptualizing her face, retrieving it from its isolated position as "a single stigmatic trait"[24] so that it no longer symbolizes some generalized inferiority, a deficiency of will or character, a failure to control the body—in short, what A. G. Gowman once termed a whole "gestalt of disability."[25] If not looking at her reflection makes Grealy a temporary exile from her corporeal self, it also allows her to relinquish what she describes as "the framework of *when my face gets fixed, then I'll start living*" (221) and thus to attend to other features of her subjectivity. Finally unable to depend on yet another operation to solve her feelings of inadequacy, she must incorporate her face, in a kind of literal way, as a member of her body, to experience embodiment as inextricable from her self. "A part of me . . . that had always been there," she writes, begins at last "to speak" (221).

In a well-known moment from her essay "Professions for Women," Virginia Woolf names one of "the adventures of . . . professional life" as "telling the truth about my own experiences as a body" (288).[26] Her confessed inability to "solv[e]" this problem, to make the female body visible by authoring rather than objectifying it, to grant a woman's corporeal experience a kind of truth status, becomes Woolf's legacy to later autobiographers. Narrating her past in the specific terms of living with illness, Grealy wrests what Leigh Gilmore calls "the agency of re-membering"[27] from hegemonic discourse and textualizes her body back together. But the effect—and, I think, the very purpose—of her "manifesto"[28] is not to guarantee a unified female body but, rather, to keep the "story" of the female body in motion, to show how the "truth" of particular bodies is open to revision. "Telling the truth" thus becomes a necessarily revolutionary act, a question not of establishing an essential femaleness but of "reconstruct[ing] the world," as Gilmore argues, "from a subject position not based on exclusion, violent differentiation, or the compulsory masking of identities."[29]

Grealy's face is an inescapable component of her identity, but its meaning is neither inevitable nor imprisoning. Grealy sets physical disease against cultural dis-ease, suggesting that the material conditions of surviving cancer and bodily "deformity" help her to discover something about living as a woman in patriarchal culture. In this sense both the body writing and the body described become thresholds, "neither," as Grosz argues, "—while also being both—the private or the public, self or other, natural or cultural,"[30] and thus disrupts the binary categorizations that underwrite cultural oppression. Moreover, by refusing to deflect the gaze from her face—indeed, by training her own as well as her readers' gazes steadily on the problematic of "the body" through her own physical experience—Grealy breaks the habit of accommodating a marginal self to social pressures through alternating denial and exaggeration of difference.

While *Autobiography of a Face* assures us that Grealy's face participates in the establishment of "who" she is, the text does not also try to pin down a definition of that person, or even of that face, in any closed, enduring way. Neither a story of triumph over adversity and physical disaster nor one that presumes a stable reference point, a "here" from which the story is told, *Autobiography of a Face* is an autobiography without resolution. Its ending is particularly ambiguous. In the closing scene, Grealy stages a metaphorical looking away, as if to ensure that the text, and the identity narrated therein, remains open-ended. After nearly a year of avoiding her image, Grealy finds that she has "no idea what [she] objectively looked like," and sitting in a café with a man she finds "quite attractive," she wonders what "he [was] actually *seeing* in [her]" and looks into the darkened window "to see if I could, now, recognize myself" (222–23). Lonely self-scrutiny and stark, clinical detail have characterized most of Grealy's prior descriptions of her face; here, however, she does not provide a single detail, even a medicalized one, of her current appearance. Preventing us, unexpectedly, from "seeing" her, Grealy intimates that the only gaze that matters is her own. At the same time, the implied turning-away from the window transforms Grealy's "visage" (200) from a specimen to be examined to simply one other face in a setting that is at once public and intimate. The "night-silvered glass" in which her reflection will be indistinct and the communal atmosphere of the café reflected in that glass—these too suggest that even Grealy no longer sees herself as solitary, as a solitary and contemptible body part.

Yet what of the male friend whose interest in Grealy is presented as both affirming and irrelevant? She writes that "for all those years I'd handed my ugliness over to people and seen only the different ways it was reflected back to me. As reluctant as I was to admit it now, the only indication in my companion's behavior was positive" (222). Is her willingness to look at herself, to come to terms with the face in the mirror, whatever its current contours, a result of male approbation, or is Grealy's positive reading of the man's engagement with her in itself an indication of her newfound self-acceptance? The ambiguity of this moment tells more than one story. Denying us access to her face at precisely the moment when it seems she might finally accept herself as "normal" or even "attractive," Grealy refuses to capitulate to a desire for definition and closure and so culminates her text by rupturing the very identity she had seemed so actively to seek. She writes that "in films and literature the dead know they are dead" when "they can no longer see themselves in the mirror" (222). Yet it is difficult to separate her sudden desire to look at herself in the window from the sort of romanticized encounter that has previously been the measure of her self-loathing. Do a man's attentions bring Grealy back to life? Could there be a scene of looking somewhere beyond a lonely bathroom with the door shut tight or a European café bathed in silvery light, itself the stuff of cinema?[31]

Grealy's preoccupation with how others view her visible, material presence reiterates (even if it also, ultimately, challenges) a cultural dictum about the relationship between female subjectivity and physical desirability. But I would also argue that Grealy's reclamation of an image in the mirror, of wanting to gaze at herself and to be gazed upon by appreciative others, signals an important move toward articulating her own desire. To the degree that disabled or disfigured women are encoded as asexual, Grealy's simultaneous connection to and separation from her male companion breaks through a certain barrier to an important representation of female sexuality that is quite different from her earlier, imprisoning relationships. It is this notion of breakage that Grealy brings to the fore in order to protest the cultural subject position of a disfigured woman, the paradox of being somehow nobody and nothing *but* body at once. One goal of disability autobiography is to counter what Thomson has described about the extraordinary body in literature ("literary texts necessarily make disabled characters into freaks, stripped of normalizing contexts and engulfed by a single stigmatic trait") by situating the body within the larger context of an individual's life story. As G. Thomas Couser argues, "Autobiography serves to deflect the gaze from a body that might otherwise trigger stereotypical responses."[32] By highlighting her experience as a disabled or disfigured body, however, Grealy goes one step further, not just insisting on the "ordinariness" of putatively different bodies, but also challenging readers to reconsider the entrenched notions of the body as a thing to be ignored, tolerated, or overcome by a controlling mind. Far from suggesting that Grealy ultimately transcends the weight and drag of corporeality, *Autobiography of a Face* is a declaration of inimitable embodied experience, as well as a window and a mirror in which we may recognize our own bodies, our own contingent selves.

Invisible Disability: Georgina Kleege's *Sight Unseen*

As Lucy Grealy's story makes clear, the physical self-consciousness demanded of women in patriarchal society is exaggerated for women whose bodies diverge from familiar norms. This expectation of beauty and self-indulgence makes facial disfigurement particularly difficult to bear. Because Grealy equates a worthy identity with a beautiful appearance, and because her culture signifies the shape of her face as monstrous and ugly, she concludes almost necessarily that she is unworthy, a body and self out of alignment. It is only after years and years of surgery—all those attempts to rectify the "error" of her face—that Grealy comes to recognize that changing the way she feels about herself requires a shift in perspective from within, from the inside of the body out. She learns to look at herself differently, to perceive what she sees—in a mirror, in others' eyes—from a different angle of vision. In this sense, Grealy is highly attuned to the very belief challenged by Georgina Kleege in *Sight Unseen*: that all truth can be discovered in and with the eyes, that an exchange of looks is the highest form of intimacy as well as the most potent mechanism of intimidation or power.

Autobiography of a Face and *Sight Unseen* are both accounts of conditions first identified in childhood (Grealy and Kleege were nearly the same age at the first signs of illness) and relatively unchanged since then. Their stories thus focus not on the progress of disease but on its aftermath, on the specifically visual interactions between changed bodies and culture. Both authors recount a profound desire to escape the confines of their bodies through performance, Kleege of sight and Grealy of a hyperfeminized sexuality. Embarrassed by stares but longing for an approving gaze, Grealy tries relentlessly to regulate her nonnormative body, as does Kleege, mimicking the operations of normal vision. "Offered no means of coping with my condition," writes Kleege, "(the word 'blindness' was to be avoided), I did everything I could to conceal it."[33] Both authors describe internalizing tenacious messages about normalcy that link social acceptance with an absence of identifiable difference. Ultimately, however, self-actualization in these authors' texts becomes something other than mere arrogation of looking. If Grealy's wish to be seen as a legitimate object of desire reminds us that ableism may objectify a woman with disabilities as asexual, thus complicating feminist discussions of the gaze, so does Kleege's eventual refusal to mime sightedness subvert a symbolic equation, common even in feminist theory, between vision and knowledge, intelligence, or self-control.

In the first sentence of *Sight Unseen*, Kleege announces, "Writing this book made me blind" (1). Such a proclamation establishes an important framework for this collection of personal essays, which investigate representations of blindness and sight through the conceptual lens of Kleege's own partial vision. The book's opening gambit invokes an entrenched cultural prejudice that reads illness as a kind of punishment, a sign of mental weakness or moral lapse. The implication that Kleege might have "made herself sick" by writing links her visual impairment with the unfeminine self-indulgence of art, even as it seems designed to instigate readers' pity for her diminished capacity. The author's physical limitation becomes the mark of her psychological overreaching and the proof of her audience's difference from her. Yet Kleege summons the myth of disability as otherness and failure only to disrupt it. Declared legally blind due to macular degeneration at age eleven, Kleege did not literally "go blind" during the composition of the book, but her statement underscores the relationship between self-creation and writing that is a key component of women's autobiography of disability. As Frank argues, quoting Paul Ricoeur, "The self only comes to be in the process of the life story being told: 'the *subject* is never given at the beginning' of a narrative."[34] Kleege suggests accordingly that only through the construction of *Sight Unseen* was she able to discover new, positive meanings for blindness and thus to claim a blind identity on her own definitional terms. Calling herself "blind" is not a capitulation to enfeeblement or helplessness but, rather, an act of defiant self-re-creation.

Kleege's story foregrounds the conflictedness of disabled subjectivity in a culture that privileges abled-bodied independence, the paradox of having to accept marginalized status along with the pressure to conform and perform "normally." The internalized stigma of blindness, Kleege argues—the "burden of negative connotations and dreaded associations"—encourages blind people "to sham sight" through technology and adaptation (19), even as those very efforts serve as a reminder of their failure to meet culturally agreed-upon designations of normality. Kleege writes that as her own vision began to deteriorate as a child, she learned quickly to disguise her difficulty reading books and blackboards and recognizing distant objects by mimicking the body gestures, the tone of voice, and even the facial expressions associated with sightedness. She thus raises questions about how a culture determines the limits of "normal" behavior, appearance, or physical ability and about how we understand and experience illnesses that do not render a person obviously or visibly disabled. Though Kleege's visual acuity is less than 20/200 (the barrier of legal blindness), she is nonetheless able to "pas[s] as sighted" in certain social situations (12); at the same time, she calls herself "imperfectly blind" (150), as if to suggest that what sight she has actually debars her from full participation in the category of blindness. In this way, Kleege's liminal condition shows us how the boundaries of identity are both highly arbitrary and easily disturbed.

Perhaps more importantly, however, *Sight Unseen* confronts a sighted reader's complacent trust in the certitudes of perception by situating the so-called norm on the margins of Kleege's own visual experience. Her descriptions of what her eyes perceive and how she actually looks at an object challenge a normative sense of the "right way" (96) to see. Because her form of macular degeneration leaves a very large "blind spot" in the middle of her vision, Kleege must "move [her] attention off center, viewing the world askance" (104). She holds objects an inch from her face, sliding her eyes from one edge to another in order to see with her peripheral vision. She stands "a foot" away from (93), then edges "closer and closer" to (94), huge canvasses in museums. Her "flawed vision" (147) necessitates a kind of literal "close reading" or Nietzschean slow seeing—two of the text's controlling metaphors. All this slowing-down and moving-in defies the notion that "seeing is both instantaneous and absolute" or that "sight provides instantaneous access to reality" (96). If the only proper way to see "is to take something in at a glance and possess it whole, comprehending all its complexities" (96), Kleege suggests, then her sidelong way of looking, "circumambulat[ing]"

(104) objects, becomes an ideological metaphor for displacing the eyes as the source of power and eyesight as a guarantor of knowledge and identity.

At the same time that she shunts vision to the side, Kleege introduces herself as a paradoxically authorized gaze. Neither the freak show spectacle who must protest her basic humanity to readers (what Kleege describes as the "conventional goal of blind autobiography" [3]) nor a hero whose will and fortitude defeat the defects of the body, Kleege repeatedly and confidently focuses her attention on her readers, speaking directly to and seeming to stare directly at them: "Look at me when I'm talking to you," she demands. "Do you really see all that you say? . . . Aren't you projecting your own expectations, interpretations, or desires onto my blank eyes?" (138). In one way, such provocations empower Kleege as the origin of language and meaning: her vision is panoptical (she knows where one's gaze is directed) and capable of undetected spying; she can control where one looks and even what impression one might have of the view. But the display of monological visual power is deceptive; Kleege's manner of looking moves her—and her readers—to the margins, where meanings are discovered rather than imposed. *Sight Unseen* redefines the meaning of blindness not so much by attempting to establish an equivalency between vision and blindness but, rather, by "disabling" sightedness itself, undermining its epistemological stability. "Vision involves more than merely aiming the eyes at a particular object," Kleege writes (2), but her aim is not to invoke notions of "insight" or "wisdom" that purport to compensate for the affliction of blindness. Rather, Kleege uses her gradual, tactile, relational way of seeing to illustrate that "there is no one way to look . . . no optimum vantage point or viewing condition" (147). Hers is a gaze transformed, a look whose approach to the stuff of the world, and whose sense of its own power, offers an entirely new dynamic of seeing.

In the first several essays of *Sight Unseen*, Kleege complicates cultural stereotypes about blindness and vision by demonstrating her facility for a variety of "sighted" activities. In "Blind Nightmares" and "In Oedipus' Shadow," Kleege presents herself as a skilled semiotician, deftly unpacking representations of blindness in literature and film. In "The Mind's Eye," she details her penchant for art museums and her unusual way of looking at paintings. In each of these instances, Kleege transforms a conventional understanding of what it means to be blind or sighted: how has a "legally blind" woman seen the movies and read the books she describes? What exactly does she "see" at the museum? Where other writers tend to generate a critique of dominant paradigms of disability strictly through personal experience, Kleege begins her story with an extended interpretation of culture's stories about blindness and vision. Beginning with Oedipus and ranging through texts as divergent as *Jane Eyre*, the 1967 film *Wait until Dark*, and Monet's water lilies, Kleege situates herself as just one other looker, as a participant in the visual world, a teacher as well as a partner in the project of "seeing." In short, she makes us viewers *together*, eliding herself as the object of our attention while simultaneously using her visual perspective to argue for the limitations of sight as one's sole or primary means of knowing the world. Kleege stretches the limits of identification with her readers, avoiding the dual seductions of voyeurism and sympathy —indeed, for much of *Sight Unseen* we are not looking at Georgina Kleege at all but, rather, at habits of looking themselves.

The cumulative and strategic effect of Kleege's discussion of movies and literature through two chapters is clearly to dissociate her from characterizations of the blind as "supernatural or subhuman, alien or animal," "different," and "dangerous" (28) and of blindness as symbolic of "fragility and helplessness" (55), "divine retribution" (71), or "the complete loss of personal, sexual, and political power" (69). But displaying her dexterity as a cultural critic allows Kleege not simply to protest the invalidity of such negative stereotypes; more to the point, she *proves* through her own performance of intellectual analysis their single-minded and reductive attitudes about loss of sight. Kleege makes her case less through personal outcry than through a scholarly marshaling of evidence, dismantling "facile assumptions about blindness" (65) by exposing the underlying cultural anxieties that motivate those assumptions in the first place. Narratives about blindness "are not about blindness at all," as Kleege suggests (58), but rather about a need to guarantee the privileged status of the sighted—a need which, in its turn, emerges from fears about the fragility and unpredictability of embodied identity. In what Susan Wendell has called "the flight from the rejected body,"[35] disability signifies all that must be carefully guarded against by normative corporeality: "tragic loss, weakness, passivity, dependency, helplessness, shame, and global incompetence." Kleege's staging of herself as an interpreter of myths of blindness thus serves as a specific refutation of the kinds of associations Wendell enumerates; far from weak, passive, or incompetent, Kleege takes charge—she surveys the ideological territory, she infiltrates, she squares off against an imagined reader's resistance to any suggestion that sightedness is less than immediate and unfailing. "Why not break this absolute dependence you have on your eyesight?" she queries (32). "The sighted can be so touchingly naive about vision" (96). If blind women in movies are "nothing but need" (51), requiring the assistance of male heroes to rescue and protect them, it is Kleege herself in *Sight Unseen* who seeks to "save" sighted readers from cultural misapprehensions about blind identity.

Positioned at the start of *Sight Unseen*, Kleege's deconstructive examination of blindness in film and literature deflects attention away from Kleege herself—from the "personal" or intimate details one tends to associate with the autobiographical mode—to such an extent that we lose "sight" of Kleege altogether, at least temporarily. One might forget that her own vision is at stake here, too—even that she herself is "blind," so thoroughly are reading and moviegoing associated with sightedness. Not only do these chapters demand, therefore, that stereotypes about the blind be reexamined; perhaps more pointedly, Kleege also puts pressure on the category of sightedness. "Blindness"—as a trope, a symbol, an event that must be interpreted and invested with meaning—is situated in the culture rather than the individual author, and Kleege further insists that whatever diminishment a blind person experiences is a function of social relations rather than personal insufficiency. Rejecting sustained autobiographical narrative at the start of her text, Kleege thus enacts on the page the sort of "favorable depiction" of blind people that she fantasizes might someday be possible in film: "Blindness would become invisible," Kleege writes, because "a 'realistic' blind person on screen would have so mastered the skills of blindness that there would be no need to draw attention to them" (57). Kleege's phrasing here—the "skills of blindness"—mimics Nancy Mairs's claim for disability as a threshold onto unfamiliar modes of erotic intimacy with her husband; impaired vision dissolves into just one other form of normal behavior. To speak of the skills of *blindness* rather than the skills of seeing is to disturb the hierarchical binary, figuring blindness not as tragic diminishment but as something *anyone* could learn to do, even as a kind of expertise or virtuosity. Indeed, Kleege encourages her readers to "practice" blindness as a way of decentering sight and relinquishing their monological—and ultimately anxiety-driven—grip on vision as one's primary mode of contact with, and sense of rootedness within, one's environment.

Only when we enter a Matisse exhibit with Kleege does her unique way of seeing come to the fore of her narrative. Kleege describes her behavior in museums in highly physical terms, as a kind of dance: "I perform a slow minuet before each painting, stepping forward and back, sweeping my gaze from edge to edge" (95). Such a procedure seems sequential and partial, resulting not in the instant intake, the global impression that the sighted claim to experience, but something more interactive, involving the whole body's motion in the process of looking.[36] As such, Kleege's sight is neither complacently unquestioned nor singular but, rather, dialectical and relational. Because she proceeds so methodically, Kleege forces a sighted reader to slow down, too, and to reconsider thereby the very process of making meaning out of what one sees. To see slowly is to resist the idea that one can "see" wholly and instinctively, that through seeing one achieves mastery over the phenomena of the world. From up close, Kleege observes details that casual viewing "overlooks"—texture, thickness, size, and color. "The most 'realistic' eye" in a painting "may be no more than a swirl of brown with a thin comma of white laid over"; Monet's water lilies are "crusty" rather than "liquid"; and abstract paintings have "depth and form" from two inches away (94). Reading such descriptions, one might begin both to imagine what Kleege sees and to remember one's own impressions of what painting looks like, an overlap that serves less to reify Kleege's identity as "impaired" than to upend a dominant belief in a single, correct way of looking—always to be understood as a correct way of "being."

Kleege, then, is "master" of vision and blindness alike, both instructor and student of the dynamics of looking and interpreting what can be seen. Resisting the inspirational narrative and cautious about positioning herself as "instructive spectacle, useful to everyone but [her]self" (90), she keeps readerly attention focused on the ambiguities and deceptions of sight generally, not the anguish or struggle of losing her sight in particular. Yet there is one "sighted" activity Kleege emphatically cannot participate in: eye contact. Where *Sight Unseen* starts from the premise that Kleege "find[s] it easy to imagine what it's like to be sighted" (3) because the dominant culture—from infrastructure to ideology—is so fully oriented toward the sighted (the marginal always knows the center), the chapter titled "Here's Looking at You" admits to feeling "confus[ed]" (122) by the "mystery" (124) of eye contact. Macular degeneration makes it impossible for Kleege to pick up facial details or even to perceive the totality of a person's face in a single glance. "When I try to look someone in the eyes," she explains, "he disappears" (124).[37] Since the same "off-center gaze" that troubles her fellow museumgoers makes her appear "shy, distracted, suspicious, bored, or untrustworthy" (124), Kleege "fakes" eye contact, aiming her eyes and face in the right direction, "perform[ing] tricks" (126) with her eyes that mimic the concentrated intimacy, the assertiveness or honesty, associated with a direct look.

That Kleege's experience of "see[ing] and feel[ing] nothing" could be interpreted as "the most significant visual exchange" (125) with another person throws into question the privileged cultural and theoretical status accorded an exchange of looks. (One imagines Kleege meeting Grealy—how might Grealy's perception of herself change in a face-to-face encounter with Kleege's off-center gaze?) "Here's Looking at You" repudiates the idea that because they are "excluded from [the] constant, kinetic interchange" of eye contact, the blind "must take the sighted's word" for its importance and trustworthiness (131). Kleege focuses her discussion on what eye contact is believed to reveal—the "truth" of a person's psychical or ontological state—as well as on the contextual data that contribute to our assessment of the "genuine" emotion allegedly communicated by the eyes. What the sighted attribute solely to eye-to-eye understanding, for instance, Kleege explains as a function of the entire face and body: stretched skin, widened eyelids, light reflected off the eyeballs, furrowed brows, and twitching lips. Again, the effect is to shift the reader's perspective away from the eyes themselves and onto what surrounds them. Compared to the specular exactness claimed by the sighted, Kleege admits that she "focus[es] too much on the peripheral details" (128) for her to appreciate fully the significance of eye contact. Yet what lies at the periphery of vision is precisely Kleege's concern in *Sight Unseen*. Calling attention to the stage of looking—all the details from body posture to setting to desire and projection—Kleege suggests that the presumed guarantees of visual contact are, on one hand, partial and gradual and, on the other, comprised of myriad pieces of information that *supplement* what the eyes alone exhibit. Thus by conveying to her readers all that presses into a scene of looking from the surround, Kleege explodes any idea that we have access to, that we can "know," the other's "interior" just by looking into his or her eyes.

As a result of what Kleege cannot *see*, the essay concentrates on what *she* "knows": the physiology of "the visual system" (128); the artificial strategies (airbrushing, dilating eye drops) employed by actors and fashion models to maximize the specular effects of their appearance on film; the sighted habit of employing metaphors that "point to the eyes . . . as the site of all significant experience" (131). At the same time, however, Kleege also repeats such words and phrases as "apparently" (134, 137), "I assume" (133), "I'd like to see" (132), "I've heard tell" (136), and even "I miss the point" (129). These terms seem to emphasize the cultural displacement of the blind. As one who cannot make eye contact, Kleege doesn't "get it," and thus she speaks tentatively; she seems cognitively "blunted," out of the social loop. Yet the fundamental pressure point here is less blindness than sighted arrogance about eye contact, with all the psychological, erotic, epistemological charge of that phrase held under scrutiny.

Kleege situates herself in a sighted milieu where stories are trafficked as truth, a world where people uncritically "tell" the appropriate narratives of cultural myth. The doubt and uncertainty implied by "apparently" or "assume" pertains not at all to Kleege's limited understanding, then, but instead level the author's skepticism against what people insist they can discern from the eyes. By figuring the certitudes of eye contact as the product of a kind of rumor mill, Kleege interrogates one of sighted culture's most sacred forms of accessing another's true self, refusing to take for granted—to take anyone's word for—what constitutes meaning, significant experience, or identity.

A discussion of the local, interpersonal event of eye contact, then, becomes a critique of technologies of understanding, of culturally sanctioned mechanisms of interpretation and assessment. Kleege foregrounds how sighted ideology reduces knowledge and meaning to the single action of seeing, wholly subsuming the participation of our bodies, our expectations, and our desires into the mythologized behavior of eyes. She concedes an evolutionary and biological basis for the importance of vision (citing, for example, mother-infant mirroring and the predatory advantage of forward-directed eyes), but she refutes the symbolized, romanticized, poeticized assumptions about eye contact that deny legitimacy to other forms of making contact with the world. (Again, consider Grealy's claim to be able to "see" something meaningful in the looks she receives from others.) The sheer "diversity" (136) of the stories Kleege recounts about the impact of eye contact reveals more, finally, about sighted people's belief in its authority than about any real access it has to "reality." And if power cannot be said to reside in one's ability to see, then power itself must become open to reclamation, and identities constructed within certain cultural configurations of power are in turn available for rewriting, revision. In effect, Kleege looks back in this chapter and performs her own version of eye contact with her readers. "Pull the wool off your eyes," she commands us. "Tell me what you see" (138).

If it is possible to see in a different manner—off center, askew, up close, and side to side—*Sight Unseen* also argues that we can "see" with a different part of the body. To contest sight as culture's dominant mode of knowing (a structure that necessarily assumes the blind as less than fully human or grants them supererogatory and highly idealized "insight"), Kleege defocuses the eyes entirely and shifts to the hands, examining various forms of touch as a powerful form of knowing and relating to the world. Janet Price and Margrit Shildrick have argued that "our sense of touch is every bit as important as, if not more important than, sight in mapping out the morphology of our bodies and of the spaces in which we move. . . . Touch, unlike sight, is quintessentially an interactive sensation. . . . Touch frustrates hierarchy, and crosses boundaries rather than creates distance."[38] In a scene that dramatizes this idea exactly, Kleege relates an early memory of her father, an artist known for large-scale sculpture, helping her to weld together pieces of metal: "My hand moves inside my father's hand. His index finger lifts and points. I look where he points. I draw the flame to the point. . . . Like most of our conversations, this one was essentially wordless, conducted hand-to-hand, my small hand inside his" (163). The scene accumulates images of both real and symbolic connection—the fused scraps of metal, one small hand clasped within another, daughter to father, human to metal, idea to "form and dimension" (163)—that reflect a central preoccupation in *Sight Unseen*. To be "hand in hand" with the world is to refuse a subject position defined by static hierarchies of gender and health that equate women with receptive passivity, physical difference with helplessness. Though she was not yet blind in the scene above, the metaphor of welding shapes one of *Sight Unseen*'s central propositions: American cultural myths of self-reliance and isolate identity privilege male able-bodiedness and condemn intersubjective relations, caretaking, and disability as signs of—or thresholds onto—regressive dependency.

In contrast, Kleege argues for reciprocity and mutuality, for "conversations" between people and between people and things in the world that unite body and idea, hands and eyes, words and movement. Kleege suggests that communication does not derive solely from sight (that, indeed, it may not even require sight) and that it is only through the mutual interaction of embodied selves that the myriad seams of reality and identity stay "fast and lasting" (163). To quote Sarah E. Chinn, Kleege utterly "unseat[s] the visual from its perceptual throne."[39] Relationality, in Kleege's articulation of it, informs everything that she does—from seeing and reading to teaching, writing, and making art—in a way that challenges both reductive models of female identity as selflessly oriented toward others and others' feelings *and* feminist wariness of need.[40] Importantly, the scene of welding with her father emblematizes a relational experience in which meaning emerges from active partnership rather than domination or mastery.

The quintessential manifestation of this dialectical phenomenology, the most potent instance of "hand-in-hand" contact with information and meaning, is Kleege's decision to learn braille, a process she begins only as an adult.[41] Reading braille is profoundly physical, involving the whole self from fingertips and arms through the shoulders and into the head, brain, and mind. Reading this way, Kleege reactivates her body in communication with the world, empowering her hands in the place of her eyes. But she does more than propose hand reading as secondary compensation for the loss of sight. "Close reading" had once signified Kleege's literal proximity to a computer screen or a printed page—she describes herself as "the physical embodiment of close reading" (198)—and therefore measured the distance between Kleege and "normally" sighted individuals, whose eyes "process as many as a dozen [characters] at a time" compared with Kleege's "three" (199). But despite her wry analogy to the textual habit of "dwell[ing]" (197) closely over textual detail (Kleege was a Yale undergraduate and writes that she "felt physically well-suited, if not predestined, to be a close reader" [198]), the liberating possibilities afforded her by braille have little to do with New Critical interpretive practice or ideology. The tactile reading of braille allows Kleege to rediscover a way of being in the body that her struggles to read with her eyes had forced her to relinquish. With her eyes, Kleege is in fact an inefficient reader; with braille, she reads more quickly, with less strain and greater mobility. With her hands at work, Kleege can in fact move *away* from the page, letting her body uncoil, stretch out, and relax: "The frantic uncertainty of reading print was gone. And there was no pain. . . . I was serene, floating" (204). Moreover, hand reading has the unexpected effect of disguising Kleege's visual impairment. Comparing the logistical problems of giving public readings by sight to the ease of reading by braille, Kleege writes that "[her] blindness is less visible to [her] audience" (227). In a paradoxical way, reading braille makes Kleege both more and less "blind"; it is one of the "skills" of blindness that indicates her difference from the sighted world even as it strenuously resists negative connotations of failure or inadequacy.

Reading braille thus carries an even more political valence in that it serves to mark identity: "The way we read defines who we are" (217). To choose braille, to read not with the eyes but with the fingers, is to seem to regress to a benighted state of incapacity and to openly identify oneself as disabled, to repudiate the promise of low-vision aids and thus of "progress"—but it is also, accordingly, to reject sightedness altogether and so to defiantly claim disinterest in trying to be or seem "normal." Because Kleege does have some sight, because she can, however "imperfectly," read with her eyes, her decision to learn braille inspires resistance and anxiety from those who are threatened by her apparent indifference to a sighted way of life. "Braille is a part of the dim and dire past, not the desirable present," Kleege explains; "my desire to learn braille cast me as an eccentric Luddite" (215). The issue is less old-fashioned recalcitrance about technology, of course, than it is the choice of "blind" behavior over sighted, a willingness to "be seen" as blind when gadgets and machinery could allow her to mimic the practices of the sighted. Kleege makes the point that reading braille has to do with more than just convenience, physical comfort, access to materials, or lower costs; a far more confrontational desire to challenge the dominance of the norm is at stake here, a call to widen the array of ways of being in the world and of articulating subjectivity. "The first time I read my name in braille," Kleege remarks, "made me muse on identity again: 'This is me in braille' " (217–18). Reading braille thus effects a shift in Kleege's sense of herself as a person and as blind; far from confining her to a state of diminishment, braille is generative, creating new possibilities, surprising her with the discovery of an unfamiliar but no less legitimate self. Braille enables Kleege to move back and forth across the divide between ability and disability, to transgress and thus to destabilize that boundary. “Me in braille” is just one more self, one more version of Georgina Kleege.

“Up Close, In Touch” recounts Kleege’s pursuit not only of braille but also of the life of Louis Braille himself, including an odyssey to the Braille museum at his birthplace in Coupvray, France. Kleege details the accident that blinded Braille as a child and his later perfection, as a teenager at the Paris Institute for the Young Blind, of a system of coded dots. She acknowledges her admiration for Braille’s “strength of character” (225), his willingness to take enormous risks in the face of institutional resistance to adopting his new system (a resistance ultimately due, Kleege implies, to sighted fear about the ramifications of empowering the blind with the ability to read). Identifying with Braille because he “stood up to sighted authority and said, ‘What you offer is good. What I offer is better’ ” (225), Kleege in turn indicts her own culture’s oppressive myths of normalcy and impairment. And by ending with Braille’s story, *Sight Unseen* wraps itself back to the rhetorical mode with which it began: making use of cultural representations of blindness in order to uncover the power dynamics and ideological anxieties that contribute to their perpetuation.

Braille’s life narrative becomes significant at this particular juncture in the text for several reasons. By emphasizing Braille’s inventiveness and lingering over the crafty subterfuge whereby students utilized his system despite the threat of expulsion from the school, Kleege implicitly counters the very stereotypes of blind helplessness that hindered Braille and his peers. The story also provides a historical context for Kleege’s insistence on learning braille and on her own refusal to fully accommodate herself to the dominance of the visual. Braille’s system, and his insistence on its usefulness, resonates with Kleege’s own project in *Sight Unseen*; she too defies cultural authority by telling an alternative story of blind identity and by creating a new language with which to articulate a blind and female subject. As we read about Kleege’s discovery of Braille and his refusal to accept defeat in the face of cultural pressures against his new language, we have been situated in Kleege's own position, witnessing *her* invention of a new vocabulary with which to spell out the world and herself within it. And she reminds us powerfully that no identity is ever unattached to others in the world; far from superseding her voice or story, Braille's narrative is adamantly Kleege's—she is the mediator, the translator, the bilingual interpreter, the legatee of the freedom of braille, and the creator thereby of her own new story.

Kleege argues that the linear structure of conventional blindness autobiographies reaffirms the idea that blindness can be separated from the "self" as an affliction one overcomes; a narrative of transcendence and resolution "presupposes that blindness is somehow outside oneself" (4). Describing her own book as a " 'coming out' narrative" (5), she suggests that the radical intent of *Sight Unseen* is to claim blindness as constitutive of identity in ways that are surprisingly, unfamiliarly positive. The three sections of the text proceed from the opening discussion of "Blindness and Culture" through "Blind Phenomenology" to "Voice, Texture, [and] Identity." In one way, this sequence seems to move us steadily "inward," ever closer to some "authentic" Kleege. But I would argue that the trajectory of Kleege's text is in fact deliberately anti-linear and nonprogressive; *Sight Unseen* charts a mock-journey or quest that presents the self not as an isolate individual triumphing over cultural forces but, rather, as something one accumulates in contact with the stuff of culture. In its gesture toward the typical life-path structure of men's self-writing, *Sight Unseen* also exposes what is usually left invisible in canonical autobiographies: the influence of cultural mythology, the expectation of a "normal" body, the triumph of mind and will over the body and the circumstances of birth. Culture is thus not so much a secondary "background" against which Kleege's singular subjectivity stands out in high relief but, rather, the very material from which she explicitly fashions a sense of self.

Sight Unseen follows few of the generic patterns of Western life writing; its parameters are neither a masculinist public domain nor a feminized domestic sphere. Kleege's investment lies more with deciphering how people see than with the telling of her own story, and she thus subordinates her childhood and "interior" experience to her adult, active participation in a sighted world. The fact that Kleege's essays are less personally revelatory than other autobiographical writing by disabled women (compare Mairs's and even Grealy's more relentless anatomization of their shame, sexual longings, and acquiescence to patriarchal lessons) calls particular attention to the dynamics of gazing, raising questions of access and authority; Kleege lets us "look" only so long, and at only a narrow compass of her life history. Asking, "Incompetent, dependent, potentially unruly, sexually deviant—is this really how the sighted see the blind?" (57), Kleege situates her project in the context of what Wendell refers to as the "disciplines of normality." If inhabiting a world that privileges sight requires Kleege to disidentify with herself as blind, then writing herself into a blind identity means having to create new and acceptable versions of blindness that contest inhibiting stereotypes. The goal seems neither to prove equality with the sighted nor to announce her triumph over impairment but, rather, to dislocate her readers, to encourage not so much identification between readers and author but instead a greater awareness of *every* embodied self's location in a particular cultural milieu.

It is therefore curious and also telling that Kleege's relationship with her father is the only intimate one to figure prominently in *Sight Unseen*. The text devotes a chapter to him, titled "A Portrait of the Artist by His Blind Daughter." Why is the father singled out, when Kleege is so circumspect about any other significant relationship? (Her husband, Nick, and her mother, also an artist, are mentioned but do not factor as "characters" to nearly the same degree.) The father serves here as what Paul John Eakin has called "the *proximate other*," that figure ("most often a parent") whose relation to the autobiographer so defines the life lived that the story of self can only be told as a partial biography.[42] It is possible that the father's death protects him and Kleege alike from the dangers of misrepresentation. But whatever ethical concerns may underlie this portrait, two important and intertwined thematic issues also motivate its inclusion: patriarchal authority and the broken body of the father. Kleege states that she "inherited [her] flawed vision" (149) from her grandmother, who developed the more common form of age-related macular degeneration, and that the linchpin of this connection is her father, through whom the "defective gene" passes (150). These two other impaired bodies establish a familial legacy of responding to illness in ways that reinforce the agon of mind and body, defining consciousness as if it were at the mercy of an unruly body—unless it can be subdued through enormous force of will.

Kleege explicitly describes her grandmother as a hypochondriac who used illness "to manipulate the people around her" (149). Partially sighted, like Kleege—or "imperfectly blind"—the grandmother was suspected of "faking" incapacity, of disguising how *capable* she actually was, so that her health problems became a sign of what was assumed to be psychological weakness. The father had "doubts about the severity of his mother's blindness" and read physical impairment as proof that she was "dependent, fearful, and needy" (150). This resentment of and resistance to his mother's ailments is bound up with Kleege's father's own childhood infirmities—asthma and other respiratory problems—and his mother's anxiety about the severity of these conditions, which Kleege describes as "almost completely debilitating" (151). Kleege's father learned not only to suspect sickness in others as deceptive and manipulative, then, but also to deny physical limitation in himself. Kleege writes that he deliberately transformed himself into "an extremely athletic adolescent" (151), and she specifically links the scale and muscularity of her father's artwork to his determination to overcome any vestige of the "sickly" child that his mother feared he was (and, we are to assume, very nearly produced in him).

Kleege's own vision problems are thus shaped by an environment of distrust and detachment from the body. Kleege admits that she internalized a sense of guilt about her "flawed vision" (150) and exaggerated her self-sufficiency to protect her father not just from the bad feelings associated with her "defect" (150) but from his sense of personal inadequacy or defectiveness as well: "If I could preserve the illusion of normalcy, I would remain unflawed" (150). In the Kleege family, the body becomes the source of falsehood and denial, demonized as an instrument of interpersonal treachery or suppressed as an obstruction to proper gendered behavior and parental approval. If Kleege's father's relationship with his mother is inflected by suspicion, Kleege's with her father serves as an index of

the way in which disabled women often experience their anomalous bodies as obstacles to specifically *male* approval and desire. While her father's effort to deny bodily weakness merely reiterates masculinist norms of singularity and strength, Kleege's similar effort signifies a problematic association between denial of self and the need to please an authoritative father.

Kleege's father renounces his illness to move away from his mother (presumably heightening her worry and therefore linking health and autonomy with repudiation of the mother); Kleege disguises her illness to move *toward* her father, assuaging *his* guilty feelings and subsuming her needs into his. When she writes that her father "resisted any impulse he might have felt to disable [her] with paternal protection" or that her blindness "never limited his expectations of what [she] could do or become" (151), such claims seem somehow disingenuous, particularly because Kleege also states that her father had a kind of morbid curiosity about her ability to "mask [her] lack of sight" (151). While the father may have respected and stimulated Kleege's intellect, his fascination for her ability to "fake" sight—for the "artifice" of healthiness—nonetheless imposes on Kleege an explicit association between intimacy and normalcy. Kleege writes that because "complaining" about her condition "would only make [her] more troublesome and less lovable" (207), she impersonates sightedness: "It was . . . easier to pretend that I saw what they did" (208); "I could only draw a version of what he saw" (151).

Disability repeats itself not only genetically but also ideologically, circulating in families who take their cues from cultural attitudes toward gender, illness, and generational conflict. "A Portrait of the Artist" shows us that art is similarly relational, that it is created not by the "vision" of the solitary genius but rather by the many layerings of social dynamic. The chapter begins by announcing that Kleege and her father "disagree[d]" (139) about eye contact, suggesting again that "visual experience is relative" (139) and thereby initiating an extended meditation on the various connections between seeing, disability, and art. The father's giant sculptures take shape in direct reaction to Kleege's grandmother's attitudes toward bodily ailment. In turn, Kleege's art signifies an explicit break from her father's denial of both his own illness and her blindness. Her way of writing —the fact that she *is* a writer and not, say, a dancer—emerges from her need to tell the story of what she sees, to intervene into familial and cultural tale-telling about blindness and gender. In its discussion of art, family, and illness, the chapter actively blurs a series of binary oppositions, deconstructing the boundaries that separate father from daughter, the disabled from the norm, the literal from the representational. Kleege's "portrait of the artist" is thus also a self-portrait, exploring the familial and social constructions of blindness that inform her identity as a writer.

When Kleege tries to describe exactly what she sees, for example, she paints in words, passages as clearly and lyrically rendered as if she were describing an actual painting or writing poetry. Yet she confesses that "words are only the restless prowl around and around the thing I want to name, a spiral search from the periphery toward the center. But words are at least a point of departure" (153). In a parallel movement, Kleege's father returns to painting late in his life (too weakened from cancer, emphysema, and tuberculosis to continue his metalwork) and produces small abstracted pieces that resemble the "splinters of color," the "pulsating shimmer" of Kleege's own vision (159). Words and painting: each is instigated by physical collapse and by a desire to acknowledge both the simultaneous failures and continuity of the body. Kleege writes of one of her father's paintings, "I could hold it over any image and say, 'This is what I see.' It's not quite right. . . . But it's close enough. A point of departure" (159). The repeated phrase—"a point of departure"—joins words and painting in a shared understanding that no medium can make stable and solid what is ever threatening to come apart. The polysemic swirl around an absent center—words that only haunt the edges, "slashes of color" that "spiral" inward as if into the depths of a "cone" (159)—invoke the same "central black hole" (153) of Kleege's vision, the "frayed" cells of her retinas (155). These metaphorical eddies are precisely the point: there is no transcendental signified, no "truth" at the center that writing, painting, sculpting, or "perfect" vision could ever hold firm. All forms of storytelling, Kleege implies, from family legends to cultural mythology, are only a point of departure, endless beginnings that initiate inconclusive journeys. It is the attempt to travel that matters, Kleege has us understand, and the willingness to keep one's head turned toward the margins, toward the vibrant colors and shapes that occupy the periphery of our vision.

There is a subtle distinction between Kleege's somewhat guarded text and Lucy Grealy's more overtly "confessional" one. Through much of *Autobiography of a Face* Grealy is a prisoner to the gaze, but she also takes a risk that Kleege does not, letting us look not just at her face but at her own subjection to cultural stereotypes. Whatever temperamental differences might play into the authors' willingness to reveal intimate detail, I would argue that ideological considerations also undergird the respective levels of self-scrutiny in these two texts. That Kleege's text looks so consistently *outward* may suggest the position of a blind woman in a sighted world, attuned not only to her appearance but to the very operations of seeing and perceiving as well. Kleege writes that the "obsessive self-preoccupation" expected of blind women in cinema would "label a sighted woman as a dangerous vamp" (55). But Grealy's situation suggests otherwise, that coercive myths equating beauty and worth *do* instigate a self-preoccupying mentality in sighted women. It is perhaps corporeal difference generally, rather than blindness itself, that underlies the frantic effort to achieve culturally approved ideals of beauty or sexual attractiveness. Difference is a liability that must be corrected for, covered with "prettiness" or sex appeal.

From their unique perspectives, then, Grealy and Kleege articulate both sides of the subject-object dynamic, complicating our understanding of what it means to be seen and to look, to be the object of derisive stares or gratified gazes as well as the subject of a presumably masterful vision. Kleege unravels the binary that would marginalize her as defective even as she claims a disabled surface (braille, cane); Grealy heals the breach of self and rejected body even as she provokes thought about how we define what is and is not beautiful. Grealy's rapprochement with the face in the window is akin to

Kleege's account of learning to read braille and of deciding to carry a cane, and the culminating pride with which she "announce[s] [her] blindness without apology" (227). Together, *Autobiography of a Face* and *Sight Unseen* demonstrate the tension prevalent in disability narrative between identifying as disabled and simultaneously resisting the stigma associated with disability. In effect, each text does both: pointing out the ways in which their conditions are different, requiring certain kinds of apparatuses, treatments, surgeries, and so on, they also call attention to how their conditions are signified culturally. Acknowledging the body as "different," they then question the fictional and discursive terms by which we understand the self-same, inclusion in the world of the normal. Each author rejects, finally, her own acts of regulating and repudiating her body, mounting a revolt against the tyranny of the visual.

3 sexual selves, community allegiance

Connie Panzarino & Eli Clare

I have been exploring how the lineaments of anomalous bodies map new relationships between gender, selfhood, and social expectation. Disability appears in the texts discussed here not as the negative half of a binary that writers hope to transcend (which would do little to effect real change in attitudes toward gendered and corporeal difference) but, instead, as a wedge that pries those oppositional terms apart, revealing the fictive stability of normative categories. But what happens when disability and gender are only two of multiple forms of difference, and perhaps not even the most salient? If, as so many disability activists have argued, mainstream feminist theory has elided the concerns and experience of disabled women, what do lesbians and queers have to say about disability studies?

The representation of impairment or disfigurement in the works of Mairs, Grealy, and Kleege is concerned with problematizing a binary matrix that constructs female subjectivity as both failure and ideal, the inferior underside of a masculine norm as well as a mythologized collection of largely unattainable attributes. These writers contest regulatory (and often contradictory) narratives that promote beauty, sex appeal, and marriage as the determinants of a successful female existence and according to which disabled women are necessarily construed as failures, less than whole, and even vaguely inhuman. They voice potent protests against the invasive and violent effects of patriarchal ideology, demonstrating how contorted selfhood can become within the framework of enforced, reductive roles. The dissonance they experience derives in part from the gap between what they are taught to desire (male approval, some phantasmic standard of beauty), their own sexuality (each is straight), and who they have been taught they are (undesirable, broken, sick, dependent). A woman's worth is to be sought in the nature of her attachments to men, the very arena from which she may be debarred by disability or physical difference. The result is uncomfortable contradiction: *desire men*, heteronormative culture instructs, even as it shunts anomalous bodies to what Judith Butler has called "those 'unlivable' and 'uninhabitable' zones of social life"[1] that lie beyond the borders of the dominant able-bodied subject. Who is the subject of such desires as a disabled woman might have, and how does she experience the urgencies of desire given her experience of a body marked by shame?

The writers discussed thus far have answered such questions differently. Nancy Mairs excoriates her youthful implication in fairy tales and myths of romantic union, but she also describes a series of extramarital affairs as symbolic of the entanglement of power, identity, and embodiment that she struggles to resolve. Lucy Grealy records her sexual behavior as a simultaneous capitulation to and defiance of both the "truth" of her face and an association between being lovable and sexually appealing. Georgina Kleege says nothing explicit about her sexual life but presents herself as a "normally" married woman as she critiques the pressures on blind women to look pretty, to attract and/or depend on men. Each writer enters the terrain of sexuality in order to splinter the connection between a legitimate sexual identity and able-bodiedness; from Mairs's unabashed descriptions of sex with George to Grealy's café conversation to Kleege's offhand mentions of her husband, the broken or impaired female body no longer signifies sexual deviance or lack. But to some extent, these narratives of self-actualization are still grounded by men; husbands and past or potential lovers locate the self-representational project in something familiar, acceptable, legitimate. The point is not to mistake individual relationships with men for the broader political and philosophical complexities of patriarchy, to be sure. Yet to a degree, these writers negotiate their sense of themselves—as women, as rejected bodies, and as sexual agents—within a heterosexual paradigm that, while it may frustrate or contort their desires, does not mark the desire for a male partner per se as abnormal.

For the lesbian or queer life writer of disability, the relationship between identity, sexuality, and the impaired body is inflected somewhat differently. Building on Adrienne Rich's foundational critique of the naturalness of heterosexuality, several recent studies have argued that able-bodiedness also, to quote Robert McRuer, "masquerades as a nonidentity, as the natural order of things."[2] In turn, McRuer argues that heteronormativity assumes and requires a nondisabled body; compulsory heterosexuality is compulsory able-bodiedness—or, in McRuer's words, "heterosexual bodies are distinguished by their ability."[3] This bundling of able-bodiedness with heterocentrism suggests a structural affinity between queer and disabled figures as the necessary stigmatized others against which hegemonic embodiment secures itself. Homosexuality and disability share a cultural history as medical pathologies, subject to treatments designed to regularize a disruptive and unruly body. Each has served discursively to metaphorize the other; both are associated with deviance, and both represent nonnormative sexuality. A discussion of disability in the context of homosexuality thus underscores the pressure exerted by dominant paradigms to conform along multiple axes of identity. But given a body each of whose various marks becomes the sign and guarantee of shameful others, such a discussion also highlights the difficulty of disentangling gender, sexuality, and disability as equally relevant but not collapsible features of selfhood.

The conjunction of queerness and the sexuality of people with disabilities is threatening not simply to the institutions of heterosexuality and able-bodiedness, however. If feminism generally has not addressed the experience and concerns of disabled women, so too have lesbian and queer communities tended to elide the matter of disability, as the disability community has tended to assume a somewhat defensive posture vis-à-vis gays and lesbians. Alison Kafer contends that Rich's theorizing about heteronormativity obscures her ableism: not all women, Kafer argues, "are similarly and equally affected by compulsory heterosexuality."[4] Heterosexism may mask its ableism, but so too do some articulations of radical lesbian protest. At the same time, homophobia emerges in a disability community weary of being deemed unnatural for anomalous corporeality and thus wary of "queer" behaviors. If, then, as Kafer puts it, the "sexuality of people with disabilities is understood as always already deviant" by dominant cultural paradigms, same-sex practices "merely magnify or exacerbate that deviance,"[5] and in a queer movement invested in presenting itself as " 'deserving' of heterosexual privilege," "those who are queer and disabled find themselves . . . more marginalized than ever." The cultural message to the queer disabled person, as one critic remarks with some understatement, is that "your sexuality . . . is inappropriate,"[6] and another complains that disabled lesbians "feel terrifyingly isolated."[7]

Where Mairs, Grealy, and Kleege take a primarily solitary stance on the autobiographical project, Connie Panzarino and Eli Clare experience themselves as multiply constituted through internally fractured community identification, and their texts—Panzarino's *The Me in the Mirror* (1994) and Clare's *Exile and Pride* (1999)[8]—articulate precisely the difficulty of identifying oneself as part of politicized or activist groups that take an unfriendly view of some other aspect of selfhood. "Community," as I argue elsewhere, does not inevitably provide safe harbor or respite from repressive identity narratives; as suggested above, even progressive movements exert pressure to conform to certain compulsory identifications.[9] The particular challenge Panzarino and Clare meet in their life stories is to self-name from within their complex negotiations with dominant and alternative cultures alike, as well as to welcome readers from potentially uncongenial positions into their texts. Though their rhetorical and structural tactics in response to that challenge differ, both authors reveal surprise at and frustration with a kind of border patrol that demarcates acceptable from devalued selves even in groups committed to plurality. Panzarino, a pioneering disability rights activist as well as a lesbian whose plea to other disabled and gay people is to "love yourselves and each other" (260), figures herself the constructive interloper, prompting new forms of understanding and recognition between gay and lesbian and disability communities. Clare, who confesses openly to feeling "not disabled enough" for the disability community and declares that "we need all the allies, lovers, community, and friends we can gather,"[10] fashions a less stable, more diverse, polymorphous subjectivity, pushing her autobiographical act toward new grammars of self-representation.

These writers thus dispute the closure that identifying oneself would seem to guarantee. Not only naming but continually renaming themselves, Clare and Panzarino use what Leigh Gilmore has described as the metonymic possibilities of autobiography, "the endlessness or extendibility" of self-representation. Rather than focusing on autobiography in terms of metaphor, where the text is seen as "mirroring an essential sameness" (the text equals the self), Gilmore encourages a shift toward the more associative movement of metonymy. In a metonymic conception of autobiography, self-representational texts are connected but not equivalent to the author, serving not to stand in for the self but, rather, as associative gestures at the "meaning" of identity that could potentially shift across multiple texts and versions. In this context, the "truth" that autobiography tells cannot be determined by reference to something in the life of the author that "simply is" but, rather, derives from "the claims of contiguity wherein the person who writes extends the self in the writing."[11] Thinking of Panzarino and Clare in terms of metonymic extension or expansion suggests not only that their texts cannot be reduced to the raw data of their lives but also that the various parts of themselves cannot be collapsed into one another to form one unbroken identity. The texts—and, perhaps more importantly, the selves to which they refer but are not identical—are densely layered, at times even propulsive.

To get at the divisions and contradictions of their subject positions, we might thus also think of Panzarino and Clare as engaging in metonymic relationships with the various groups to which they would claim allegiance. If they cannot be reduced to the texts that name them, neither can they be encompassed by such limited categories as lesbian, disabled, female, dyke, or even queer. Yet eschewing static markers of identity does not prevent either writer from embracing group membership for the way in which a sense of solidarity assuages the insults and injuries (psychological and, for both of these writers, physical) leveled against them by homophobic and ableist others—including, most egregiously, their parents. In these memoirs, gender and sexual identity cannot be unbraided from the logistical, social, and bodily effects of disability, and self-narration emerges from the interplay between self-recognition and community pride.

The Specular Disabled Self: Connie Panzarino's *The Me in the Mirror*

Born in 1947 with spinal muscular atrophy (SMA) type III, Connie Panzarino grew up in an era when "disabled" was primarily defined as lack of productivity in the workplace. As Panzarino soon discovers, however, her "ability" to work is narrowly determined—by whether or not she can access a stairs-only building, for example—and obstructed by byzantine social service policies that make her ineligible for funds to support the personal assistance she needs in order to work outside the home. As early as her teens, Panzarino begins advocating to protect the rights of the disabled (her first victory results in construction of a wheelchair ramp at her neighborhood library). She goes on to participate in a series of groundbreaking legislative efforts, including the drafting of more than ten bills and policies with local representatives, the formation of several disability rights groups, and the filing of a lawsuit against Caspar Weinberger, then secretary of Health, Education, and Welfare, to amend the definition of "disability." *The Me in the Mirror* details such political activity as one of the most significant counteragents to the association between disability and inertia or incompetence and to the notion that disability is a personally tragic event, located "within" the individual body. From a young age, Panzarino resists accommodating herself to the prejudices of her environment, striving instead to force that environment to adjust to the physical and economic requirements of the disabled.

Panzarino is susceptible, nonetheless, to the pressure of cultural narratives about the body, female sexuality, and proper roles for women. Her memoir devotes considerable space to the difficulty of reconciling self-perception with the particulars of her condition: the loss of muscle strength in her neck and torso, the gradual paralysis of her arms and hands, and the inability to swallow certain foods. The fantasy of being able-bodied begins in childhood, when painful braces and exercises for her legs, inattentive parents, loneliness, and a sense of dislocation from her "maddening," "immobile" body (23) combine to produce the image of "another 'Connie,' " one who tries to convince Panzarino that she can walk (20–21). The "me" in the mirror of this text is thus a composite figure, both a projection of Panzarino's girlhood self-loathing and desire to be "normal" and a woman whose acceptance of herself is initiated and reinforced by her political achievements. The work of "seeing" her disabled self (recognizing herself *as* disabled) oscillates between these poles, as the hard-won self-affirmation that comes, paradoxically, from identifying publicly as a disabled person gradually dispels the little girl's withdrawal into isolation and shame.

Because the signs of disability began to manifest when Panzarino was only seven months old, her narrative focuses more fully on childhood than many of the texts discussed in this book. She describes growing up with amytonia congenita (the original name for SMA), detailing the emotional and financial burdens that disturb the household, the problem of finding adequate caretaking and assistance, and her parents' erratic and often abusive behavior. The opening chapters of the memoir establish the interlacing themes of guilt and blame, forming the backdrop against which Panzarino's later social activism will take shape. Returning again and again to traumatic scenes of disagreement about how to treat her condition, Panzarino calls attention to the interpretive conflict that the disabled body instigates. ("Disability," write David T. Mitchell and Sharon L. Snyder, "inaugurates the act of interpretation.")[12] She is the "unexplainable" (29), the marred child whose dysfunction casts a pall of shame over the family, but also a "bright" (55) girl fully capable of assessing the needs and signals of her body. Straining against her parents' expressions of frustration—even disgust—at her condition, Panzarino presents herself as at once compliant with that assessment and rebelliously convinced that "everybody else was weird and that [she] was fine" (27). In this way, *The Me in the Mirror* spotlights what happens when families follow the cues of medical and spiritual establishments, regarding disability as "something terrible," an error to be "fix[ed]" (27).

Unlike the fragmentary and circuitous paths followed by Nancy Mairs, Georgina Kleege, and (as I discuss below) Eli Clare, Panzarino's narrative pattern in *The Me in the Mirror* is more conventional. After a brief prologue detailing her adult work as an art therapist—an overture that establishes her professional competency—Panzarino begins the tale with infancy, documents her fortitude and resourcefulness through many years of struggle against societal ignorance, and ends with a utopian vision at Beechtree, a farm she establishes for disabled women. This linear structure, with its triumph-over-adversity thematic, would seem to graft an unconventional story onto a traditional narrative form. As G. Thomas Couser notes, the "radical and permanent dysfunction" of paralysis "cries out for strong compensatory narrative paradigms," and many stories of disability do symbolically repair physical dysfunction by detailing an author's impressive achievements—a rhetorical model that construes the writer as what Couser calls the "Inspirational Disabled Person," a supercrip "who overcomes impairment through pluck and willpower."[13]

But a different way of thinking about Panzarino's choice of a tightly controlled narrative sets the forward motion and the thick detail with which she tells her story against the loss of self-representational control that results from her disability. In *The Body Silent*, his noted account of paralysis from a spinal tumor, Robert F. Murphy writes that "as the price for normal relations, [the disabled] must comfort others about their condition. They cannot show fear, sorrow, depression, sexuality, or anger, for this disturbs the able-bodied."[14] In Panzarino's case, the normative social decorum Murphy cites is compounded by a family that frequently ignores her most basic bodily needs, thus ensuring such emotions as anger and fear but also making her wary of expressing those feelings to the adults upon whose care she depends. In her construction of a text that seems almost overly attentive to sequence, specificity, and cohesiveness, Panzarino may be not so much capitulating to worn paradigms that uncritically assert rhetorical control as offering a critique of nondisabled attempts to control her unruly body through definitional and descriptive imposition. Self-determination becomes an especially urgent textual goal for Panzarino in response to a pervasive sense of unreality that stems from her parents' hostile, accusatory response to her impairments.

The theme of failure dominates the first part of the book, addressing the impact of religious and medical models of disability on both individual and family psychology. The belief that the disabled body is a sign of sin, an irreversible consequence of parental misdeed, coincides in the Panzarino family with an unswerving trust in the "doctor-gods" (28) who view young Connie's body as a thing to be corrected, disorderly flesh over which both child and parents must exercise their will. Moralized blame and rehabilitative "intervention"[15] thrum an ominous beat through the early chapters, as exercise consistently falls short of the hoped-for results. "When I couldn't do the exercises," Panzarino writes, "my father said I was lazy and my mother lost patience and hit me" (46). Not surprisingly, Panzarino internalizes the ineffectiveness of the exercises as her own ineptitude: "I had failed. I still couldn't walk. . . . I also felt guilty for failing" (41). "I felt so often that I had failed her," Panzarino says of her mother; "I failed her again" (28). "I didn't know why she was tormenting me, but then I did know; I had failed. Again, I thought, this was my punishment for failing to walk" (45). This repetition of self-blame, abject as it sounds, levels a potent indictment against societal prejudices that isolate and stigmatize the disabled individual. What has truly failed in this scenario is not Panzarino's legs or feet but a system so trained on restoring a broken body to functionality that it ignores the elaborate structures of prejudice and fear that conspire to signify anomalous bodies as tragically flawed.

Panzarino spares little sympathy for her parents' passive acquiescence to medical authority or for their insensitivity to her despair and exhaustion. She is put through a series of painful—and ultimately ineffectual—exercises thought to improve flexibility and muscle strength, despite her obvious inability to move in desired ways. The regimen is standard protocol for the era, and Panzarino's parents abide by the dictates of doctors, which, by promising to regulate and even reverse the immobilizing effects of SMA, simply reinforce their disappointment when Panzarino "fails" to walk. In one such harrowing scene, Panzarino is laid down on the floor and told to roll herself across the living room, a task that her arms and torso muscles are too weak to accomplish. She recounts repeated attempts to convince her parents that she cannot propel herself, appeals that are both precipitated and followed by their dismissal of her cries that she "can't do it" (44). Twice, her father contorts Panzarino into awkward positions on the floor, saying, " 'See, you can do it!' " and then "walk[ing] out of the room, leaving me on my side" (44). Panzarino's mother joins in: " 'Come on, you can do it. Don't be such a baby.' Mom pushed just enough for me to gain the momentum to flip over onto my back. I tried to catch her eye as she . . . left the room and went back to cleaning the kitchen" (45).

Panzarino internalizes these acts of parental intrusion and rejection—two sides of a single normalizing attitude that treats dysfunction as a lack of will—as punishment for the crime of muscular weakness. The significant friction of the scene derives from the contrast between Panzarino's relative motionlessness on the floor, the ineffectuality of her vocal exertions, and the combined effect of her parents' peremptory remarks and abrupt actions. The adults enter and exit the living room again and again, emphasizing both their independent motion and their connection to each other, while Panzarino, as if banished to the floor for an undefined transgression, "rocked and pushed and panted" in a desperate effort to move that ends in "exhausted," rage-induced sleep (44–45). Her inadequate body becomes an overdetermined site of feeling: shame impels her to "bit[e] my arms," anxiety makes her stomach "hurt," and she wakes up "burning with pain" (45). As if in direct response to her physical inertia, Panzarino "wailed," "cried out," "began sobbing," and "screamed and cried out loud," but her parents belittle her, calling her "lazy" and "snapp[ing]" at her cries of distress (44–46). The scene triangulates the disabled child, longing to walk to please her parents and soothe her anguished sense of ontological failure, and nondisabled adults whose trust in a certain paradigm of "normal" mobility occludes their readiness to acknowledge Panzarino's legitimate personhood. Her noisy articulations thus produce only exasperated disregard; she is less a viable subject than an unwieldy set of nonfunctioning limbs.

Panzarino depicts her relationship with her mother, her primary caretaker, as an agonistic contest, the most fraught of her early bonds. Alternately loving and cruel, so humiliated and fatigued by her daughter's condition that she lashes out physically as well as emotionally, Ann Panzarino is the text's representative of stereotypically disparaging attitudes toward disability. In a discussion of the impact of disability on early mother-infant experience, Adrienne Harris and Dana Wideman suggest that the mother's capitulation to negative cultural myths about disability can produce a "diminishing of identification"[16] between mother and her "damaged" baby. Panzarino describes an entangled relationship marked by both an absence of identificatory connection with her mother and a level of attachment that confuses the distinction between self and other. Relying on her mother for her most basic functioning and movements, Panzarino becomes excessively attuned to her mother's moods; she learns to be on her guard against her mother's potential irascibility and behaves with preemptive docility: "At the age of four, in order to make my world safe, I knew I had to make my mother happy" (30).

Panzarino implies that the degree of physical closeness with her mother necessitated by her condition further collapsed the boundary between their bodily selves. She writes that her mother was "so intensely tuned to my needs that I think she often didn't know where her wants began and mine left off. . . . If she was thirsty or hungry, she would assume I must be too. . . . It was hard to know if I could ever exist separate from her" (51). In one scene, Panzarino describes her mother's reluctance to let her play with neighborhood kids—one of many instances where the belief that the disabled child is fundamentally sick, fragile, or "other" prevents creative adaptation to that child's range of motion and gets rewritten as the disabled child's own guilty inferiority to the group. Both Panzarino and her mother experience her difference from the others as painful embarrassment, which for Panzarino becomes a problematic form of sympathetic, and highly physical, identification with the mother whose cues she observes so intently: in her words, she "couldn't tell whether they were my tears, or my mother's. I was sitting on her lap, our bodies pressed together" (29).

Panzarino thus absorbs and mimics her mother's ambivalent response to her, learning that her disabled body requires infantilizing overprotectiveness but that it is also a source of disgust, the cause of her mother's "turning away" (29). As if reduced to the collection of demands her body constantly makes on others—to be held, to be repositioned, to use the bathroom—she is also dissociated from the sensations of that body by a caregiver who repeatedly co-opts her own assessment of her needs. This is made particularly clear in scenes describing the exercises Panzarino is forced to endure. When she complains about the discomfort of propping up her feet in a futile effort to prevent muscle contractions, for instance, her mother retorts, " 'It doesn't hurt that much. Besides, you need to get your feet straightened out or you'll never walk' " (17–18). In another misguided attempt to stimulate her circulation, Panzarino's feet are submerged in first very hot and then very cold water, "back and forth repeatedly." Despite the fact that "it felt like hell" and "shocked [her] whole body," Panzarino is denied the capacity to evaluate and define her own bodily experience: "My mother said it wasn't painful, and then got mad at me when I cried" (17).

Even more violent outbursts tend to erupt in response to the issue of Panzarino's personal care. Though she was not incontinent as a child, she could not transport herself unaided from wheelchair to toilet. In one particularly egregious scene, Panzarino describes her mother's reaction to this need, which she suggests was provoked by the ambiguous overlap of function and inability:

> Something hit me across the face and continued hitting me on my arms and legs. . . . "Mommy, Mommy," I cried, until I realized it was Mom hitting me.
>
> Time seemed to stand still as the blows kept coming. She picked me up and carried me to the bathroom, saying, "You're so ungrateful. You don't care about me. I hate you! I hate you! What do you think I am, a slave? You don't appreciate me. You don't

> deserve anything." . . . She put me down hard into my crib and left, slamming the door behind her.
>
> "Mommy," I sobbed. I was terrified. I would die without her. . . . I cried and shouted for her endlessly, "I'm sorry, I'm sorry." . . . My heart ached for me and for her because I loved her, and I thought she hated me. (30–31)

This exchange exemplifies a binary logic that codes the disabled figure a narcissistic taskmaster, willfully and self-indulgently manipulating the pity of everyone around her to hold them in sway to an exaggerated helplessness. The mother sounds like a petulant child, irrationally shouting down an unfeeling, unperturbed parent. At the same time, Panzarino makes clear her sense of profound, existential dependency on her mother's uncertain willingness to provide basic care. In this crisis of maternal abandonment, mother and daughter are caught in a contest over responsibility and interdependence that strikes at the very heart of a cultural response to disability as an indecorous and ultimately unforgivable display of the body—its uncontrollable processes, its capacity to defy order by continuing to function even as it relentlessly breaks down.

This scene also gives the lie to what Murphy has claimed of the effect of disability on familial relations when it is the child who is "stricken." Describing his interviews with disabled people, Murphy argues that "the dependency of disability overlapped and reinforced the normal dependency of children, deepening the parent-child tie. . . . The relations of family reciprocity became stronger and the parental role mellowed, its disciplinary features softened."[17] Panzarino's situation seems quite the opposite. Far from being integrated into a cohesive family unit, Panzarino seems to lurk on the periphery, even as SMA overwhelms the parents' response to her. Such behavior is produced in part by the combined pressures of religious and medical discourse around disability. Panzarino explains her mother's behavior as a direct result of religious guilt; she reports having "overheard" her mother telling a friend that "she had asked a priest why this was happening to her child. He told her it was her fault or my father's fault because they must have sinned"

(28). The onus of responsibility for Panzarino's condition is leveled squarely on the parents by their most trusted moral adviser, and it is hardly surprising that in an Italian Catholic family in the early 1950s, the mother assumes the full weight of the catastrophe and projects her guilt onto her daughter.

This accords with what Harris and Wideman have said of the "contradictory position" of the mother of a disabled child: "She is empowered to act by the culture but is scapegoated as the primary problem in instances of pathology."[18] Panzarino seems to sympathize with her mother's withdrawal as at once a buck against the requirements of the normative maternal role and a symptom of the prevailing attitudes toward disability that encouraged her to treat her daughter's SMA as a failing to be overcome. Yet Panzarino is also clearly concerned to demonstrate how immediately her mother's capitulation to those pejorative narratives slid into her own sense of liability; she takes on her mother's sense of failure as her own burden to minimize the threat that her mother represents. The overlay of patriarchal and ableist expectations makes for an especially vexed dynamic between mother and daughter, as each finds herself inappropriately accused, so to speak, with the fault of bodily inferiority. In Panzarino's case, self-blame compensates for the anguish of parental repudiation, paradoxically stimulating a heightened sensitivity to, even compassion for, those who treat her badly.

Perhaps this is why Panzarino imbues her younger self with an unlikely degree of developmental and psychological maturity. She avows that she "talked fluently and clearly" at seven months old (63) and writes that after being examined as a one-year-old by doctors who "couldn't find anything wrong," she "figured [she] had passed the test and [that] nothing was wrong" with her (15). In the scene discussed above, where she is not yet four years old, she writes that her heart "aches," as if with precociously insightful empathy, for her abusive mother. And as if in imitation of her mother's insistence on knowing best about Connie's physical needs, the adult Panzarino often records her mother's feelings without acknowledgment of the inevitable guesswork involved (e.g., "My mother was torn . . ." [63]). In another passage, she is the medical spectacle being examined by "a crowd of doctors" who "pointed to various parts of [her] body and flopped [her] arms and legs around." When one of the physicians announces that "it's so hard with these children. The only enjoyment they have is eating," Panzarino claims to have "wondered what he would do if he knew how good it felt to rub [her] legs together" (58). She is just eight years old.

My aim here is not to dispute the accuracy of Panzarino's childhood awareness of herself and her surroundings or to make an obvious point, reiterated by many scholars of autobiography, about memory's inevitable refraction of events over the distance of years. Beyond authorial reconstruction or embellishment, the display of self-consciousness counteracts what Panzarino presents as an ongoing contest over the meaning of her disabled body and the reliability of her body's sensations. Given her dependency on a mother who openly questions the veracity of her bodily signals (accusing her, for instance, of requesting bathroom assistance just to get attention), Panzarino begins to doubt her own perceptions: "I thought there was something wrong with my mind," she writes. "After being contradicted so many times, I didn't trust my own sense of reality" (115). The acutely observant "I" that narrates *The Me in the Mirror* thus directly refutes the undermining impact of skeptical authority figures. If her mother can declare "sarcastically" that she " 'never know[s] when to believe' " her daughter's testimony (52), the autobiographical Panzarino attempts to turn the tables through narrative command, as if the sheer volume of detail she amasses and the precision with which she seems to remember could guarantee the irrefutability of her tale.[19]

If the anomalous body of disability inspires an interpretive scramble to contain the threat it represents—what Mitchell has referred to as "explanatory compensation"[20]—*The Me in the Mirror* offers its own version of Panzarino's experience in a way that explicitly opposes both the influence of the mother and the discursive power of (primarily male) doctors and priests. Panzarino's narrative covers gaps in memory, minimizing ambiguity and alternative perspectives in its quest for legitimate self-authorship. It is not so much that Panzarino submits her text as the single and uncontestable truth of herself but, rather, to invoke Gilmore's notion of metonymic autobiography, that she writes a far more flexible kind of self than the one to which she was confined as a child by familial and institutional prejudice. The insistence on self-consciousness at very young ages works against what Panzarino records as persistently disempowering messages, while her admissions of self-doubt and self-hatred serve the implicit purpose of indicting those ideological structures that characterize a disabled girl as unworthy—of religious devotion (53), sexual attraction (81), and work or education (89). Though her assertions of youthful insight might not be entirely believable, the effect is to bring readers into collusion with the adult writer, as if to suggest that we, along with the author, are getting one over on those figures whose fear and prejudice conspired to conflate an unruly body with an unsavory character.

Panzarino's abundantly self-reflexive, self-insistent text also seems initiated by her own deliberate suppression, in response to her mother's anger, of her body's signals. When a second daughter is born with SMA, the Panzarino household becomes even more volatile, the mother even more prone to violent outbursts provoked by now two daughters' physical demands. Having to use the bathroom, in particular, becomes an occasion for resentment and fear, and Panzarino devotes considerable space to this issue throughout the narrative. She writes that whereas her younger brother Frankie "got hit because he was bad—because he broke something or said something nasty to my mother" (64), she and Pidgie suffer their mother's blows because of bodily requirements beyond their control. Rarely insolent and certainly not physically rambunctious, Connie and Pidgie are nonetheless figured as uncontainable flesh; in Panzarino's words, "We all got hit for talking back to our parents, but Frankie never got hit because he had to go to the bathroom." "If she got mad enough at me," she writes of her mother, "I was sure she would kill me" (64). Maternal rejection strikes at the heart of who Panzarino understands herself to be ("It didn't seem like I had a disease. . . . I *was* a disease" [40]), and she learns to equate survival with denial of her body's most basic needs.

Her mother is not the only factor in Panzarino's habit of willfully ignoring her body. An entire chapter addresses the problem of having to hold her urine at school because there is no one to assist her in the transition from wheelchair to toilet: "They said they would allow me to go half days so I wouldn't have to go to the bathroom at school" (75). Given no choice but to accommodate herself to a bureaucracy that fails to provide adequate facilities or support, Panzarino limits her intake of fluids, thereby minimizing her bathroom use but also endangering her health. The open discussion of bathroom behavior—hardly the stuff of "polite" autobiography—points up the consequences of construing disability as a matter of individual responsibility. The problem is made to seem Panzarino's, rather than the system's; it is her own body, relentless in its production of waste yet recalcitrantly immobile, that bars her entrance into a regular routine of schooling. When Panzarino comments ironically that she is rewarded with an extra class for her "good urinary behavior" (79), she makes a familiar point that even the most apparently private matters (forms of access the nondisabled take for granted) are deeply embedded in ableist attitudes and infrastructure.

Flaunting narrative decorum, *The Me in the Mirror* frequently addresses such topics as a way of underscoring the idea that disability is relational, a function of the interaction between bodies and social practices. It is precisely the point that bodily functions are a source of difficulty and exposure for Panzarino—but not because an indecorous focus on physical experience is inherent to the disabled experience. Rather, what constitutes the exaggerated "presence" of the disabled body is in part the orientation of "personal" care rituals toward the nondisabled (the personal *is* political, but in far more ways than feminism itself has recognized).[21] Panzarino puts her body in play more than any other writer under discussion here, calling attention to it as it sweats, gains weight, chokes on some types of food, and begins to menstruate. Far from disguising the inevitable processes of her female body, Panzarino readily acknowledges the frustrating inescapability of "my fat body that had to pee even when I didn't want it to" (55). (Her phenomenology is not just "visceral" but gynecological and even scatological.) But in so doing, she suggests the collision between corporeality and discourses of normality that regulate the body's peculiarities. Panzarino situates the telling of her size, shape, function, and condition within stories of the disabled person as "some dangerous thing" (78), "the enemy" (150).

One of the most potent aspects of this narrative strategy is her description of sexual and erotic enjoyment—from masturbating to playing spin-the-bottle to her growing interest in both boys and girls—which emerges early in the text as an arena of self-directed experience. While several of the writers discussed here display their sexual activity as an antidote to prejudice against disabled people's "entitlement to pleasure and to sexual life,"[22] only Panzarino levels autoeroticism specifically against the notion of disabled sexuality as an unthinkable contradiction in terms. She writes openly about masturbating in her wheelchair as a young girl, rubbing or squeezing her legs together to distract herself from having to urinate (56, 58). Initially linking self-stimulation with the injunction against bathroom needs, enforced by her parents and school authorities, that impels her to disregard her body's impulses, Panzarino layers the pleasurable response she can produce in her body with her attempt to minimize that body's disruptiveness. Emphasizing that her body is particularly problematic in a social environment that fails to adjust to the variances of physical difference, she refigures that body as a source of private—but of course also defiantly public—gratification.

There would seem to be no more private—one might even say embarrassing—topics than "masturbating . . . for getting rid of diarrhea cramps" (56), going to a laundromat in "a little smock shirt" and "just a pair of underpants with my Modess pad" (161), or suffering because her "clitoris was broken open and bleeding" from a "bunched up" skirt (221). Yet more than shock value is at work here. The graphic descriptions serve as what Carol Thomas has called "evidence that 'the micro' is constitutive of 'the macro.' "[23] In each of the instances listed here, fundamentally at issue is whether or not Panzarino receives, or can afford to supply herself with, sufficient assistance for transportation, household chores, personal hygiene, and so forth. Clearly invoking entrenched myths about both female and disabled bodies as excessive, unseemly, even grotesque, Panzarino confronts her audience with the ramifications of such oppositional rhetoric and restyles the microcosmic moment as potentially interrogative of social codes that equate being "physically helpless" (112) with what Susan Wendell refers to as "global incompetence."[24] Panzarino sets the comparatively high level of aid she requires against the social narratives that particulate and cordon off the body, along with the many ways in which she determines her experience and manages her environment.

If failure dominates the early chapters of the memoir as the primary symbolic conception of disability, much of the later text is concerned with detailing an extended battle for control through which Panzarino constructs a politicized and feminist disabled identity. Her discussion of sexual partnerships dovetails with a focus on work and political activity as contested sites of interpretation about what disability means and how disabled communities can most effectively form and work for change. As a student at Hofstra, she helps to organize PUSH (People United in Support of the Handicapped), a group whose actions include representing disabled students in Washington, D.C., and initiating programs for the disabled both on campus and in the community; still living at home, she remains dependent on the uneven attentions of her family, particularly her mother. In this juxtaposition of locales, "disabled" is a highly contextual descriptor, an assertion of productive political visibility in one situation but a marker of incapacity in the other. Panzarino describes herself shuttling uneasily back and forth between these definitional poles, citing control as the crucial distinction between them. "I wanted and needed," she writes simply, "more control in my life" (124).

Work, both academic and political, allows Panzarino to "feel good about [her]self" and to effect identifiable change, both ideological and socioeconomic, in the lives of the disabled. Romantic and sexual activity, however, is more troubled terrain, and much of the text pursues a quest for romantic love and heterosexual marriage. Despite an early interest in girls (such as "cute Linda with the blue bow in her hair" [66]), Panzarino is socialized to view boys as the appropriate object of desire, and she is indeed "turned on by boys" (91). At the same time, disability bars her from inclusion in the liaisons of her high school friends. She writes, "I realized they thought that since I was physically different, I shouldn't have a boyfriend or even be interested in boys. They never asked me if I wanted to get married or have babies, although they asked each other questions like that all that time. . . . I couldn't tell them that I wanted to be married some day, because I knew they didn't think anyone would want to marry me. . . . [I] dreamed of being married" (81). Later, in college, "becoming an adult" exacerbates her confusion about the intersection of disability and normative female roles: "It was difficult to figure out how or if I could become a wife, mother or working woman and still be disabled" (124). Here, a disability consciousness jars with feminism: Panzarino wants what feminist activists would have trained her—quite overtly, in the late 1960s—to be suspicious of.

Alongside confessions of being immersed in dominant paradigms about love, however, *The Me in the Mirror* narrates disabled sexuality as both legitimate and antiromantic. In one of her first encounters, she is kissed by a fellow "radical activist" (102). The scene is at once comic and pointed in its challenge to idealized romantic perfection: "All of a sudden he leaned over and kissed me on my mouth. It was so hard and so fast, he knocked me off balance and my head fell back. I couldn't lift it up again and neither could he, so we had to wait for the volunteer. It was awful! I was so embarrassed I wanted to die. The next time Jim kissed me, and all the times after that, he put his arm around me first, to give support. Practice makes perfect" (103). In such a moment, the notion that intimacy is a purely dyadic and private event is challenged by the peripheral but necessary presence of the volunteer; Panzarino simultaneously dispenses with the idea that a call for help signifies an existential condition of helplessness. Panzarino can acknowledge embarrassment without capitulating to defenseless vulnerability, and at the same time she figures herself and her partner as taking command of their situation; indeed, what looks at first like physical limitation becomes a threshold onto even greater intimacy, as "practice" requires further kisses, and the logistical innovation of Jim's arm increases their physical closeness. "Support" is a double-edged word here, connoting both reinforcement for Panzarino's neck muscles but also, less obviously, a degree of attunement between Panzarino and Jim; bodies and emotions are fully intertwined. Further, the scene interrogates the slippage between disability and "failure" through its compression of time. The first disappointment is quickly submerged in the "next time" and the happy repetition of "all the times after that," making sexual encounter an ordinary, repeatable event.

Panzarino's first serious relationship is with Ron Kovic, author of *Born on the Fourth of July*. Originally high school classmates, Panzarino and Kovic meet at the disabled students' office at Hofstra, after Kovic returns from Vietnam. Panzarino credits Kovic with "broaden[ing]" her "political world" (154): where her activist energies are initially trained on "local officials, local libraries and school districts," Kovic's outspoken antiwar position turns her political awareness toward a broader system of inequity and oppression. Panzarino suggests that her involvement with Kovic brings to a head her own conflict with the political attitudes and domestic habits of her parents. When her father derides Kovic's protest of the 1972 Republican National Convention as a " 'disgrace' " (155), Panzarino associates "not giving up on Ron, or [her] beliefs" with "find[ing] a way to live on [her] own" (155). In some ways a typical tale of a young woman bucking against the restraints set by her parents, *The Me in the Mirror* demonstrates in such moments how thoroughly the matter of independent living is bound up with widespread values that dictate the cultural response to difference and to social critique. Panzarino implies a link between the hostility that provokes her father to warn her not to "even talk to" Kovic and an ableist world that assumes both the ease of self-sufficient living and the right to claim political superiority.

Panzarino describes her relationship with Kovic in the dual terms of social activism and sexual discovery. The text suggests a structural similarity between disabled veterans "protest[ing] the mistreatment of Vietnam veterans by the government" (168) and Panzarino looking at her "whole self naked in a mirror" for the first time (166). Both are acts of dissent against dominant political ideologies and the policies they endorse, and both aim to consolidate the efficacy of activism by dismantling the internalized self-hatred that acts in concert with social marginalization. Panzarino's self-appraisal is marked first by shame and then by surprised acceptance. "Somehow it felt wrong to look at myself," she admits (166), but then "[I] was surprised to see that I was not as deformed as I thought I was. Something changed inside me." This "me" in the mirror, unlike the childhood spectral image she thought could walk, is at once a person with SMA and a woman who takes the initiative in sexual encounters. The day after her transformative mirror-moment, she tells Kovic that "I wanted to make love with him" (166).

As in the previous instance of kissing Jim, Panzarino presents her desire here as active and confident. In the explicit scene of lovemaking that follows her "forward" (166) request to Kovic, Panzarino combines a relatively unremarkable description of their act ("We started kissing. . . . He sucked on my ears. He pressed my face into his chest" [167]) with a more clinical explanation of the bodily particulars that influence what they do ("He didn't have any feeling in his penis and it was hooked up to his urinary bag"). The combination denaturalizes conventional romanticism as well as emphasizes the degree to which the participants in any sexual encounter are situated in complex individual, physical, political, and social histories. Even the apparently passive form in which much of the scene is written (e.g., "He put my hand on his nipple") has a subversive effect, not so much implying that Kovic takes command or behaves coercively than representing the unique erotic choreography of these particular two bodies. Paralysis and muscular weakness are hardly an impediment to sexual satisfaction. With two attendants nearby in the event that Panzarino might need to use the bathroom, she and Kovic "ma[k]e love for hours."

The relationship with Kovic allows Panzarino to foreground the intertwining of politics, sex, and disability, to demonstrate the impact of each on the individual experience and cultural evaluation of the others. In many ways, however, a familiar tale of heterosexual power relations plays out here, with Kovic engaging in a series of affairs with other (nondisabled) women even as Panzarino is "trying to be the good wife" (195). Somewhat unselfconsciously, Panzarino attempts to dismiss these liaisons as insignificant, despite their longevity: "His relationships with able-bodied women never lasted more than *a year or two at most* and usually only lasted a few weeks, while his relationship with me was constant" (195; my emphasis). A stereotypical confrontation over commitment is presented as the antecedent to Panzarino's nascent attraction to women; in the moment of discovering that Kovic has moved out of their shared apartment, Panzarino "can't believe [she] kept looking for love for so long from someone who was so incapable of giving it to [her]" and realizes how much she longs for "an equal relationship" (205). "Flooded with images" of her mother and other "beautiful able-bodied women" hampered by normative expectations for women and beset by conflicts with the men in their lives, Panzarino "feel[s] strong and angry" and sheds the belief that "[her] very being depended upon whether [she] could become a wife." Within a few pages, she has slept with Maura, a friend and previous attendant.

The Me in the Mirror obviously subordinates the possessive inequities of traditional marriage to the equal partnership imagined to obtain in lesbian relationships, where women know "exactly" (209) how to please each other and perfect "understand[ing]" characterizes their interactions. "I didn't want to be 'owned' the way one is when they're married," she writes. "When it then became the trend for lesbians to make commitments and have marriage ceremonies, I cringed. . . . Yet I have had many committed lovers who have come close to that partnership" (254). Rejecting prejudicial attitudes against disabled sexuality as well as anything that smacks of conventional heterosexuality or patriarchal marriage, Panzarino describes her relationship with longtime partner Judy as one of a high degree of attunement and respect: "We were completely there for each other financially, spiritually, emotionally and physically, but did not own each other. We made mutual decisions with one another based on what was better for each individual. We at least strived to support one another even when we personally disagreed with the other's choice" (254).

In this sense, the depiction of Panzarino's sexual identity would seem to operate according to a relatively static binary of sexual experience and lifestyle. Given more recent explorations (such as Eli Clare's, discussed below) of transgendered identity and forms of sexual behavior that exceed the boundaries of the straight/gay paradigm, this model may strike readers as reductive, outdated, or even essentialist. Yet whatever the conceptual limitations of Panzarino's framework in this regard (clearly informed by mid-1970s feminism), her focus on disabled identity and disability rights works to fracture rather than to uphold structural binarisms. Panzarino discovers that the lesbian community is unexpectedly unwelcoming to her due to her condition; far from being embraced into a mythically accepting sisterhood, she is initially received with "condescension and lack of support" (211), "rejected for [her] body's imperfections and forced by others' assumptions to live as if [she] couldn't love" (212). As Shelley Tremain argues, "What constitutes 'lesbian experience'" in an ableist society does not include "disabled dykes, our bodies, or our sexual practices." Nondisabled dykes, according to Tremain, whether theorists, activists, or personal attendants, too often neglect the struggles of "their disabled sisters," perpetuating a sense that their unique experiences and needs are trivial or "not truly 'political.'"[25] Given Panzarino's hard-won notoriety as a disability activist, her exclusion from the lesbian community comes as an especially hurtful surprise.

While her relationship with Ron Kovic broadens her political vocabulary and her brief interlude with able-bodied Maura teaches her that disabled women "are oppressed in this culture not only because they are disabled, but also because they are women" (202), Panzarino suggests that she must rely on herself to understand and articulate the multiple subject position of disabled lesbian. This accords with Tremain's contention that the intersection of disability and lesbianism produces a "conceptual impossibility": "Ableism structures lesbian, gay, and queer politics," while "white heterosexualism . . . dominates the disability rights movement."[26] Panzarino sets her resulting sense of marginality against claims of her expert knowledge. Among nondisabled gay women, she is "not seen as someone to make love with" (212–13), but as the leader of workshops on both ableism and homophobia, she becomes a pedagogue of sorts, an educated authority. Panzarino frequently occupies this role in her own text—in dialogue with other voices that merely express bewilderment, frustration, and rage, she is the rational one, the one who "explain[s]" (213). This acts as rhetorical leverage against the troubling effect that disabled bodies can have, no matter how progressive or alternative the audience. But she also "pushes the limits," in Tremain's words, of dyke identity through frank accounts of her desires and sexual activity.

For instance, in a workshop on body image, Panzarino joins other disabled women in being "angry about how our bodies had been looked at by doctors, by men, by family and by other lesbians" (222), and in the pages of her text, she declares that she "wanted to be sexual" (221). As the weakening effects of SMA progress, Panzarino eventually "could no longer use [her] own hands at all" (234). As with Kovic, however, the physical condition that makes it "hard for [her] to be an active sexual partner" (235) becomes an opportunity for inventive erotic play. First acknowledging the validity of "grieving" the new loss of movement, Panzarino writes, "I learned to use my mouth, my breath and my creative voice to accompany my lovers in touching themselves" (235–36). Such a description effectively shifts the locus of sexual pleasure away from genital exclusivity and resituates it across bodies that can receive and give pleasure in unfamiliar ways (Cixouvian polymorphous eroticism resituated and rewritten); moreover, it exemplifies the simultaneity of self and other in the threshold space of sex. Though less mobile at this stage than during her relationship with Kovic, in this account Panzarino appears to take a more active role, "learn[ing]" and "us[ing]" rather than having parts of her body "pressed" or "put" by the other. Importantly, she names her breath and voice as key components of her capacity to please other women: she writes her pleasure on the bodies of her lovers.

Panzarino's offhand references to attendants in more than one scene of lovemaking, her repeated discussion of the need to be lifted on and off toilets at both school and work, and her mention of being assisted with such work-related activities as dialing phones and filling out forms further exhibit an explicit union of feminist with disability rights perspectives. One of the central concerns of *The Me in the Mirror* is the struggle against laws that deny adequate funding for what Panzarino calls "life support" (178). As Jenny Morris has argued, "The disabled people's movement has, so far, failed to give enough prominence to . . . the private world of the family and personal relationships," subordinating "caring relationships" (the putative domain of women and thus not worthy of activist energies) to a focus on "participating in the public world of work."[27] Panzarino resists such a dichotomy. A disability sensibility *and* a feminist sensibility are evident throughout her text, where sexual relationships, the gynecological and scatological habits of her female body, and her highly assertive political activities join the interests of women and the disabled alike, blurring the distinction between public and private, personal and political. By including attendants in her description of every part of her life, for example—from bathroom to office and from sex to sit-in—Panzarino suggests how inextricably linked gender and disability are, and how each is affected by social myths of independence and the primacy of the rational mind.

From her first experience in school, doing well enough that "they allowed another disabled young person to attend" (79), to forming such groups as Disabled in Action of New York and the Disabled Lesbian Alliance to being spotlighted in New York's daily *Newsday* for her "fight" against "the injustice of the law" (178), Panzarino emerges as the hub of "a grassroots movement for workers with disabilities" (179). This positioning serves two important rhetorical purposes: first, it offsets the portrayal of her dependence on a "desperate" (144) and angry mother, who seems to begrudge Panzarino's increasing autonomy despite the pressures of caring for two adult daughters with SMA. Second, it specifically links Panzarino's individuation from her mother's contradictory needs with her assumption of group identity. Affiliating with other workers, women, lesbians, and disabled people—typically as an organizer and leader—provides a sense of shared purpose and political efficacy that contests the hegemonic inscription of disability as a matter of individual fault. *The Me in the Mirror* records multiple, intersecting efforts to achieve a sense of "interdependent" identity through work, sexual expression, and community activism, each of which entails thinking creatively about how to accommodate physical difference and a redefinition of what it means to survive on one's own.

This may explain why Panzarino's younger sister Pidgie appears relatively infrequently in *The Me in the Mirror*. Like Lucy Grealy's exclusion of her twin sister, Sarah, throughout *Autobiography of a Face*, Panzarino exhibits a need to separate from a sibling whose similarity to the self threatens a sense of viable individuality. Panzarino writes explicitly that "as she grew older," Pidgie "became a threat. There was no one in the whole world that was like me. I was unique. I was different, and while that was a problem for some people, the difference also made me special. Pidgie was the only other person in the whole world that looked anything like me. She moved like me, she used the bedpan like me. . . . She was brilliant like me" (131). While elsewhere Panzarino voices a desire for a reflective look, a visual exchange with "someone like me" (62), the relationship with her similarly disabled sister heightens the already extreme tension and competition with their mother. In Panzarino's words, "The boundaries between my mother and myself became more blurred and more complex ever since the addition of my sister" (131–32). Textually distancing herself from Pidgie, then, serves the purpose of disentangling the boundaries of self from a mother whose rough handling and shaming behavior has profoundly damaging psychological consequences. This is particularly clear when Panzarino takes the position of more fully "actualized" disabled person vis-à-vis her sister, "want[ing] Pidgie to get the right attitude about herself as a disabled person" and "encourag[ing] Pidgie to be assertive" (131).

If the "right attitude" is defined in part as believing oneself to be worthy of independent living in the context of reliable personal assistance, then it becomes vital for Panzarino to separate from a mother who deems her sexuality "sick" (226) and with whom she still feels "six months old, except that now [she] could talk and pay rent" (149). She suggests that seeing themselves in each other is difficult for her and her sister not so much because they represent each other's past and "future realit[ies]" (132) but, rather, because such mirroring recalls their mutual "helplessness" in specific regard to their mother. The point is not that Panzarino rejects the specular reflection of a disabled self; to the contrary, as I have been arguing, she identifies strongly with various groups of disabled people throughout her life. The issue is rather needing to defend a sense of viable subjectivity from a mother whose demeaning influence metonymically represents pervasive cultural attitudes toward disability and difference. In this sense, Pidgie becomes an opportunity for Panzarino to assert authority as a member of a cohesive and politically powerful disabled community. *The Me in the Mirror* does not refuse to look in reflecting surfaces; instead, it seeks arenas in which looking will produce a mutually constitutive recognition and respect.

The fullest expression of such a community is Beechtree, a farm in upstate New York that Panzarino establishes as "a space where disabled lesbians can live free from homophobia and ableism" (225). Much like the haven for artists and lovers that Katherine Butler Hathaway envisions in *The Little Locksmith*, Beechtree holds out the possibility of sexual, artistic, and political expression apart from "power imbalances" (230) of patriarchal and nondisabled ideologies. Panzarino writes that "equity was an important theme at Beechtree. . . . Living at Beechtree was about not just accepting disability or difference, but celebrating it" (230–31). While the impulse to eschew the oppressions of an able-bodied, masculinist world does at times manifest as separatist retreat (with the women at Beechtree "[getting] in touch with Mother Nature" and rewriting "God as a Goddess" [232]), Panzarino's account maintains its focus on breaking down the social barriers that seek to hold marginal groups at bay. The loving and equitable environment at Beechtree serves as a potent contrast to the abusive home life of her childhood. Where she once felt "anger at my whole self" (125) largely due to her family situation —in itself a function of deeply entrenched cultural fears about anomalous bodies—she ultimately directs that emotion at the appropriate source: "I wasn't angry about being disabled, I was angry about not being able to get what was available to make me able to function better with my disability" (235).

The "me in the mirror" thus transforms from a kind of hallucinatory specter, a fantasy of wholeness, coordination, muscular strength, and independence, to being the self-created figure that resides within the text. "Being happy with my disability," Panzarino writes, "became my declaration of total rebellion against what society expected and what my family had prepared me for" (161). *The Me in the Mirror* constructs Panzarino as what Margrit Shildrick and Janet Price call a "fully self-present," if also revisable, individual.[28] Shildrick and Price contend that disability does not precede its observation; it becomes a meaningful entity only through the evaluative measuring and critical self-gaze inherent in the medical model. To put the issue slightly differently, writing the self offers "new ways of understanding what knowledge is and how it is produced."[29] As Carol Thomas has argued, "What disabled women say about their own lives" is a crucial component in correcting "over-generaliz[ed]" and "universalistic accounts" of disabled women's experience.[30] Paradoxically, then, Panzarino does in some sense create her disability (as Kleege's text makes her blind)—but to counterdiscursive effect. While her narration does not operate according to an open-ended ambiguity that refuses to be stereotyped or stabilized, it does nonetheless write an alternative version of lesbian, disabled subjectivity—one whose subversiveness lies in the thick texture of its ordinary life.

Queer/Cut: Eli Clare's *Exile and Pride*

"Until very recently," writes Alison Kafer, ". . . there have been few representations of the sexual experiences and desires of disabled people by disabled people, particularly disabled queers."[31] While such recent anthologies as *Pushing the Limits: Disabled Dykes Produce Culture* and *Restricted Access: Lesbians on Disability* seek to rectify that dearth, the publication of a book-length text like Panzarino's—one that intertwines an unapologetic portrayal not just of the joys and accommodations of queer disabled sexuality but also of the chilly reception a disabled lesbian might encounter from her various communities—is still relatively infrequent. Eli Clare's *Exile and Pride* extends both of those narrative tracks from the vantage point of a slightly differently politicized atmosphere. While Panzarino reveals the tensions within and between such categories as disabled, lesbian, or woman, she nonetheless affirms her solidarity to these groups; they provide a kind of stabilizing force for her. Clare is more restless, less willing to shape herself to the contours of any available versions of selfhood. Her sensibility is informed by recent post-structuralist formulations within the queer and disabled communities, and *Exile and Pride* does not overtly attempt to integrate the various aspects of Clare's experience.

Neither disability, sexuality, race, class, nor regional identity can be called ground zero of Clare's identity, but hyphenated designations do not fit particularly well, either. As an androgynous, physically and speech impaired, feminist, "redneck" dyke, Clare presents —and courts—a definitional conundrum, which *Exile and Pride* at once addresses and represents by imagining "new ways of being something else entirely" (128). The "polyphony" of her text, as Susanna Egan suggests in a different context, "serves to replicate the instabilities" of Clare's social, political, gendered, and embodied position, disrupting "conventional expectations" and enacting the "emerging identities" that Clare seeks to inscribe.[32] *Exile and Pride* respells its author's name, presenting her as Eli rather than Elizabeth Clare, and for Clare, the autobiographical project is largely devoted to a sense of not being at "home" anywhere, including her body—which has "never been singular" (137). Clare begins writing from an "ever-present sense of displacement" that is bound up with "the intersection of queer identity, working-class and poor identity, and rural identity" (44). She foregrounds these at times irresolvable crossings, speaking of "the body as home, but only if it is understood that language too lives under the skin" (11).

Exile and Pride is a kind of architectural blueprint detailing the cultural construction of the "empty house" (131) that is her body, "stolen" by "abuse and ableism and homophobia" (132). But if it describes the history of subjectivity at the confluence of oppressive discourses, *Exile and Pride* also stands as Clare's "reclaimed body," wrested back from the "stereotypes, lies, [and] false images" (131) that multiply ostracize an ambiguously gendered, working-class, rural queer with cerebral palsy. Clare foregrounds the insufficiency of any given term to account for her (as well as all the others with whom she declares solidarity), and her text works toward positive and self-defined images to counteract the "shame," "silence," and "isolation" (91) imposed upon disability, queer sexuality, and working-class identity in a patriarchal culture. "Without pride," Clare writes, "individual and collective resistance to oppression becomes nearly impossible" (91). By presenting herself as a composite self in which no one piece is ever dominant, Clare aims at a form of identity open to retelling and recombination, one that defends against the stasis that can result not only from the essentialism of prejudice but even from the autobiographical act itself.

Coming-out story, trauma narrative, disability treatise, environmentalist manifesto—*Exile and Pride* does not move fluidly, like Clare herself, from one point to the next. A kind of structural jerkiness pervades the text, as if to manifest both the "jagged edge" (11) that demarcates one group from another, the accepted from the outcast, and self-love from self-loathing, as well as the "stop-and-go clamber" (4) of Clare's own gait (illustrating Arthur W. Frank's point exactly, that bodies give illness—and, I think, disability—stories "their particular shape and direction").[33] And perhaps more profoundly, formal discontinuity embodies the text's larger claim about the conceptual inadequacies of naming: to create a coherent narrative whole is to smooth over the awkward repetitions, the inconsistencies and randomness of life, just as the bandying about of identity categories like lesbian, woman, and disabled pretends to an illusion of sameness that elides real diversity.[34]

There is, therefore, no unified "I" in *Exile and Pride* to access, only rupture, a proliferation of perspectives and stories. The representational strategy is one of pastiche; Clare writes identity as mosaic, an accumulation rather than a steady progression "forward" toward some truth or core of selfhood. Indeed, at the end of the book—the point at which we are prepared, given the conventional dictates of self-writing, for closure, for a sense of having "gotten to know" the autobiographical subject—Clare is at her most disruptive, broaching a definition of herself that denies words rather than capitulating to or comfortably residing within them. Far from claiming "I am," Clare concludes *Exile and Pride* by saying only what she is not, radically confounding all attempts to label her and leaving us with more questions than answers about the intricacies of identity—and about what it means to say that anybody "is" anything.[35]

Importantly, many of the tales in Clare's text are difficult to tell because of their internal contradictions—their ideological impossibilities, as it were. She is a feminist "hick" (135), a fierce environmentalist who still feels loyal to her childhood in the logging towns of rural Oregon. She was brutally abused as a young girl by her father and his friends (stated in the text as abrupt fact, rather than serving to organize the narrative), the same men whose way of life "taught [her] the hills and woods" (125) and to whom she maintains an ambiguously gendered identification as "an almost son" (126). She had difficulty acknowledging her sexuality in the face of the "real, actual, institutionalized asexuality" of the disabled, in a world that reads same-sex desire as deviance and the disabled as "genderless, asexual undesirables" (119). Uttering so many secrets at once is the textual equivalent of what Clare proclaims as her queerness, a term that designates not the woman-identified lesbian existence celebrated by Panzarino but, rather, the totality of Clare's barrier-bending opposition to the severe inadequacy—and the oppressive violence—of patriarchal ideologies about the body, sex, and the environment.[36] "Queer" and "cripple" are "words to shock . . . words to resist internalized hatred, words to help forge a politics" (70). In turn, Clare's text performs hybridity, its accretion of segments mounting a structural argument against, in Julia Watson's words, "the privileged discourse of Western identity politics that autobiography has helped to create and sustain."[37]

Thus "exile" and "pride" signify the ostracizing power and the transformative potential of language, as well as the disorienting and determining impact of bodily difference. If exile is both a metaphysical and a geographical place to which a person like Clare is banished (by cultural norms of physical ability and appearance and of gender and sexual behavior, as well as by her own political beliefs, which impel her to flee her violent upbringing in working-class Oregon), pride is a textual and a philosophical way back, both cause and effect of rewriting the strict binaries that govern Western ideologies of identity. Clare states that "the lessons of who is dominant and who is subordinate" are "drill[ed] . . . into the bodies of children," but at the same time, those bodies are "not merely blank slates upon which the powers-that-be write their lessons" (129). The body exerts its own pressure—"the sensory, mostly non-verbal experience of our hearts and lungs, muscles and tendons, telling us and the world who we are" (129)—but it also eludes static, oppositional definitions. In this way, Clare's body becomes a source of meaning, but it does not provide a stable ground from which sex, gender, or disabledness ineluctably emerge; as Gilmore argues, "The body is usually thought to provide compelling, even irrefutable, proof of sex and gender, and ultimately of unique identity."[38] To the contrary, Clare's corporeal difference renders the limitations of language and cultural codes strikingly obvious: so ambiguous is her body, she proclaims, "*You don't have pronouns yet for us*" (128; emphasis in original).

Disability and gender inextricably entwine in *Exile and Pride*, with each other, with discourse, and with cerebral palsy. Because, on the reductive stage of gender performance, femaleness is characterized by mannerisms determined by the able-bodied, the particulars of Clare's condition—her "heavy-heeled gait," her "halting, uneven speech," and "the tremors in [her] hands, arms, and shoulders"—literally mark her "as either genderless or a teenage boy" (131). But where other writers protest against the specifically *defeminizing* effects of ableist ideology, Clare writes that the negative assumptions about her based on disability—that she is "ugly and clumsy, unattractive and undesirable" (118)—created a space in which she could actually heed her "childhood sense of being neither girl nor boy" (129).[39] The language of gender ambiguity is reiterated throughout the text, continually denying any firm assessment of Clare as a woman. She speaks of her "quiet, bookish, tomboy self, neither girl nor boy" (130), invokes her "boyhood pleasure" (126), claims that as a child she was "not at all sure of [her] girlness" (129) even as her father's abuse confirmed "in no uncertain terms that [she] was a girl" (126), and names herself, finally, as "not-girl-not-boy" (130). In the interstices of the sexed body, compelled to conform to "natural" anatomical definitions;[40] the cerebral palsied body, unable to conform to masculinist and ableist conceptions of gendered behavior; the classed and regional body, at home with the landscape and small-town pace of Port Orford, Oregon, but exiled by the economic hardships and cultural isolation of rural existence; the abused body of a girl who takes refuge in a sense of boyness; the body out of control, violently subdued by patriarchal law—from the discontinuity of all these, Eli Clare "enter[s] as a not-girl-not-boy transgendered butch" (137), "some third, fourth, fifth gender" (134).[41]

Clare's self-representational agenda thus entails eschewing not only gendered signifiers (masculine and feminine) that do not accommodate either her disability or her sexuality, but even the ontology of "woman," which she calls "too small" (137). Like Panzarino's expansive practice of self-naming to "illuminate the contradictory, multiple construction of subjectivity"[42] ("writing articles and letters on disability, feminism, sexuality and lesbianism," for example [*The Me in the Mirror*, 239]), Clare's "neither girl nor boy" and "not-girl-not-boy" respell the possibilities and imagine new identifications, new combinations. But unlike Panzarino's piling-up of presences (Panzarino is willing to say "I am"), Clare writes herself, in part, through negation. Her strategy of resistance to hegemonic ideology works not only through opposition but also by exposing the absence of terms, concepts, and stories to account for her existence " 'in between' " (132). Eve Sedgwick has argued of coming-out stories that "the double-edged potential for injury in the scene of gay coming out . . . results partly from the fact that the erotic identity of the person who receives the disclosure is apt also to be implicated in, hence perturbed by it."[43] But what *Exile and Pride* threatens to disturb goes beyond the secure boundaries of the sexuality of its readers. Clare's body—which she repeatedly describes as "stolen" by such "lies and thievery" as "divisions of labor" and "images of masculinity and femininity," and by "racism, sexism, classism, ableism," and "notions of 'real' men and 'real' women" (130)—deprives her audience of easy recourse to both biology and discourse as a firm basis for *any* form of identity, thus challenging not only the link between the body and "erotic" identity but any certain sense of being either male or female, healthy or sick, able or disabled, straight or gay.

It is in the context of shattering binary thinking that Clare's environmentalism becomes involved with her questions about gender and disability. *Exile and Pride* devotes considerable attention to drawing explicit connections between disability, gender, class, and queerness,[44] but Clare's commentary on the economics and politics of the timber industry is the least integrated component of the text. How is clear-cut logging, specifically, enmeshed with being a queer gimp? Though the relationship is left unstated, Clare suggests that the aggressiveness of the logging and salmon industries in the Pacific Northwest *and* passive, uncritical environmentalism are equally underwritten by the kinds of attitudes that perpetuate the cultural invisibility of disability and queerness. In a discussion of the "propaganda" (22, 23, 24) disseminated by industry and parroted by local educators, Clare writes,

> My classmates and I were taught by teachers who worked for schools funded largely with timber taxes; by U.S. Forest Service rangers and their brochures; and by industry-supported textbooks, displays, slide shows, and tours. The point isn't simply that we, like schoolchildren across the country, were taught half-truths about trees and salmon. Rather we learned even more fundamental lessons, that trees and salmon are endlessly renewable commodities. This view of the natural world, which puts clear-cutting, replanting, and hatcheries at its center, conveniently supported the two industries, logging and fishing, that sustained the towns we lived in. (24)

Two sets of relationships are obscured by the idea that logging is "good" (22) for the ecosystem: first, the slide from corporate bottom lines to "truth" or "values," and second, the intricate intersections of nature itself—the fact that clear-cutting negatively affects the habitat and behavior of deer, salmon, and other wildlife (23). By "naturalizing" its domination over the land, industry sustains a myth of human guardianship over the earth, deeply embedded in "right-wing," Christian thinking (25), that construes the world as both infant in need of tending and a "warehouse of resources" readily available for human use.[45] Severing one element from another, such ideology compartmentalizes the environment in a hierarchical way that maintains strict boundaries between "civilization" and "nature," allowing for and even guaranteeing what Walker Percy calls the "many-tissued package" of natural objects.

Clearly, the frustration of the "activist," "socialist with anarchist leanings" Clare (21) over conservative economic policy is thickly intertwined with her anger at oppressive social attitudes toward human "others" who are, like the environment, seen as separate, wild, and worthy of overmastering. But the more subtle thread of her argument has to do less with the broad stroke of the environmental question ("what white people have done to North America for 500 years—laid the land bare in the name of profit and progress" [26]) than with so-called environmentalists themselves. Again, this issue is bound up with class and regional location. Paradoxically but perhaps not unexpectedly, Clare does not discover an environmentalist platform until she leaves Oregon; it is in the city that she "stop[s] taking the familiar plants and animals of the Siskiyou National Forest for granted" (25).

But she also realizes that pat, liberal attitudes toward the earth are no less distancing and hierarchical than the industrialist position she left behind and are perhaps worse for disguising anthrocentrism as a love of "nature": "White urban reverence of tree spirits and Mother Earth," Clare demurs, is "a reverence often stolen from Native spiritual traditions and changed from a demanding, reciprocal relationship with the world into something naïve and shallow that still places human life and form at its center" (25). Romanticizing nature—merely citing its beauty, majesty, grandeur, or sublimity—does little to dismantle the perception of the natural world as something "other" from humanity, a unified, undifferentiated entity wholly and essentially separate from human life. While presented as earnest concern for the environment, this "fuzzy, romanticized version of nature, combining memories of Walt Disney nature movies with . . . occasional summer vacations to overcrowded national parks" (25) derives, fundamentally, from the same mindset that views trees and fish as marketable and renewable commodities. To appreciate nature from afar, as John Daniel has argued[46]—to "love" nature without seriously engaging with it or understanding ourselves as a part of it—is to collude in the belief that it can also be mastered.

A truly rigorous environmentalist stance, then, is one that respects difference and diversity while also acknowledging human existence as one other form of life in a thriving, interlocking network of natural processes. And it is precisely in this context of a "demanding, reciprocal relationship with the world" that disability and queerness reenter, if implicitly, Clare's discussion. The kind of mentality that stands behind capitalism (categorical, linear, fearful of ambiguity or open-endedness) is linked in the text not only to the depredations of logging, fishing, and hunting but also to attitudes that militate against corporeal difference—as in the imposition of "genital surgery . . . on intersexed people" to uphold the "mutually exclusive definitions of male and female" (128), or the commodification of disability and racial difference in American freak shows, which transformed anomalous bodies into "freaks, savages, and geeks" (71). In the face of such material ramifications of the ideological suppression of difference, Clare demands "systemic changes" (44). For any wholesale shift to occur in how we figure ourselves and our world, she argues, we must scrutinize our complicity in the ideology of capitalism no less than rhetorically inflammatory activism that keeps boundaries in place and perpetuates stereotypes (the logger as "brute," for example, or the disabled as helpless and in need of benevolent protection). And "we must be conscious of who the 'we' is" (59), acknowledging the ways in which the particulars of subject position directly influence our perception of social, political, and economic structures. The sustained critique here addresses the dangers of implicatedness, the way any seemingly private choice ripples into a larger ideological system, but also, less obviously, how a kind of thoughtless paternalism can pervade even apparently progressive coalitions.

Exile and Pride brings a similar analysis to bear on the medical model of disability. In the medical paradigm, the disabled body is pathologized as "defective" and seen as requiring correction, treatment, or cure. Disability is held to reside solely within the body and is thus the responsibility (the fault, the affliction) of the individual, as well as a puzzle for doctors (perhaps heroically) to solve. This dynamic implies that a life that continues to be disabled despite medical attention is so damaged as to be not worth living, and any effort on behalf of the disabled that addresses social, material, or logistical issues rather than providing a cure is seen as "boring," even pointless.[47] Many scholars have pointed out that the exaggerated push for cures—most notably exemplified by Jerry Lewis's muscular dystrophy telethons—disguise deep-seated horror at anomalous bodies as "the compassionate desire to prevent or stop suffering."[48] In an extended reading of images circulated by such disparate venues as advertising, public service announcements, telethons, pornography, and the health care industry, Clare suggests that representations of the disabled as both dependent children and objects of investigation play on widespread reactions to corporeal difference as if it were both pitiable and morbidly fascinating. She stages a provocative juxtaposition, worth quoting in full:

> Imagine a group of straight men raking in the bucks for women's rights by portraying women as pitiful and tragic individuals who lead unbearable lives by virtue, not of sexism, but of their femaleness. Or imagine straight people, who purported to advocate for gay/lesbian/bi people, raising money by reaffirming the cultural belief that homosexuality is a devastating but curable condition. These situations would be intolerable; queer and feminist activists would rise up in revolt. But this is exactly where disabled people find ourselves. Nondisabled people, like Jerry Lewis, who purport to be working in the interests of disabled people, turn their backs on disability oppression, rev up the stereotypes of tragic and helpless cripples, and pour the bucks into research rather than civil rights. And disability activists are rising up in revolt, naming the telethon a pity festival and challenging the disability charity industry head on. (107)

In a manner akin to that of preservationists who purport to respect the land while appointing "civilized" humanity the protectors of an idealized natural world, the frantic search for cures grants the nondisabled a privileged cultural status vis-à-vis the disabled, who—in their dependent and infantilized state—remain "on the margins," "isolated and shunned" (106).

If pietistic compassion stimulates oppression as much as normative binarism does, both are prolonged by representations of difference as the sign of essential separateness and untouchability, whether in an idealized or subordinating manner. Thus disability, the environment, and queerness come together around a problematic lack of accurate images, which it is *Exile and Pride*'s purpose to rectify. As one example, Clare writes, "Sometimes nondisabled folks ask me what I would do if I could take a magic pill and wake up 'normal'—that is, without CP. They always ask in such a way that I know they believe my life to be unbelievably hard. I like telling them that for me having CP is rather like having blue eyes, red hair, and two arms. I don't know my body any other way" (106–7). In effect, the text strives to make each of its constituent identity markers—class status and rural background, sexual orientation, gender, disability, and ecological activism—*believable*. Each is merely one among many "features" of an individual life, requiring accommodation and attention, perhaps, but not correction or pity. Disabled and "enabled" (67), queer and straight, female and male, and the "natural" and the "human" are fictional opposites masking a continuum of human experience, what Mitchell and Snyder refer to as "divergently functioning organisms," "dynamic humanity," and bodily "elasticity."[49] In her insistence on making visible so many instances of abjectness—on making the "outside" the place from which she speaks and exhorts others to action and representation—Clare trespasses on the edges of legitimate subjectivity, unfixing the "truth" of self even as the body materializes in all its constitutive significance. "Disability snarls into gender. Class wraps around race. Sexuality strains against abuse. *This* is how to reach beneath the skin" (137).

In a lengthy section titled "Freaks and Queers," Clare surveys the history of American freak shows to explain why she has not, as other disabled people have, appropriated the word "freak" to "shape pride" by invoking and then defying the legacy of carnival performances as "freak, monster, pet dwarf, court jester, clown" (100). For Clare, "freak" calls up other kinds of performances, too (ones over which the disabled have perhaps even less control than their appearances at freak shows).[50] These include the objectifying display of disabled children before teams of doctors, students, and other specialists to observe their various peculiarities; the parading of the disabled on telethons that stimulate viewers' horror, fascination, and guilt; and more personally, the routine and unabashed stares of strangers at Clare's "trembling hands" and "jerky movements" (94) and the taunts of "*retard, monkey, defect*" (91) or "*retard, monkey, weirdo*" (94) she heard in classrooms and schoolyards. Like Nancy Mairs, Clare catalogs both the hateful and the euphemistic terms in common parlance—handicapped, disabled, differently abled, physically challenged, gimp, crip, retard—and differentiates between words of "solidarity" (68) and those that "tell a wishful lie" (69). "*Cripple* makes me flinch," she writes, ". . . but I love crip humor, the audacity of turning *cripple* into a word of pride. Gimp sings a friendly song, full of irony and understanding. *Retard* on the other hand draws blood every time" (69). This is no mere "semantic game," as she emphasizes (68); language penetrates the body itself, informing and delimiting our conceptions of what counts, of what "is."

Terms that define and exclude; slang that signifies membership—Clare picks and chooses her vocabulary, detailing the broad social legacies at stake in the use of any epithet, and she draws her own boundaries. Importantly, the discussion of language reorganizes affiliations and exclusions on Clare's own (literal) authority. For instance, paralleling the history of disabled and queer experience in American society, she counters the objectifying and pathologizing of queer people as "freaks of nature" (96) with the notion of pride: "By making *queer* our own, it becomes less a bludgeon. We take a weapon away from the homophobes. *Queer* . . . is a coalition-building word" (96–97). But beyond straightforward telling, Clare also performs a manipulation of language that simultaneously establishes a "we" while diminishing the antagonism of "us" and "them." In discussing the diversity of the queer community, she speaks of "dykes, faggots, bi's, and trannies" (97) or tosses off shorthand like "l/g/b/t" (96, 97)—terms that denote Clare's intimacy with and inclusion in the groups she mentions. The history lesson about the exploiting, criminalizing, and medicalizing of "freaks and queers" necessarily involves all of Clare's contemporary readers, while her examination and use of certain words may very well exclude some of them. In this way her acts of naming rechart the landscape of embodied identity, spell new possibilities of connection and desire, and confuse the boundaries of inside, outside, the legitimate, or the real.

In an analysis of the unnamed, ungendered narrator of Jeanette Winterson's 1992 novel *Written on the Body*, Leigh Gilmore asks,

> How, within the discourses of self-representation, do names signify identity? What does it mean for a name to identify a subject—to gender it, sex it, make it real? What are the definitional limits of "sex," "gender," and "sexuality" as evidence of the "identity" of an autobiographical subject? . . . Gender and sexuality do not reduce to each other nor do they confirm *an* identity for the narrator. . . . What might seem so ontologically *there* as to defy the need of representation becomes, in this text, difficult to name.[51]

Such questions certainly address the problematic of *Exile and Pride*, whose author presents herself via a neutrally gendered name, refuses the nouns that mark gender, and describes herself as a transgendered dyke. But they also bring into perspective the interplay between Clare's radical, queer identity and Panzarino's woman-identified celebration of body and erotics. For neither Clare nor Panzarino do gender and sexuality reduce to each other, nor do they guarantee identity in any predictable or unified way; indeed, as Clare demonstrates, gender itself is a highly contestable category.

Both authors similarly challenge the ontological certitudes of a sexed body; "female" is too small for Clare and too narrow for Panzarino to inhabit without further elaboration. Names and gender are held to guarantee veracity, but both refuse to stay put in Panzarino and Clare: neither *Exile and Pride* nor *The Me in the Mirror* opens with the simple claim, "I am a woman named . . . ." Who then is the "I" who speaks, the woman whose self-naming defies paternity but for whom identity emerges from group affiliation, rather than a culturally privileged autonomous self? Who is the "I" whose body is neither transparent nor silent but instead visible and vocal, "spastic" (*Exile and Pride* 94) and asymmetrical, marginalized by race and class? The concepts of woman, body, desire, sufficiency (a "good enough" body and self-sufficiency, independence) are mutually constitutive as well as explosive—disability transforms and is transformed by the meaning and experience of gender, sexuality modifies disability, and so on.

How much transformation, finally, can a single autobiographical text be said to effect? In reference to scenes of coming out as a gay person, Sedgwick has deplored "how limited a leverage any individual revelation can exercise over collectively scaled and institutionally embodied oppressions."[52] But, as I have been arguing, personal narrative enters the cultural conversation as what Reyna Rapp and Faye Ginsburg refer to as "*unnatural histories*, visions of lives lived against the grain of normalcy."[53] Rapp and Ginsburg argue strongly for an enlarged social "fund" of knowledge, disseminated in part through the personal narratives of people with disabilities, that counters how disability is narrowly defined by medical discourse. While Rapp and Ginsburg are primarily addressing prevalent assumptions about quality of life that mediate reproductive choices, their point about the political as well as interpersonal consequences of limited information about life with disability also pertains to matters of sexual agency. The kind of self-naming in which Panzarino and Clare engage works against a stripping away of definitional control from the subject common to the medical model as well as against the scarcity of autobiographical writing that directly addresses the experience of lesbian or queer sexuality in the context of disability (and vice versa). This accords precisely with Wilkerson's point that "everyone can learn more from paraplegics and quadriplegics about the extensive possibilities of human sexualities that depart from heterocentric and phallocentric norms."[54] Both writers also attempt to redraw the boundaries of community to encompass multiple differences.

The last paragraph of *Exile and Pride* not only answers the call for new stories that rewrite the history of gendered and disabled experience; it also literally re-members, constituting unfamiliar bodies and recombining gendered and sexual identities in a proliferation of types. Clare longs to "sit with butch women, femme dykes, Nellie men, studly fags, radical faeries, drag queens and kings, transsexual people who want nothing more than to be women and men, intersexed people, hermaphrodites with attitudes, transgendered, pangendered, bigendered, polygendered, ungendered, androgynous people of many varieties and trade stories long into the night. . . . Bold, brash stories about reclaiming our bodies and changing the world" (138). This kaleidoscopic scene of bodies, sexualities, and identities evokes the celebration of women that characterizes the ending of Panzarino's memoir, where she writes of giving a speech on disability and ableism at a National Lesbian and Gay Pride March in Washington, D.C.: "I faced the murmuring crowd of three hundred thousand people gathered at the morning rally. . . . Their energy was enormous and took me by surprise. . . . I felt like a treasured member of a great throng, and we all agreed" (258–60). Like Panzarino's vision of a thrumming corporeal mass that is at once collective and individuated, Clare's fantasy presents the body as unfixed and transformable, while also confirming the centrality of the body—however it may be experienced or narrated—to subjectivity. But where Panzarino imagines a specifically female and unified merging, Clare depicts an exchange that is both more variegated and more overtly concerned to insist on the liberatory potential of self-writing: her litany of peoples swapping the stories of their bodily difference is a celebration of the limitless possibilities of embodied experience, but it is also an exhortation, to herself and to others, to tell.

4 alternative motherhoods

Denise Sherer Jacobson & Anne Finger

The disabled woman made mobile by a wheelchair or scooter, with a cane or brace, defies humanistic fantasies of bodily wholeness in an especially visible way. Her uncanny assemblage, her hybridity as a figure both organic and mechanical, presents an embodied self without distinct borders, one whose functioning is to some degree inseparable from the accoutrements of technology. Physical integrity takes on new meaning in the context of a body only ambiguously differentiated from the apparatus that helps it to move. Given an entrenched cultural association between disability and the monstrous or inhuman, this imbrication of animate and inanimate forms (a troubling of categories whereby the human body is partially inert while the equipment is in motion) would seem to exaggerate the preternatural, alien presence of the disabled individual. As I have been discussing throughout this book, the perceived helplessness and childlike dependency of disability contribute to societal discrimination against disabled women as participants in meaningful work and intimate relationships. But it is perhaps the specifically mechanical aspect of some bodies—disturbing those myths of maternal care that idealize the soft, fleshly "naturalness" of breasts, arms, and laps—that most inspires resistance to disabled women as mothers.

Feminist theorizing about embodiment has, of course, contested maternity and nurturance as essentialized or instinctive components of female identity and has attacked the ideologically motivated anatomizing of women's bodies that separates parts from the whole (such as the womb) so as to render those parts available for legal control. Feminist critiques of myths of motherhood have similarly focused on the tendency to represent women in terms of isolated parts construed in the polarized terms of ambivalence: breasts that feed and then withdraw gratification, or vaginas that signify life and death, safe haven and consuming need. As many have pointed out, contradictory beliefs about the healing and pathologizing properties of women's bodies are thoroughly intertwined with fantasies that romanticize mothers as all-powerful beings but also demonize them as solely responsible for the failures of childhood. In a discussion of reproductive rights, for instance, Susan Bordo points out that the "ideology of woman-as-fetal-incubator" is simply the other side of the "cultural archetype" coin whereby mothers are feared as "cold, selfish," and "evil"; the focus on a single body part coincides with active suppression of a legitimized female "personhood."[1] As disability theorists have argued, subjectivity is embodied, but its full meaning cannot be accurately defined by or contained within a single, negatively imagined physical trait. And it follows that disabled mothers find themselves in an acutely difficult position, striving to be fully acknowledged as persons rather than a set of mythologized, vilified body parts.

Recent feminist theory has responded to the self/other basis of Western ideology about women and the body by seeking to unravel binary logics altogether. In Donna Haraway's famous "manifesto" on cyborgs, for example, the "antagonistic dualisms" of Western thought are replaced by the alienated, internally fragmented body of the cyborg—"theorized and fabricated hybrids of machine and organism," "a creature in a post-gender world," "resolutely committed to partiality, irony, intimacy, and perversity," always displaced and partial, a visible protest against notions of integrity and wholeness.[2] Haraway's proposition that "in a cyborg world . . . people are not afraid of their joint kinship with animals and machines, not afraid of permanently partial identities and contradictory standpoints,"[3] suggests an affinity between the posthuman subject and a disabled body only indistinctly demarcated from its mechanical aids.[4] Diane Price Herndl makes this link between cybernetics and disability explicit in an essay discussing cosmetic reconstruction after breast cancer; Herndl writes that having her "skin lifted," her "tissue removed and rearranged" makes her "alien to [her]self forever" in a potent "disavowal of the whole idea of the normal."[5] Such ideas have radical implications for rethinking the intersection of maternity and disability, two forms of embodiment that, because they blur the conceptual boundary between otherness and the self, both produce and lie hidden behind paradigmatic cultural delineations of normality. "Up till now," Haraway claims, "female embodiment seemed to be given, organic, necessary; and female embodiment seemed to mean skill in mothering and its metaphoric extensions." The cyborg world, by contrast, is "a monstrous world without gender."[6]

There would seem to be exciting theoretical possibilities in an alliance between the hybrid bodies of disability, motherhood, and the cyborg: an openness to the strange presence of difference within, an unsettling of the self/other binary that undergirds patriarchal and able-bodied attitudes toward both motherhood and physical dysfunction. The fear of dependency that encodes disability as helplessness and weakness, an affliction that implies a kind of dispersed, whole-self "sickness," and mothers as dangerously powerful and strictly other might be profitably reconsidered from the perspective of bodies whose very "nature" it is to be unstable, constantly obscuring the dividing line between human and machine, able and impaired, integrated with technical aids yet fragmented by scarring, paralysis, or pain. This is Lennard J. Davis's "dismodernist subject": "disabled," "completed by technology," "partial, incomplete," and "wounded."[7] Such bodies encourage a way of thinking about mother-child relations, for example, not in terms of an originary oneness that, necessarily renounced, must be forever sought in others but, rather, as a subject-to-subject relationality that begins with the very first involvement of a mother with her baby—in gestation, in fact. The encounter with what is other to the self that disability impels and the cyborg materializes *is* motherhood, and to conceive of subjectivity in terms of a produced rather than natural embodiment—to think of all embodiment as more or less prosthetic—is perhaps to lessen the mystified breach that holds motherhood and disabled women so insistently apart.

While there are important points of contact between "posthuman" and disabled reconstructions of identity, however, problems arise insofar as the language of fragments and alienation reiterates the very subject position many life writers of disability have struggled to discard. To scorn the notion of bodily "integrity," for instance, as an ableist and ultimately coercive instrument of social regulation may also be to overlook the ways in which the lived experience of disability so often involves punitive cultural messages that isolate the impaired or "different" body part, instilling a sense of physical incoherence. Lucy Grealy demonstrates the self-severing that can happen as a result of scarring when she writes that "the lower half" of her face, its contours radically altered by cancer and multiple surgeries, "canceled out the beauty of the upper half" (*Autobiography of a Face* 157). Anne Finger, whose story of post-polio motherhood I discuss below, describes a similar feeling of internalized bifurcation: "My body is split in half: the good and the bad. . . . My left leg was my good leg, my right leg was my bad leg."[8] While the textual selves that such writers create do not inevitably hearken back to naive assumptions about organic wholeness and self-acceptance, neither do they turn entirely away from the possibility of reconciling those parts of themselves cordoned off as "bad" or from the need to reintegrate, in some fashion, a self forcibly split apart by cultural myths of beauty, ability, femininity, and health.

To fetishize a postmodern feminist rejection of "normal" may also be to obscure the way in which *not* always being constructed as "other" matters to disabled women striving to articulate what Finger calls a "regular" identity as a mother (156). Disability studies exposes the dividing lines between able-bodied and disabled, beautiful and monstrous, and male and female as fictive and ideological, but it also questions the assumptions that sometimes lie behind that very act of exposure. The political gesture of identifying oneself as posthuman, for instance, may signify quite differently for the person already accorded the status of human than for a woman with disability, taught to associate certain bodily particulars with freakishness and lack. Many disabled women voice an urgent desire to claim those very qualities deemed stereotypical and delimiting by feminism: beauty, sexual appeal to men, nurturance, and even a maternal "instinct." In her examination of reproductive rights debates, Bordo acknowledges that "feminists may be made queasy . . . by the idea of emphasizing the experiential significance of pregnancy and birth, out of a fear of the conceptual proximity of such notions to constructions of mothering as the one true destiny for women."[9] The same might be said about feminist reaction to some disabled women's very vocal insistence on identifying as eager, even conventional mothers. Yet Bordo's argument—that the ideology of women as naturally and fatedly maternal can best be subverted by "the construction of a public, *feminist* discourse on pregnancy and birth"[10]—also holds true for women with disabilities, whose experience of themselves as mothers (hopeful or in actuality, adoptive or biological) is informed by the mixed messages that emerge from patriarchal *and* feminist attitudes toward women's reproductive choices, the reproduction of disability, and disabled women's capacity to care for others.

The question I pose here, then, is what happens when disabled mothers write about themselves, composing new stories of origin that disrupt traditional myths of motherhood, feminist suspicion of the pressures of normative mothering, and ableist fear of replicating disability. If the authors discussed thus far write in some degree to dispel cultural ignorance about—and hostility toward—the fact of women with disabilities being actively sexual, the narratives of Denise Sherer Jacobson (who has cerebral palsy) and Anne Finger (who contracted polio as a child) demonstrate that the putatively "appropriate" and less threatening social role of heterosexually married motherhood is no less fraught with contradiction and misunderstanding. Indeed, disabled women are regarded with perhaps even more vehement opposition when they attempt to assume the culturally sanctioned position of mother. Jacobson and Finger must confront challenges from the various cultures in which they reside: a patriarchal society that promotes motherhood as proof of a woman's success, an ableist world that stigmatizes women with disabilities as both incapable of providing adequate child care and insufficient models for "normal" behavior or activity, and feminist groups in which both having a disability and wanting to mother may be regarded with (perhaps unconscious) skepticism, distrust, and even hostility.

As activists such as Michele Wates have pointed out, disabled mothers' desire to do the ordinary (to do what the nondisabled do as a matter of routine) is often held up as evidence of exceptional courage and fortitude, while the very same desire may also be received with a kind of shocked territorialism, condemned as a sign of irresponsible self-indulgence, on one hand, or a capitulation to patriarchal ideals, on the other. Jacobson's *The Question of David: A Disabled Mother's Journey through Adoption, Family, and Life* (1999) and Finger's *Past Due: A Story of Disability, Pregnancy, and Birth* (1990) recount the social and emotional struggles of women whose bodies mark them as paradoxically maternal and barren at once and what happens when their interests in reproductive and disability rights do not precisely agree. This chapter, in turn, seeks to explore the ways in which these texts present the disabled mother as an ordinary but also carefully considered role. By challenging a range of assumptions about what it means to be a "normal" mother, Jacobson and Finger redefine motherhood, rethink maternity and disability alike, and critique a cultural tendency to perceive both of these experiences as solely private matters, thus ignoring the politicized social relations that inform disabled women's lives and identities.

A Question of Trust: Denise Sherer Jacobson's *The Question of David*

Denise Sherer Jacobson has been a prominent figure on the disability lecture circuit and a member of Berkeley's renowned Center for Independent Living for many years. Yet her memoir of adopting a disabled baby invokes this professional status only a few times in more than two hundred pages, and always in a way that reinforces rather than dispels what Jacobson elsewhere cites as deep-seated feelings of helplessness, passivity, and submissiveness. For example, a brief mention of the "celebrity status"[11] she and her husband, Neil (who also has CP), enjoy as a result of speaking at disability-related conferences is quickly subsumed by the arrival of their baby David. In this scene, Jacobson emphasizes not their aplomb as public speakers but the stress and uncertainty of being the disabled parents of an "at risk" child. Later, Jacobson juxtaposes the ease with which she talks about disability before classes of health professionals (doctors, therapists, and pharmacists) with the anger and bitterness she fails to express when Neil's family, meeting David for the first time, behaves insensitively (150). Indeed, throughout *The Question of David*, Jacobson seems studiously to avoid presenting herself as a professional regularly sought out for her expertise; instead she narrates a subject beset by self-doubt and struggle.

Yet the minimization of her public persona as an advocate for disability rights may serve an important rhetorical purpose in Jacobson's tale of disability and adoption. Motherhood, in this text, is neither a "natural" nor a private event. Jacobson's decision to adopt a baby—even her willingness to undergo the radical change that parenting necessarily entails—is scrutinized and implicitly condemned by strangers and family members alike. The sheer effort of will and physical strength involved in everything from filling out the adoption application to changing David's diapers activates a legacy of self-doubt, originating in Jacobson's painful memories of growing up with cerebral palsy. Complicating matters is the fact that David himself exhibits early signs of CP, which provokes further memories not only of uncomfortable tests and exercises Jacobson underwent as a child but also her awareness of being a burden on her own parents. "Was I ready for a baby," she writes, "a disabled baby? Would I have to relive my own experience of childhood—the demanding therapy, the 'special education,' the loneliness of a child not being accepted by the nondisabled world? (I still dealt with that same loneliness in adulthood)" (11). Despite her desire to take it on, motherhood is a shattering experience for Jacobson, disruptive and disorienting, so that however full a sense of herself she may have had as a woman, an adult, and a person with CP *prior to* David, the challenges associated with adopting him evoke long-standing anxieties and stimulate new questions of whether or not she will be able to redefine herself as a mother.

To a large extent, then, not responding to certain situations with nimble poise is exactly Jacobson's point. Nothing has prepared her to mother David—not just because real motherhood must inevitably be different from the cultural myths that attach to it but, more importantly, because Jacobson herself is different from the cultural myths that figure mothers in very specific physical and psychological terms. As Wendy S. Harbour puts it, "Sometimes it's tough just to get past the birth control in our heads[:] the little thoughts and fears and stereotypes about our own disabilities that make us wonder if we'll ever make decent moms." And Michele Wates adds, "There is a . . . tendency to blame disabled people for being so *irresponsible* as to have children."[12] Perceived as asexual and childish, deformed and "sick," disabled women are held to lack the dexterity and maturity to mother, and their desire to do so is frequently met with skepticism and even contempt. In a very real sense, a disabled woman may be unable to pick up her baby, make eye contact, drive to a doctor's office for routine exams, or speak to her baby without slurring her words. Yet only recently (and still rarely) have either the medical or the social service communities responded to disabled women's challenges that such points of difference not be held as evidence of their inadequacy as potential mothers. When Jacobson writes that she "bring[s] out the patronizing side in many people" for whom disability signifies "childlike innocence" and a lack of "common sense," or that her "slow, seemingly labored speech" tends to inhibit conversation with strangers (34–35), she begins to demonstrate how difficult it will be for her to be taken seriously as a parent.

Both of the scenes in which Jacobson explicitly refers to her professional identity also foreground what becomes a kind of leitmotif throughout the text: a feeling of estrangement from Neil. Jacobson repeatedly differentiates her writerly sensibility from Neil's "logical" one (105), but more than a temperamental disparity is at stake here. Adopting David seems to bring into stark focus their habitual reactions to "the ugly emotions" (105), the "guilt, hurt, and anger" (150) that disability can produce, perhaps most intensely within the family. Adopting David summons acute anxieties that both Jacobson and her husband experienced as children, so that in situations of stress, both recapitulate long-standing emotional patterns. Jacobson states explicitly that Neil retreats into a defensive intellectualism (a stereotypically "masculine" response to threat) that deflects attention away from his impaired body, a distancing mechanism that inhibits working through the aftershocks of familial rejection and resentment. At the same time, she exaggerates what is repeatedly characterized as her own propensity for hysterics. In the many and ambivalent discussions about how much and what sort of emotional response is warranted in the face of resistance to disabled parenting—which involves an oblique narrative about Neil's desire for a traditional wife who will assume primary care of the baby as well as management of the myriad logistical "details" (13)—Jacobson's public and professionally competent self seems to disintegrate.

Jacobson thus suggests that the emotional impact of internalizing negative messages about her capability may be more disabling than anything having to do with the practical realities of her physical condition. On some level, Jacobson herself doesn't fully trust that she will be a good mother—and those scenes in which she records her acquiescence to Neil's wishes, remoteness, or interpretation of events seem designed to illustrate how acutely the prospect of mothering provokes an old habit of relinquishing decision-making power to the institutional authorities who governed her experience of disability: parents, doctors, social services. If having a child requires, therefore, that both Denise and Neil confront the ways in which being disabled is interpreted *and experienced* as a kind of extended childhood, then the writing of the text constitutes Jacobson's effort to confirm her adult identity and to redefine both motherhood and marriage to include the specific contours of disability. The story of David rejects received truths about "mother nature," about the nature of caretaking, self-sufficiency, and "appropriate" emotional responses to an environment ill-equipped to accommodate disabled parents. Through the intersection of mothering and disability, Jacobson attempts to reorient her readers' understanding of both, while at the same time managing her own feelings of insecurity and inadequacy.

As one way of establishing the relationship between Jacobson's history as a child with CP and her new role as a mother with CP, *The Question of David* juxtaposes negative cultural attitudes toward disability against the way in which disability becomes a point of connection and understanding between mother and son. Jacobson's own CP was viewed as a tragic calamity: "At four years old," she writes, "I already knew what I looked like in other people's eyes: a pretty child who could hardly walk or talk, who had to be carried up and down stairs and fed, and schlepped to doctors and therapists. I was viewed as a tragedy by well-meaning family and friends who pitied my mother and admired her devotion to me" (64). Disability entails—because it is understood to signify—loss of control; taking David to physical therapy sessions, Jacobson "fight[s] back the memories" of enduring childhood as "a disability, never a person" (117). After a difficult visit with both families, Jacobson reports that the Sherers and the Jacobsons "had never been able to accept the concept of disability as anything less than a cross to bear" (155).

But Jacobson complicates uncritical assumptions about what constitutes disability by insisting on the specificity behind the globalizing term and by citing certain physical characteristics as welcome points of similarity between her and David. For instance, when a therapist claims that David might be "severely disabled," Jacobson protests against the tendency to compress a range of symptoms into one term: "How many disabled babies had this woman ever come across? Maybe in St. Louis they didn't have enough of a variety to compare and contrast. I've seen babies with cerebral palsy who couldn't hold their heads up or suck on a bottle. . . . *Severely disabled?* David? Alert, well-nourished, gurgling David?" (37). Such a remark has multiple effects: Jacobson presents *herself*, rather than the pediatric physical therapist, as better equipped to assess David's condition, thereby reminding us that disability is in part a subjective term, determined by the experience and beliefs of the viewer, rather than essentially or stably "in" the body. And she interrupts a cultural tendency to reduce the particularity of physical conditions to a single, pejorative category. Of herself, Jacobson remarks that "being classified as severely disabled felt so inappropriate. It pigeonholed me based on the outward appearance of my cerebral palsy, not on my ability" (38).

Like Nancy Mairs, Jacobson claims that the very apparatus that earns her the label of "severely disabled"—her power wheelchair—is in fact distinctly *em*powering: "I'm much more 'able' than I ever was on crutches," she writes (38), and what's more, "I feel and am much more autonomous and independent using it" (19). What might have been a bleak evaluation of David's condition thus becomes, in the writing of the scene, an opportunity for Jacobson to dispute the authority of the so-called experts and the vocabulary of prognosis ("severe" according to whose frame of reference?). Recounting the therapist's claim that David is "exhibiting an overactive Moro reflex," Jacobson turns the sign of "abnormality" into a source of familiarity (the Moro reflex is a newborn's characteristic response to being startled, such as the sensation of falling, by flinging its arms sideways and flexing its fingers). "I smiled knowingly at David. We had something in common!" (37). Jacobson is the adult narrator here, able to discern and identify, not the frightened girl who went "kicking and screaming" to Bellevue Hospital when she was barely older than David himself (117).

Just after Jacobson declares herself an insider and an agent, and not an invalid or isolated outcast (she has access to a certain domain of knowledge and experience, she enumerates "all the things [she] can do" [38]), she writes that she "wanted to say something" to the physical therapist examining David, but didn't. "I had the feeling that nothing I would be able to articulate at the moment would have made any difference in her prognosis of David. Besides, I feared that it was not safe to express my dissenting opinion until David came home" (38). Jacobson is "playing nice" here in part because she and Neil have not yet been granted custody of David. That concern has a legitimate basis: because they have disabilities, Denise and Neil worry that their petition to adopt David will not be approved, and thus Jacobson is motivated to appear accommodating. But more pertinent to her self-representation is the marked contrast between what Jacobson *writes* and what she *does*. Only in the text does she articulate her disagreement; only here does she allow herself to be contradictory, assertive, even defiant. In the moment, as she reports, she primarily feels afraid. Dissension is not simply impolite; it is *dangerous* (this is reminiscent of Connie Panzarino's fear of upsetting the mother upon whom she depended for basic care). More than learned passivity (which Jacobson describes as "second nature" [155]) is involved; she is also capitulating to a powerful belief, held over from childhood, that she "had to be nice." "I was in no position to risk abandonment," she writes; "I could not afford to express my sadness, pain, and anger" (183). Jacobson exhibits here what Arthur W. Frank might refer to as an "*ethic of recollection*," where the life story becomes "a moral opportunity to set right what was done wrong or incompletely."[13] Far more than a reportage of events, then, *The Question of David* becomes the arena in which Jacobson can transform submissive and compliant behavior into scenes of self-confident, resolute expression.

Jacobson repeatedly stages such passages, amplifying the tension between the worst vestiges of growing up with CP and her use of language to write a counternarrative of validity and self-assertion. Describing a situation in which she is "scolded" by a "twenty-something-year-old" day care worker who comes to fetch David because of another mother's forgetfulness, Jacobson writes, "In automatic reflex, I apologized for the inconvenience, profusely. . . . A few minutes afterward, my anger bloomed. How dare that little twerp admonish me! I hadn't asked her to come. She volunteered. . . . Guilt began seeping through; maybe I was partly at fault. . . . Even so, what right did she have to treat me like a little girl, and why did I feel like one?" (184). In this rapid-fire litany of conflicting emotions, Jacobson utilizes the autobiographical space to tell a different story—to express "ugly," even insulting thoughts ("that little twerp") to question her unthinking acceptance of being somehow to blame for inconveniencing someone else, and to demonstrate how frequently she experiences being disabled as a form of disenfranchisement and shame. The fact that Chris, the day care assistant, infiltrates Jacobson's private space, chiding her "in the living room of [her] home," further emphasizes the denial, by the nondisabled, of a disabled person's sense of legitimacy and control. In turn, however, Jacobson's creation of a textual space in which to level her critique against Chris directly resists the infantilizing attitudes toward disability that Chris's behavior exemplifies.

An even more intensified instance of this dynamic occurs when Jacobson recounts her and Neil's decision to fire their housekeeper, an Israeli woman named Chavallah. Denise and Neil are mutually dissatisfied with Chavallah's irresponsible behavior, yet in her initial description of the scene, Jacobson describes herself as childish and unable to control her emotion, while Neil is a cool and detached mediator. Importantly, the triangulation at work here positions Neil as the father-in-command, Jacobson as the unruly girl, and Chavallah as the able-bodied figure whose inconsistent ministrations to the household underscore the importance of what Jenny Morris describes as "receiv[ing] assistance in an empowering, rather than a disempowering, way."[14] When Jacobson expresses her displeasure with Chavallah, the housekeeper—"a jungle cat circling its prey"—lambastes her as "spoiled," "selfish," and "stubborn" and addresses herself to Neil "as if he were her ally" (104). In the moment of confrontation, Jacobson writes, "anger and hurt choked my throat, just as it did when I was younger" (104). She is like a schoolgirl being taunted on the playground, "scream[ing]" at Chavallah, "You're a liar. You're a liar," words that would seem to corroborate Chavallah's condescension. Perhaps more egregiously, Neil's intervention into what is very nearly depicted as a stereotypically female "cat fight" exhibits his rhetorical and emotional control: "When my husband . . . finally had enough, he raised his hand. 'The fact is, Chavallah, this is her home' " (105).

But in the pages of the memoir, Jacobson layers a different narrative over her presentation of the details of this imbroglio. Here, she expresses rage about the many times *she* has accommodated Chavallah's needs; here too she reveals how angry she is at Neil for retreating into the role of disinterested negotiator rather than being an active advocate for his wife or—more pointedly—an equal participant in firing Chavallah. On the page, Jacobson constructs a clear-thinking and self-possessed subject capable of admitting her limitations but also of observing the ways in which others, particularly Neil, fail to acknowledge their complicity in shunting the disabled woman to the periphery. In the moment, it is Neil who takes possession of the house for Denise (in a way that seems to silence her); in rewriting the story, Jacobson is both architect and proprietor—the autobiography becomes the "home" that Jacobson could not speak up for when she was in the throes of anger and hurt. Announcing her inability *then* to adequately voice her resentment against Chavallah becomes a way of doing so *now*, in a forum perhaps more emotionally and politically efficacious than a fight in the kitchen. And here too she renders herself a less than acquiescent wife, responding emphatically to Neil's single comment: "*That was it? That was all he was going to say on my behalf?*" (105).

The autobiographical space thus works to subvert some of the more traditional gender roles that Denise and Neil play out in their dealings with each other and with home care workers. In a similar way, Jacobson uses the space of the text to reconstruct entrenched beliefs about child development and the mother-infant relationship. Her discussion of David's experience at day care, for instance, raises important questions about how we gauge "normal" toddler behavior. Reporting the director's complaint that David is "unresponsive" and " 'unsocial' " (185), Jacobson counters the apparent proof of her child's disengagement with evidence of resourcefulness and ingenuity, asking, "How could my experience of David be so different than Jean's?" (186). Far from " 'spacy' " (185), at home David is "a self-sufficient little guy" who "could get his own bottle from the refrigerator" and "his own bowl for cereal," a boy who "thought a lot" and helps Jacobson solve such puzzles as how to open a package encased in cellophane (186).[15] That David's quiet demeanor, cleverness, and ability to play alone are read by Jean not as signs of autonomy or maturity but, rather, as antisociable disinterest underscores how thoroughly an association between disability and defectiveness can permeate one's assessment of behavior. Jacobson suggests that David is primarily guilty by association with her and Neil, rather than as a result of his own actions—which might seem far less remarkable in a child of "normal" parents. While it is eventually determined that David does have a form of language delay, Jean's "diagnosis" of his behavior as maladaptive inappropriately pathologizes him, failing him on two counts: Jean neither interprets David's behavioral style as an acceptable form of difference from other children nor responsibly investigates what might really be at stake in his tendency to avoid speaking. Jacobson's portrayal of this scenario thus makes two related juxtapositions. Against Jean's "false assumptions" (186), Jacobson is again the more accurate judge of David's behavior, and in contrast to Jean's putatively authoritative observational skills (she "had a good reputation" and "a waiting list of children" [186]), Jacobson's version of events takes precedence, garnering readerly support. Here in the memoir, she is author and mother at once, creating a textual David for her readers—an appealing, sturdy, intelligent "little guy."[16]

Scenes such as this, in which Jacobson portrays herself as taking charge of definitional authority, depend for their impact on our awareness of her lingering feelings of inferiority. While the desire to authorize one's voice has been a source of both momentum and self-censorship for many contemporary female autobiographers, Jacobson's is an especially compacted sense of illegitimacy. As she puts it, "I often struggled to convince myself that I had a right to be heard and, more important, that I had something worth saying" (183). Suffering less from any effects of CP than from what Susan Wendell calls "a powerful internalized disciplinarian" wielding "shame and self-hatred" as its instruments of punishment,[17] Jacobson has learned to suppress her opinions, desires, and needs. Used to being condemned as "selfish and inconsiderate" (67) whenever she expressed hurt or anger, she continues to have "difficulty seeing [herself] as being an equal in a relationship" (69), frequently "ignore[s] [her] own instincts" (76), and "struggle[s] to overcome passivity" [98]). Though the existence of the book stands as a dual victory—over the dire forecasts that she would "be a vegetable for [her] adult life" (73) as well as the loss of writing space and time that David's arrival causes—assertions of weakness nonetheless pervade the narrative, implying the persistence of self-doubt in spite of Jacobson's writerly control.

But to frame this another way, that chorus of internalized critical voices generates its opposite: the self-assured woman of good instincts who affirms her side of the story. Jacobson's strong and determined persona (the one who stage-manages the story, not the one so often spotlighted in individual episodes) directly contravenes the image of her as fearful and inadequate; yet the latter is necessary precisely because *The Question of David* is, fundamentally, a story of triumph over unrelenting self-doubt. Importantly, Jacobson refuses the "supercrip" paradigm of disabled experience, in which praise for accomplishing the ordinary masks (because it is effectively the same as) animosity toward the "unordinary."[18] Jacobson's achievement is not that she overcomes the damage inflicted by CP in order to become a mother; it is rather that she perseveres in that desire in the face of social skepticism, no less than her own misgivings about herself. In that sense, the reiteration of just how profoundly she doubts herself makes legitimate and meaningful those moments when she prevails—as when she finally attends to her "intuition" (186) and removes David from Jean's nursery school.

When disability and maternity intersect, the "ordinary business"[19] of mothering collides with the extraordinary body of CP in a combination that may be difficult for both subject and onlookers to accept. Jacobson's process of acknowledging herself as a legitimate mother is inseparable from coming to terms with CP, because motherhood stimulates a reawakening of a tenacious and primitive anguish about being seen as "a raving cripple" (208). In a particularly pithy illustration of the friction between fantasies of "normality" and the reality of having CP, she records her mother's need to "keep up the momentary fallacy that, as it was often phrased, 'there looked like nothing was wrong [with] me.'" "It used to please my mother," she writes, "whenever my teacher would remark on how 'normal' I looked sitting quietly at my desk" (122). But if adult self-authorization entails refusing "to defeat a very integral part of who I am" (122) and accepting her disability, becoming a mother simultaneously necessitates that she refuse being "disabled"—by which I mean the stigma of disability and cultural pressures against disabled people becoming parents. The conundrum Jacobson's text seeks to resolve is that empowering herself to be "who she is" means quitting the struggle to meet ableist standards of embodiment, while at the same time realizing that disability and motherhood are not mutually exclusive—identifying herself in terms of CP without also capitulating to those constructions of disability that exclude the possibility of mothering. Michele Wates has described many disabled parents as "hankering after 'normality,'"[20] but what Jacobson longs for is to be validated as a mother *and* a disabled person, with "disability" and "maternity" as separate but interlocking identities, rather than "disabled" modifying a prior and putatively stable category of "mother."

Against such efforts as her mother's to normalize her and deny disability, Jacobson positions the realization—both the recognition and the bringing to fruition—of her parenting skills. She refers more than once to her "instinct and intuition" (183), but something more than "womanly" or "emotional" attunement to her surroundings is at stake. Toward the end of the day care episode, Jacobson indicates what *The Question of David* fundamentally strives to achieve: "As I looked back over the last three months of grappling with my own indecision, I started to realize that what other people thought or said wasn't as important as I was brought up to believe. . . . David had to come first! I had to trust that I knew what was best for him. He had to know that he could count on me" (191). The urgent address here is directed toward David, but of course it is Jacobson's own readers who are given to understand that she "knows best"; what other people think *does* matter, insofar as complicating a pervasive cultural ideology that prohibits the overlap of disability and maternity is one of the book's most primary agendas. *We*, as much as David, must know that Jacobson can be counted on, that her ideas are good ones, that she is dependable, and that she makes responsible decisions. I do not mean to suggest that Jacobson's text is defensive or apologetic; to the contrary, where she once exerted herself to accommodate others and satisfy their expectations, the authorial Jacobson exerts control, conducting her audience toward new insight and understanding. I would argue that the narrative's foregrounding of "an issue of trust" (183) is implicitly concerned with ableist culture's trust of Jacobson—readers share the task of "believing [herself] capable of protecting [her] son" (183). Though Jacobson herself opposes "intuition" to "expertise" (27), the choices she makes for David based on her experience as a disabled person are consistently shown to outweigh the opinions of the nondisabled physicians and therapists she and Neil consult.

The Question of David thus offsets Jacobson's negative assessments of herself with episodes in which disability is the model for, rather than an aberration of, behavior and movement. For example, the very aspects of her condition that left her on the literal sidelines of childhood games become a pattern for David's learning process: constructing a Lego train with David, Jacobson claims that "[her] slowness seemed to help him grasp the concept of how to do it" (166). Disability becomes opportunity when David, still a crawling baby, uses Jacobson's wheelchair to "pull himself into a standing position" in order to be picked up (158). Jacobson suggests that having a mother "confined" to a wheelchair, far from inhibiting David's own mobility, stimulates his independence. Because neither she nor Neil can push him on a swing or stand at the bottom of a slide, for instance, David confidently approaches other adults for assistance and manages on his own to negotiate the "twists and turns" of a slide "designed to thrill daring six- and seven-year-olds" (182).[21] At the same time, David is also keenly attuned to Jacobson's range of motion; she writes that "harried mothers often approached me to ask how I managed to train David to stay within sight while they chased their kids up and down the aisles. . . . Somehow, David just seemed to know his parents' limits and his own" (182).[22]

Moreover, Jacobson is a resourceful and creative mother. When she wants to take David outside for "walks" by herself, she figures out how to maneuver him into a sling carrier called a Kacoon (though she also calls a friend "for moral support": "I already had the idea," she admits; "I just needed someone around" [132]). Time and again, Jacobson proves that she is an able and ingenious protector who maximizes her physical capabilities and manipulates the environment to make things possible for herself and David alike. What is missing is a wider network of support—encouragement from others, acknowledgment, and recognition for being something other than an object "of concern or pity."[23] This is precisely the point Reyna Rapp and Faye Ginsburg make in arguing that a narrowly defined nuclear family structure excessively complicates the "mobilizing" of the support services needed by parents of children with disabilities (and, of course, by parents with disabilities): "Caretaking of a disabled infant requires different and expanded resources" that go beyond mother and father. Margaret Lloyd has made a similar case for rethinking not only the source but also the meaning of caretaking, writing that "the successful fulfillment of caring responsibilities is not reliant on the isolated, unsupported carrying out of caring tasks"; a disabled mother's need for assistance with "*the caring function*" does not preclude her from carrying out "the *caring role*."[24]

The Question of David makes it clear just how thoroughly entangled an undermining interpretation of disablement can become in one's sense of self. Despite its resistance to stereotypes and prejudice, Jacobson's text does at times capitulate to rhetorically disparaging figurations of physical dysfunction, and there are a number of disturbing features to Jacobson's depiction of her emotions as exaggerated or even "hysterical." When Neil tells the housekeeper Chavallah, for instance, that "this is [Denise's] home" (105), he does little to disprove Chavallah's assertion that Jacobson's demands are "unreasonable" (105), because his remark merely invokes ownership, rather than setting out any sort of clear justification for those demands. "This is her home" signals important facts about Jacobson—that she lives independently, in a home of her own—but it also has a curiously patronizing effect, relegating Jacobson to a domestic sphere and implying that her ability to assess Chavallah's performance may not be fully trustworthy. And he colludes in infantilizing her, playing the father to her irrational little girl. What Jacobson lauds as Neil's "logic" seems primarily a gesture of power, as if economic priority or masculine rhetorical force simply trumps the need for honest explanation. What's more, Jacobson herself seems to perpetuate a stereotype about female irrationality, framing her conflict with Neil as a neat dichotomy between emotion and reason. There is something troubling about Jacobson's insistence that Neil is "detached and logical" (105), while she is "a hysterical woman" (104). Even as she complains that Neil "reduced a volatile situation down to one sentence," deploying his "logic" as a psychic armament in defense against Denise's "strong" and "unwieldy emotions" (105), she seems to reproduce some of the very dichotomies her text strives to challenge: male/female, reason/emotion, professional/

domestic, parent/child, mind/body. The question becomes, then, to what end Jacobson invokes stock patriarchal tropes, particularly that most vexed—and problematically corporeal—reference to hysteria.

Issues of anger and control recur throughout *The Question of David*, with Jacobson repeatedly portraying herself as struggling to manage a propensity for emotional outbursts. ("I wished I were a bull—an angry, raging bull," she declares at one point, and then, "I controlled myself" [123]). In two apparently opposite ways, disability shapes her experience of emotion—in some instances by requiring that she suppress anger or grief so as not to alienate caregivers or other social service workers, and in other instances by producing "a tantrum," cathartic eruptions of suppressed pain. References to her "infantile behavior" (105), to being "in hysterics" (119, 205), to "succumb[ing] to hysterics" (141), to her emotional responses as "*always hav[ing] to come down to hysterics*" (142), or to having "cracked" (144) explicitly locate the origin of her "dark, shadowy feelings of shame, hurt, and unworthiness" (106) in the past, when her father—rather than Chavallah—accused her of being "unreasonable" (106) or when it was her sister, not her housekeeper, calling her a "little brat" (106). In this way, Jacobson shows how familial and social attitudes deprived her of effective methods with which to deal with the swirl of "anger, frustration, guilt" (106) associated with her CP, so that current situations immediately invoke the "old tunes from childhood." By discussing the deep hold those patterns continue to have on her, Jacobson seems invested in leading herself toward a new psychological mechanism for coping with self-hatred.

Yet it is in precisely this context of self-determination that Jacobson's use of the language of madness to define her emotional life works against her stated goal of avoiding the "seduction" (106) of negative interpretations of herself. The term "hysteria" is deeply pathologizing, inevitably a characterization of women and not men, and associated not just with the body generally but, rather, with the womb—the very site of patriarchal anxiety about maternity and difference. While Jacobson attempts to interrupt a self-defeating cycle by showing how familial and institutional attitudes toward disability left her ill-equipped to defend herself against others' demands or cruelty, her language also demonizes herself out of proportion to the emotional responses she describes. Something else seems to be at stake: fear of her own body or even an implication that disability is somehow essentially connected to exaggerated emotion. Jacobson's invocation, perhaps unwitting, of the hysterical female body—with its mobile womb, its secretive interior, and its excessive symptomology—brings into view what she admits to elsewhere as her "cripophobia" (121); the disabled body, too, is marked by difference, unpredictability, a loss of control. Throughout the text, Jacobson lets us know the myriad circumstances in which her gestures are not fluid or coordinated. Her body's motion is *too* visible, too erratic, neither sexy nor maternal.[25] By describing herself as "hysterical," then, she manages to reiterate a range of stereotypes about women, the disabled, bodies, and emotion, even as she points toward the "obvious message" that disability is "a burden," the "wounding accusations," and "the yoke of blame" (106) to account for her feelings. In a curious structural linkage, the very term used to suggest the oppressions of cultural fears of disability re-entrenches cultural fear of the female body; Jacobson makes herself the embodiment of the overemotional woman, displacing her own subtle loathing toward her body onto the system of power relations and ideological narratives that make disability culturally meaningful. Given her resistance to the infantilizing maneuvers of the able-bodied, such statements as "I had reacted as I've always reacted: hysterically" (106) seem simultaneously to apologize for and prove the essentializing relationship between body and self that her text is so clearly invested in disclaiming.

Such a link is borne out when she declares, at the end of the Chavallah episode, "I didn't want my son to be crippled by the same self-doubts that still betrayed me" (107). The apparently metaphorical (and not ironic) usage of "crippled" reiterates an old connection between an irregular body and a pathology of ego. Though the ostensible message here is Jacobson's determination to teach David an entirely different understanding of himself in view of the possibility that he has some form of cerebral palsy, the conflation of "self-doubt" with "crippled" nonetheless makes use of a corporeal condition to manifest a disturbance of psyche; the misshapen body makes material the inward torture of insecurity and bad feeling. Jacobson is curiously prone to such metaphors: she writes that despair over her disability "exacerbated" her mother's "losing out" to kidney disease (36), deploying not just the metaphor of illness as battle but also the notion that a positive attitude is integral to physical health.[26] She claims that "aggravation was a way of life" for her mother and suggests that aggravation "contributed to her death because it ate her up inside" (127). In another instance, she tries to persuade Neil that it is "unhealthy" not to acknowledge "anger and sadness" and "point[s] out that his father, a man who rarely showed his anger, died of a heart attack at the age of fifty-eight" (61). Late in the text, she wonders if David's frequent ear infections are a sign of unspoken unhappiness, and she says to Neil, "Maybe he's trying to tell us something" (188).

When illness is interpreted as "a psychological event," Susan Sontag writes, "people are encouraged to believe that they get sick because they (unconsciously) want to, and that they can cure themselves by the mobilization of will. . . . Psychological theories of illness are a powerful means of placing the blame on the ill."[27] A subtle critique is at work in Jacobson's emotional etiology of sickness: her mother ought to have stood up to unthinking doctors who ominously predicted that Denise would "end up" institutionalized (36); like his father, Neil refuses to express difficult emotion at his own physical peril. Even the belief that David's ear infections have a *psychological* cause (rather than heightened exposure to germs at day care) taps into the myth of control—as if two-year-old David wills his body to produce an emotional story he is not yet old enough to tell in words (when he is, would illness then be read as a failure to express displeasure or to remove himself from a hostile environment?). Such connections shape certain fears that drive Jacobson's own narrative. When illness just "isn't," when it is made to have "use value" (a kind of whole-body sign language or an incitement to change), the random chaos of bodily reality can be denied. When Jacobson locates her mother's kidney disease and Neil's father's heart attack in suppressed anger, the arbitrariness of those physical breakdowns—as well as the loss, grief, and fear they initiated—can be safely contained in a hopeful, but also punitive, narrative of psychological control, one that seems profoundly related to Jacobson's acute awareness of being *out* of control of her body, her feelings, and her choices.

Jacobson's preoccupation with feeling like a child is intimately bound up, of course, with the "question" of David: Does he also have CP? Will she be a good mother, whatever his condition? Will she be taken seriously by other parents? When she implies that David gets sick in order to communicate to her his psychical condition, the mind/body hierarchy she invokes grants David a degree of control over his corporeality that Jacobson might wish he really had—or might wish she had—over David's body as well as her own. What the frequent references to willpower, the ambivalent descriptions of anger, and the fear of having too much or too little command of one's emotion all point to, I think, is the potency of internalized shame about being disabled. Jacobson writes that "around family, our helplessness . . . intensifies, magnifies, conjuring up memories for them and for us of being dependent children" (146). When the two families gather for a weekend visit, Denise experiences "a little girl's sadness" (152), and Neil "slumps[s]" lethargically in his wheelchair, his habitual posture of self-conscious defeat. Jacobson directly links their adult self-hatred to parental insensitivity; she argues, for instance, that Neil's negative "body image" (83) stems from the fact that his father "always told [him he] was ugly" (82), and that her own father "considered [her] a burden" (68).

Jacobson frequently cites familial disapproval of the adoption as a signal feature of her insecurity. Her sister reports that Jacobson's father and aunt are "not too thrilled" about the decision (53); when Neil tells his mother and brother, they respond with both concern and indifference. It is therefore easy enough for them to relinquish parenting control when they are with their families or, as Jacobson puts it, any "willing, nondisabled" person (155). In effect, the nondisabled world takes over the parental function, while Jacobson "recede[s] into a passive motherhood," taking "a back seat" (97–98) as David's foster mother or other home care workers perform the physical activities of mothering in her stead. Such moments raise the question of where mothering is located—in the daily tasks of bathing and feeding, in moments of holding or mirroring, in evidence of power and authority, in nurture or in DNA. Denise and Neil's own mothers are portrayed as mythically gratifying maternal figures. Lillian Sherer, in particular, is figured in terms of a nostalgic memory of presence and reliability; Jacobson's constant companion, Lillian helped her daughter write out homework, played games with her on Saturday nights, and would wake Denise "gently . . . in the early morning darkness," continuing to put on her socks long after Jacobson "could dress [herself]" (48).[28] Jacobson writes that both of their mothers acted as "interpreters and shields," "buffers" between them and the able-bodied world: "In their presence, we never had to speak for ourselves; they spoke for us, they felt for us, and they knew what was best for us" (154).

It is precisely such trust in the mother's utter capability that troubles Jacobson in her own efforts to become a mother: her ability to speak, feel, and make meaning from the world (to know what is "best") was appropriated by an able-bodied mother who assumed that her disabled daughter required such intervention. Jacobson is thus caught in a set of seemingly unworkable contradictions: her own mother's behavior was "comforting" but infantilizing, making it difficult for Jacobson to perceive herself as a competent adult or even to know how to do things for herself; at the same time, her belief about what it means to be a mother originates in her own mother's devoted but problematically mediatory style, in a fantasy that mothers need no assistance themselves. The question becomes, then, what sort of mother Jacobson can be. The description of Lillian Sherer tenderly slipping on her daughter's sock with Denise in cozy half-sleep is clearly contrasted with scenes in which Jacobson watches "someone else" give David a bath (102) or the fact that "David's diaper still took [her] so long to change" (129). Can Jacobson provide for David that sort of nurturing intimacy? Can she speak for him? Will he trust her the way she trusted Lillian? When Jacobson protests, "I was David's mother! I would always be David's mother! . . . I wanted him to know he could count on me" (155), the urgency of her repetition accentuates just how necessary it is for her to insist on her position. David is adopted, and Jacobson is disabled and moves in a wheelchair; no part of their relationship seems "natural" or whole. This situation exemplifies what Lois Keith calls "doing disability": having to maneuver oneself in an environment that does not accommodate the mechanics of disablement and, more egregiously, spending time managing "other people's preconceptions and misconceptions."[29] Jacobson is repeatedly overlooked as David's mother, as when a van service driver speaks to her housekeeper as if Jacobson were not there (116), or when paramedics direct questions to a stranger instead of Jacobson when David hurts his finger. The wheelchair, the erratic body movements, the slurred speech—these equate to baby talk, to a baby's inability to control its motions and its dependence on caregivers.

But even as she protests against this drawn-out state of child-like dependency where her desires are subordinated to those of able-bodied "parents," Jacobson overtly disrupts the notion of self-sufficiency as the pinnacle of life achievement for women or for those with disabilities. Enumerating the chores of the new housekeeper, Carrie, Jacobson wonders if David will "learn that he had to rely on someone else," if he will "think less of [her] as his mother" because she often remains on the sidelines of his daily care (129). While such worries reiterate a fear about failing to be a "good enough mother," they also effectively disrupt conventional notions of what constitutes good mothering in the first place, particularly myths of all-powerful maternal figures and of dyadic mother-infant bonding. The practical reality of her disability is that Jacobson *must* rely on others to help her care for David, but the ableist assumption that needing help to perform certain tasks is equivalent to disempowerment or a loss of self-control has been refuted by disabled feminists concerned to broaden social attitudes toward the ethics and politics of care.

As Brazilian activist Rosangela Berman Bieler has written of her own daughter's infancy, "I could not fulfil [*sic*] all her needs by myself" and so "had to share my motherhood with other people. . . . In many ways, when she was little, my daughter's image of the 'mother-provider' was shared among a few close people." Bieler suggests that the network of caretakers her daughter knew as a baby neither hampered their own intimacy nor obstructed her daughter's development into a self-confident young woman—indeed, Bieler describes her as independent and psychologically "healthy." Moreover, her use of the word "share" implies less that Bieler's dependence on others for assistance deprived her daughter of something meaningful than it invokes a sense of communal and congenial reciprocity.[30] Drawing the distinction that Lois Keith and Jenny Morris make, between "parenting," on one hand, and "the practical and physical things" that parents with disabilities might require assistance in getting done, on the other, Jacobson similarly differentiates her psychological and decision-making role as David's mother from the utilization of social services to supplement her physical tending of him.[31]

One final element I would like to highlight here as part of Jacobson's strategy of verifying that she *is* David's mother is the use of tropes of interlocking and union. To offset the conception that disability and adoption render her illegitimate, an interloper in the domain of whole and natural maternal figures, Jacobson deploys a series of romanticized metaphors of interconnection. Depicting her relationship with David as one of immediate and mutual bondedness, she attempts to dispel the overlapping connotations of brokenness, disconnection, and lack that attach to disability and adoption alike. Thus when she first meets infant David, they engage in a silent, purely imaginative conversation in which, Jacobson avows, David's "bright, steady gaze bored like a steel lance into my heart, piercing my core with a deep, painful joy" (15); later, she recalls this "first spellbinding eye contact with David" (112). Neil and David also look at each other "in a long, unbroken gaze" (90), and David settles into Neil's "sunken torso" "as if the two were made for each other" (92).[32] She asserts that David "seemed to have a radiating effect on people he hadn't even met," calling up the mythical power of babies (78), and claims, upon bringing him back to Berkeley, that "he must have known he was finally home" (95)—"David belonged no other place than in our home" (101). When a stranger remarks that David resembles Neil, Jacobson thinks, "*And I had been afraid that I would never have a complete bond with a child that didn't come from my body"* (103). Indeed, she writes that she had "little doubt . . . that David was made for us and we were made for David. The three of us belonged together" (139).

In the last paragraph of the book Jacobson reprises this belief, suggesting that all doubts and questions had already been resolved in the "very first instant David's eyes met mine, the moment when I knew that David belonged with us, and Neil and I belonged with David" (213). Repeated claims of "belonging" and of being at "home" emphasize the important fact that the Jacobsons live independently, in their own home. Such terms also seem intended to assuage a pernicious awareness of being marginalized and adrift, unlocatable within the dominant paradigms of able-bodied culture, and to anticipate the doubts of, if not her actual readers, then a society for whom disability and adoption may tend to subvert fantasies of privacy, domestic comfort, and emotional and physical connection invested in the maternal body.

A Question of Rights: Anne Finger's *Past Due*

Given a cultural environment in which both disabled parents and adoptive families are marked as unnatural, as "freakish [or] second-best families" in contrast to "authentic and normal," able-bodied, "biologically related" families,[33] Jacobson's narrative of motherhood is an especially pointed instance of what Simi Linton has described as "an account of a world negotiated *from the vantage point of the atypical.*"[34] At the same time, in its focus on the kinds of social services and personal assistance that Jacobson and her husband utilize in their roles as parents, *The Question of David* challenges the notion that child care is a primarily maternal, dyadic, and private affair, thus offering an expanded, alternative model of kinship.[35] In *Past Due*, Anne Finger, like Jacobson also a prominent figure in both the disability and abortion rights communities, tells a complex story of post-polio disability, home birth, and reproductive rights. Finger thus also uses herself as the point of reference in a narrative that is, finally, a complex social indictment—of Western culture's faith in technology and contempt for "alternative" forms of health care, of feminist ableism, of uncritical recourse to selective abortion, and of the deep-seated belief that disability must contain some compensatory "moral" to make up for tragedy. Accordingly, like Jacobson, she presents motherhood in an unexpectedly revolutionary sense. Finger argues that a truly feminist and anti-ableist society must "support the right of women *to* have children" (44), even when those women have disabilities and even when those children may also have disabilities.

Finger fantasizes pregnancy as a "dream of perfection" (20) that will somehow compensate for her sense of inhabiting a broken, inadequate body. Left with multiple scars and limited mobility after childhood polio, she imagines that having a baby will be a very particular form of self-creation or reinvention: "I wanted something perfect to come out of my imperfect body," she admits. "I wanted to make myself anew. I needed to have control over my body" (18). This language of perfection seems to tap into what Rapp and Ginsburg call "the hegemonic discourse of perfectibility disseminated by such sites as obstetric medicine, middle-class parenting literature, and, more generally, contemporary U.S. models of personhood."[36] Finger is perhaps even more vehement than a nondisabled couple seeking recourse to genetic testing to ensure "normalcy," precisely because she entertains a dream of vicariously restoring herself to corporeal wholeness through the birth of a normal child. Yet Finger's pregnancy and decision to give birth at home also explicitly resist entrenched cultural responses to disability. Finger juxtaposes her desire to have a baby against not only Nazi-era eugenics and the forced sterilizations that strove to thwart the reproduction of " 'defective' " bodies but also the "hostility" (26) toward disability that often arises in feminist discussions of abortion rights. At the same time, Finger envisions home birth as a way to recuperate the self-control she lost as a child undergoing numerous surgeries and to counteract the "climate of fear and dehumanization" (69) that often prevails in hospitals. *Past Due* is thus a story of multiple efforts toward self-determination in the face of normative social and medical attitudes about disability, pregnancy, and health care.

Finger exposes the terrible brutality of the notion that disabled people should be barred from having children, and she explicitly challenges abortion rights advocates for being "sometimes guilty of exploiting fears about disability" (24). As one way of demonstrating how fully the "private" matter of reproduction is embedded in social networks—ones that can offer support but also misunderstanding—Finger provides a thickly politicized context for her son Max's birth that includes her own previous abortion and work in an abortion clinic, her distrust of medical technology, and her activities in disability and reproductive rights groups. *Past Due* frequently records the tense conversations between women that take place at various conferences and roundtables. Early in the text, for example, Finger describes speaking before the Bay Area Committee to Defend Reproductive Rights and participating in a 1984 meeting in New York City about the controversial Baby Doe case (24).[37] In the latter discussion of amniocentesis, selective abortion, and disability rights, "differences" (29) abound: one woman is skeptical about genetic testing, while another aborted a Down syndrome fetus at five months; two women argue over the legal rights of fetuses, while another represents Catholics for a Free Choice. Finger allows this dynamic and emotionally charged exchange to unfold as if verbatim, letting women speak for—but also indict—themselves. She writes, "I am so glad I am a woman" (38). But when one of the participants responds to Finger's own tale of childhood surgeries by saying, " 'If you had been my child, I would have killed you before I let that happen' " (33), Finger also learns a difficult truth about how many so-called progressive people regard disability: "What seemed obvious to me—that a disabled life *was* worth living; that our lives weren't endless misery—seemed dubious at best to them" (25–26).

Finger's story repeatedly entails this sort of alternation between "true intimacy, born of commonality and difference, born of our shared commitment to women" (38), and the tendency among many leftist feminists to uncritically associate disability with pain, diminishment, and devaluation. The reproduction of such dialogues places in high relief what Michelle Fine and Adrienne Asch have discussed as contradictory positions "taken out of deep-seated terror and repugnance of disability and out of almost equally deep-seated—but in this case knee-jerk—opposition to the Right's attack on women and the pro-choice movement."[38] Like Jacobson, Finger calls attention to how women with disabilities are discouraged from having children or from keeping disabled infants, not because of a feminist allegiance to abortion rights, but because of ableist discrimination against disabled bodies generally.

Taking a stance against conservative pro-life arguments out of an allegiance to abortion rights can have the unintended effect of upholding an ableist worldview by failing to consider disabled fetuses viable, in a social or philosophical more than physiological sense. "Privacy-of-the-family arguments"—which claim that parents facing difficult decisions about whether or not to abort a disabled fetus or provide medical care for a disabled newborn "should be left alone," guarded against governmental attempts to protect the rights of people with disabilities—similarly disguise a fundamentally ableist agenda.[39] A potent fear of disability, Finger argues, lurks behind the pro-choice rhetoric of the women's movement no less than the sacrosanct borders of the American nuclear family. Her personal story of pregnancy, home birth, and keeping baby Max alive (whatever the mental or physical consequences of his birth experience) is thus located in a profoundly complex arena, available to the competing logics of feminism, the family, medical technology, politics, and disability activism.

Directing open-ended questions at "society," at women generally, and at feminists, disability activists, and herself, Finger rejects putatively definitive truths about disability and reproduction as well as the idealizing mysteries about birth and motherhood that serve more to obfuscate than to correct inequitable social roles and relationships. Rather, her challenge to the oppressive attitudes toward disabled bodies that appear in both feminist and patriarchal discourse is composed in a predominantly interrogative register. Asking questions not so much rhetorically as with an awareness of the complicated consequences of any answer, Finger emphasizes the possibility of rethinking disability and reproductive rights as deeply interconnected social and ethical concerns. Should women who advocate for disability rights also support the right to abortion? Do so-called birth defects "justify" abortion? Can arguments *for* the protection of disabled fetuses or babies coincide with arguments *against* right-to-lifers?[40] How should feminists trained to be suspicious of the obligation of a maternal identity respond to a disabled woman's fight for the right to parent? How does a disabled person cope with her feelings of shame or even disgust at the prospect of having a disabled baby?

Past Due proliferates such inquiries, exhorting the various communities to which Finger belongs to "link our struggles for women, for disabled people, working together . . . instead of seeing our interests as unalterably opposed" (43). Because her infant's condition realizes the very fear—the replication of disability—that underlies the suppression of disabled experience even in forward-thinking political camps, Finger inflects these theoretical questions with personal urgency, challenging assumptions about where the responsibility for disability lies and about what all facets of society define as a life "worth living" (25).[41] As Rapp and Ginsburg argue, disability needs to be "resituate[d]" in American culture beyond the nuclear family, in part so that needs might be more broadly accommodated and reliably secured.

More surprisingly, and perhaps more cannily, Finger displays her own quest for the ideal—her susceptibility to the magical thinking that a "perfect" birth might eradicate her disability and her shame. This in turn is set against the chance events of both pregnancy and disability. Something goes wrong during her labor, and the home birth that was meant to repair all the damage of Finger's past ends in a crash C-section at the hospital. Baby Max, two weeks overdue and severely distressed during the birth, suffers meconium aspiration and asphyxiation in utero and subsequently develops persistent fetal circulation, a condition in which the infant's blood is insufficiently oxygenated as it passes through the lungs. In intensive care, heavily medicated, and on a ventilator for the first weeks of his life, Max represents the "randomness," as Finger puts it, that "lies at the very heart of reproduction" (40). With cerebral palsy, epilepsy, and retardation as possible outcomes of his birth, Max brings into ironic focus the reality that disability simply happens; his situation is no more caused by Finger's disability than it is prevented by her hope that her polio might constitute a preemptive dues-paying.

Nor are Max and his mother isolate individuals; the disabilities of each become meaningful only within the intricate political and medical circumstances that Finger carefully details. That Finger refuses to place her trust in deterministic notions of design (she explicitly describes herself as an atheist) makes all the more ironic her wish that Max might magically restore something of the ease and fullness she imagines nondisabled mothers to experience upon giving birth. But it also explains the text's rejection of redemptive answers. *Past Due* does not portray Max's birth as a riddle to be solved by either the wonders of medical technology or the consolations of religion. It is narrated, instead, as a chance event that situates Finger at an uncomfortable intersection between her activist work as a disabled woman and the secret despair she feels upon learning that Max may be developmentally impaired.

Finger thus dares to articulate the fraught contradiction between education and emotion. "Did I think because I know so much," she asks, referring to her years of writing and speaking out about feminist disability issues, "that I was exempt from feelings of self-hatred?" (172). Worrying over how her husband, Mark, will respond to Max, she confesses her " 'internalized oppression' ": "I thought that he might leave us, two cripples, an embarrassment. Here comes that poor man, saddled with a gimp lover and a retard son" (136). Finger is acutely aware that her ambivalent feelings for Max derive from an ableist culture whose narratives of disability as deviance and error stimulate self-loathing and shame, yet such recognition cannot fully assuage the pain of those feelings. "Health has become the overriding metaphor for what is good in our society," Finger writes (58). Max's various illnesses thus become a gloomy portent of a life in which he may be perceived as abnormal, "[a] spastic. A cripple. Or worse: a retard" (171).

Moreover, in renewing Finger's childhood despair ("The old feelings surface," she says [172]), his condition signifies a double failure —first of the home birth invested with so much hope and existential weight, and then of the maternal identity, defined by beauty and capability, that that birth was meant to guarantee. This, then, is the collision that *Past Due* repeatedly stages—the constant oscillation between Finger's philosophical acumen and her anxiety and guilt; her love for Max, no matter the circumstances, and her fear that he might be disabled. Where she once chanted, "I don't want to be in a wheelchair, I don't want to be in a wheelchair, I don't want to be in a wheelchair" (13), the mantra now shifts to Max: "I don't want anything to be wrong with him. I don't want anything to be wrong with him. I don't want anything to be wrong with him. . . . 'I don't want to have a retarded child. I don't want to have a retarded child. I don't want to have a retarded child' " (172). She had longed for a form of replication that would soothe the hurt of a disabled childhood; she must confront instead old insecurities, the intrusion into her own response to Max of "shame" and "disappointment" (184).

How does the birth of Max, then, reshape Finger's conception of herself as a woman with disabilities, and how does the story of his traumatic birth come to refigure broader notions about disabled identity and maternity? One of the central tensions of *Past Due* involves Finger's decision to give birth at home. An obvious eschewal of conventional medical practice, home birth seems to promise a level of self-determination with regard to her body that polio—or, more exactly, social and medical reactions to polio—had prevented her from experiencing. The desire for an unmedicated, vaginal birth in the safe environment of home derives from two related concerns: Finger's worry that a hospital birth will reproduce the worst of her encounters with physicians and surgery in the past, and her belief that the technology associated with hospital births will both depersonalize her experience and put her and her baby at greater risk for complications. Finger writes that as a first-time mother and a disabled woman, she "figured . . . [she] was a prime candidate for a Cesarean" (70), and it is in large part her antipathy to "doctors or hospitals" (62), her reluctance to incur yet "another scar" (178), that ultimately encourages her to consider alternative childbirth. She argues that the sharp increase in C-sections performed in the United States signifies "a dangerous assault on women's bodily autonomy . . . a frightening extension of medical and social control over women's bodies" (182), and that "having a 'vaginal' birth rather than an 'abdominal' one was tremendously important to me" (70). In an obvious inversion of the stereotype that a disabled mother is "exceptional" rather than normal, Finger claims that she "wanted to do something that was physically courageous. . . . I wanted to do something most other women couldn't do" (70–71).[42]

Home birth is thus more than a quirky or idiosyncratic alternative to standard practice for Finger; it represents an overt reclaiming of the boundaries of her body that specifically redresses the legacy of "real terror" (68) attached to her six childhood operations. Further, the impulse to give birth in a strenuous or physically "present" way seems to symbolize triumph over both the corporeal and emotional effects of polio: not simply the atrophied muscles or hernia of post-polio, but also the sense of inferiority Finger feels in comparison with able-bodied women—the very women who so often undergo Cesareans despite their physical capacity to deliver "naturally." Finger fantasizes giving birth "in the room with the redwood paneling, with the late afternoon sun coming in through the window" (155), flanked by "lilies in the vase on the bureau" rather than "cold and metallic" machines (141), her baby's status checked not by a fetal monitor but by Laura, the midwife. The visual calm of this setting and the interpersonal caretaking represented by Laura may seem at first to depict childbirth in a problematically romanticized way; against the atmosphere of "inexplicable evil" (65) that marks Finger's previous trips to the hospital, however, such details point subtly to the ideological issues at stake not simply in having a child but in the actual logistics of giving birth.[43]

The home birth scene suggests the possibility of being attended to and soothed in an important sensory way (the light in the room, the smell of the flowers, being in her own bed, and so on), in addition to a desire to be known and respected within a community of knowledgeable and competent women (the presence of a midwife, called by her first name, implies such intimacy). The hospital, by contrast, is remembered as a cold, rigidly rule-bound environment in which the six-year-old Finger is left alone without her mother for hours at a time and given enemas and anesthesia without explanation; she eventually incurs "seven thick fat ugly scars" (68). These "clumsy stitches" (67); the "fumes" that have her "spinning downwards, swirling wildly out of control, down into some darkness" (67); the soapy enema that produces "strange rumblings . . . noises that filled [her] with shame: belches and loud, uncontrollable farts" and "liquid shit" (65)—each of these implies both an invasion of her private bodily space and a loss of bodily control for which Finger feels "deeply ashamed," "lonely and frightened" (65). "No one spoke to me," she writes, "no one held my hand" (67). Hospitals, then, and the doctors and nurses who work there, become harbingers of a loss of dignity, agents of infantilizing procedures whose purpose the young Finger does not understand.

Finger directly attributes her later work in abortion clinics (and, of course, as a disability activist) to her history as a patient helpless to protest alienating treatments or to prevent the consequences to her sense of self of physical scarring. As she writes of Dr. Friedman, whose "clumsy stitches" are inscribed upon her left leg: "It was as if he wrote on my body: 'Ugly. Piece of junk. Ruined. Doesn't matter' " (68). Just as Finger's habit of calling midwives by their first names recognizes the legitimacy of adult women cooperating in a shared project of birth, so, too, does the tactic of referring to physicians as "Dr." designate the hierarchical structure that obtains in the medical community, one that tends to idealize physicians and infantilize patients, depriving patients of experiential or conceptual authority. "Medicine," as Finger declares, "robs women of our belief in our own perceptions" (4). Frank suggests that "people who are written on from the outside have lost their voices," and that in the effort to reclaim that voice, "self-stories proliferate."[44] Like choosing to have an abortion, Finger's choice to give birth at home becomes a form of defiant life writing, reflecting a need to leave the frightened girl behind and to establish a sense of legitimate embodiment: "You are not a child any more. You are not a six-year-old who had polio three and a half years before. . . . You are a woman now. . . . I am an adult" (21–22). The shift in pronouns here from "you" to "I" signals an important transformation from the girl who was "surrender[ed] . . .

to medical control" (23) to the grown-up woman who seeks to repossess command of her health, her voice, and her subjectivity.

Finger constructs a detailed sequence of events in order to demonstrate what can happen when "obstetricians see body and mind as separate" (69). The mechanical and pharmaceutical apparatus of a hospital birth, she argues, can initiate a chain reaction of procedures that pacify the mother ("*She has been delivered*," Finger remarks ironically [72]) and put both baby and mother at risk: "One intervention almost inexorably leads to the next" (69). If the blinking lights and noise of a fetal monitor make the mother anxious, for instance, labor can stall, necessitating use of the drug pitocin. Since pitocin often exacerbates the pain of contractions, a woman may then be given painkillers or local anesthesia, which slows labor even further and can increase the chance of delivery by forceps or C-section. Finger's presentation of this scenario, replete with statistics and detailed technical information, lays the groundwork for her subsequent story of home birth by proving her capacity to make informed and rational choices. Her suggestion that it is a *typical* state of affairs lends support to one of the text's driving claims: that Western culture's faith in the technology of conventional medicine can obscure potential risks and uphold a problematic hierarchy that subordinates body to mind and in turn disenfranchises society's unruliest bodies. *Past Due* becomes, in this way, a critique of progress narratives that construe "scientific medicine" as the panacea that eradicates "the horrors of the past" (68).

But at the same time, Finger is careful to voice her skepticism about alternative medical tactics as much as conventional ones. Initially, she writes, she believed "home birth was for people who had been carried somewhat too far by the wild currents of the sixties" (62). In a segment recounting interactions with "ardent devotee[s] of natural health" (62), Finger argues that while alternative medicine may substitute the latest "herb" and "meditation technique" (63) for drugs and surgical procedures, it is nonetheless beholden to the same myth of control over the body and the same martial paradigm that underlie Western medicine's approach to illness and disability. Whether the remedy is acupuncture or antibiotics, both systems of health care tend to view disease as an "enem[y] to be battled," something to be "fought against" rather than "experienced" (63–64).[45] In taking this ironic stance on alternative medicine, Finger clearly hopes proactively to dispel accusations that she chose home birth recklessly, putting herself and her baby in danger out of a thoughtless or even immature need to rebel against the medical establishment. Her decision to give birth at home is narrated as having less to do with uncritical faith in alternative medicine's idealized notions of the "natural" than with seeking out a form of childbirth that will reunite corporeal and psychological selves and redress her vulnerability to doctors who "think [her] body is a wreck and want to slice [her] open and try vainly to make [her] 'normal' " (61).

The difficult reality of Max's home birth, however, is that something *does* go wrong. After hours of contractions and ineffectual pushing, Finger ends up in the hospital, where despite all her trepidations about technology, she is immediately attached to a fetal monitor and prepped for emergency surgery. The grueling but active efforts of labor come to a halt, replaced by a literal passive voice. Throughout the labor scene, Finger figures herself as the agent of a "relentless, animal physicality" (102): "I sit"; "I crouch on all fours" (104); "I kneel on all fours"; "I crouch on all fours and push" (108); "I squat"; "I push and push and push. I grunt and moan" (107). In the hospital, by contrast, she becomes a passive patient: "My legs are being opened and an internal monitor is being inserted into the baby's head"; "An oxygen mask is being strapped over my face"; "I am being catheterized and shaved" (111). At home she is "amazed and proud" at having "made it through the painful part of labor, without a drug" (106); in the hospital, conversely, "another mask over my face . . . I feel a needle going into my hand" (113).

Here are the dichotomies of Finger's story deliberately juxtaposed. In one segment, her body commands the action, and Finger narrates without embarrassment the crude facts of birth: "Jane and Mark move the disposable pads so that they stay under me to catch the dripping amniotic fluid and the last of my mucous plug" (104); "After each push, my asshole feels damp and cruddy" (108). In the next, she has become a child again, surrounded by aggressive doctors who wrest authority and decision-making control from Finger and her midwives alike. Finger reports that after the C-section, for instance, "the doctor with the gold chain" (113) has "given Laura a really hard time. He came out of the OR shouting at her, demanding to know if she were licensed, why we hadn't come to the hospital sooner" (115).

Underlying the trajectory from home to hospital—from the "wild," "animal self" (201) of natural birth to an unconscious, anesthetized one, and from expertise and activism to renewed dependence on the attitudes and structures of traditional medicine—is an unexpected indictment of myths of control. While Finger indicates that giving birth to Max at home was a crucial act of taking charge of her reproductive self, she also foregrounds his situation as a reminder of how little, finally, can be foreseen or ensured when it comes to the body and biology. And while she presents the "right" to abort as a nonnegotiable component of her feminist beliefs, she also uncovers a problematic slippage between the argument for women's reproductive rights and a "national obsession" with "the right to have healthy children" (42). Finger implies that relying on technology in a quest to "eliminate all pain and suffering" (41) conceals a cultural rejection of disabled bodies; what masquerades as sophisticated (even benevolent) manipulation of the vagaries of biology, she suggests, not only maintains certain members of a society in disempowered positions but also denies the inevitability—even the *desirability*—of bodily breakdowns, what Finger calls "those deaths of the old physical self that are a sort of skin-shedding" (43). Accepting disability demands not a tighter grip on what is perceived as going "wrong" in the body but, rather, a willingness to cede control and to embrace chance.

As a post-polio mother, Finger herself embodies chance in more than one way ("Perhaps it is because I had polio," she writes, "that I have always been fascinated by chance" [40]). Since neither disability nor pregnancy can be absolutely foreseen, guaranteed, or prevented, both arenas of human experience tend to be subject to the explanatory and controlling maneuvers of science and medicine. Discussing prenatal testing and the horror of disability that motivates it, Finger contends that "social pressure can work to keep people in line. . . . When a technology is available it becomes harder and harder not to utilize it—'to take advantage of it.' . . . If you don't use prenatal screening and have a child with a disability that could have been detected, a child that could have been aborted, then is it your own fault? . . . I wonder what lengths we will go to to have healthy children" (42). Rapp and Ginsburg underscore this contradiction in their discussion of technology, reproductive rights and choices, and alternative kinship structures that respond more adequately to the needs of disabled infants and their parents than a conventional nuclear family held responsible for the "problem" of disability: "The practices of genetic testing, and other genetic research," they write, "seem to promise perfectibility for those who choose and can afford cutting-edge interventions. . . . Concomitantly, other new technologies, medical and otherwise, offer another promise of expansive democratic inclusion and improved quality of life for those marked by difference from a hegemonic norm of embodiment."[46]

The full import of the role of technology in ensuring healthy newborns becomes clear after Max is born and spends the first weeks of his life completely dependent on technological interventions. Her child's reliance on the methods of conventional medicine to survive complicates Finger's mistrust of those methods as metonymic of an ableist ideology grounded in notions of control and design. But it also underscores a fundamental ethical distinction between choosing to abort a disabled fetus after prenatal screening and taking lifesaving measures with a potentially disabled newborn. The same technology that can save lives—even those lives deemed unworthy or incomplete according to able-bodied paradigms—may also be used to ascertain whether a fetus is "normal" or not, thus serving and perpetuating an ableist viewpoint.

Finger articulates her own ambivalence about the measures taken with Max: "If he dies, I will think that technology is monstrous, inhuman, a mad scientist's creation; and if he lives, I will think it is miraculous" (136). Such a statement maps out the inconsistency behind cultural attitudes toward both medical technology and disability. Granted godlike powers, on one hand, to solve the problems of mortality (pain, illness, aging, and perhaps most maddening of all, uncertainty), technology is, on the other hand, demonized when it fails—as inevitably it does, given the body's inherent unpredictability. Complex questions of responsibility and cause are at stake here. Finger points to an untenable coincidence between a fear of science run amok, futuristic invasions into the sanctity of the individual person, and a desire for technology to protect those very borders against the intrusion of disorderliness in the form of disability and disease.

Who or what, then, is at fault when life fails? How much control can reasonably be expected over corporeal experience? Is technology properly blamed when complications occur in a hospital birth, while the mother is at fault for difficulties experienced at home? Did Max's birth, for instance, go awry at home, under the care of Finger's midwife, or at the hospital, while Finger was hooked up to a fetal monitor and awaiting surgery? (Finger hints that there may have been signs of complications while they were still at home, an indictment of her midwife that she is quite obviously cautious about making in the text.) "I understand . . . the drawbacks of taking control of your own body," Finger writes; "I understand why people want to surrender their lives to someone else's power, to the power of the machine. . . . At least you don't feel this awful sense of responsibility" (201).

How we respond to bodies—what steps are followed for which particular conditions or situations—is a function of cultural belief, not "natural" but constructed. Not only the supposedly private experience of pregnancy but also the emphatically "domestic" event of home birth is available to scrutiny and judgment, and Finger articulates a worry that everyone around her wonders what she "did to" her baby. Indeed, she reports that after Max's birth, "a relative called and said: 'I can't believe Anne did that to her baby' " (200). The interplay between intimate and social, private and public, weaves a story of social relationships and patterns of behavior that compete to define appropriate ways of mothering. Accordingly, Finger establishes a textual identity that, while demonstrating its expertise on complex issues of disability and child-rearing rights, is nonetheless neither a singular authority nor unequivocal about those very issues.

If the personal is political, as *Past Due* surely insists, so too is the autobiographical relational. Finger's is one voice—frequently ambivalent and self-doubting—among many. The internalized atmosphere created by extended passages of rumination, memory, daydream, and excerpts from Finger's diary entries alternates with a more public forum, represented by the conference discussions, transcribed phone messages, and quoted dialogues with the panoply of doctors, midwives, and friends that surround Finger and her husband throughout the early months of Max's life. To the degree that Finger's voice often recedes from the position of active controller of the story, *Past Due* stresses the fact that those aspects of the story most apparently hers alone—her "home" birth, her "privacy," her identity as "mother," and her decisions regarding Max—are shaped by the demands and opinions of the larger cultural matrix.

In a similar way, the text demonstrates how difficult it is to protect the intimate spaces of attitude and belief from the pressure of social codes and norms. The highly interiorized atmosphere of the text, concerned as it is with Finger's thought process as the events of Max's birth unfold, records an individual's struggle to define experience in opposition to prevalent expectations. It also reveals the persistence of a mind/body split whereby physical disability is construed as preferable to any impairment of intellect. In a kind of litany attesting to her cognitive powers, Finger records her reaction to one particularly stimulating conference: "I think, I am so glad I am a woman" (37); "Lying there on the plane, I think . . ." (39); "I think how odd it is that I work . . ." (40); "I think of all that we have won" (41); "I mull over the things we talked about" (42); "I think too about how . . ." (43). Such repetition creates an effect of layered consciousness, Finger-the-writer representing herself as woman-who-cogitates, a mobile mind ranging around in the complex territory of feminism, social activism, and human relationships. In other moments, that ability to distill and philosophize dissipates under the numbing "fog" (146) of grief, guilt, and shame. "My sorrow has anesthetized me," Finger writes (120); "I had known everything about childbirth. Suddenly I knew nothing about what was going on" (124); "I am blank" (130). Nonetheless, thinking—and even the habit of noticing how rational thought shuts down in the throes of traumatic experience—is Finger's defense against the stigma of disability, providing an assurance of being in control even when the body behaves unpredictably.

In a certain way, *Past Due* might seem the kind of parental life writing that G. Thomas Couser describes as "unauthorized" memoir, in which "parents assume rather than request the right" to tell their children's stories, resulting in narratives that might be experienced by the children, "once grown, as violations of their autonomy, acts of appropriation or even betrayal."[47] One wonders what Max might feel reading his mother's admission of a potent fear that his disabilities will be cognitive:

> Max, those first awful days, when we didn't know if you would live or not, when everyone kept saying, "Your baby has been severely asphyxiated and we don't know how bad the damage is going to be," I had moments of not knowing whether I wanted you to live or not.
>
> I still believed in all the things I have always believed in: the rights of disabled infants, the value of disabled lives. Yes, I still believe in those. I just didn't know what I could cope with: twenty seizures a day? Inability to make eye contact? Changing diapers for twelve years? (136–37)

But if the autobiography maps Max's situation onto Finger's history in a way that situates the baby's story as inextricable from the mother's, that is part of the point Finger makes here about disability: that it is largely a social phenomenon, its meaning determined by context. The mother's telling of Max's story also reminds us that "the task of composing a normalizing narrative that can create a space of inclusion" for a baby with disabilities is, in Rapp and Ginsburg's words, "immediately thrust upon the mother."[48]

A whole set of potential losses is at stake in Max's condition, for if he does ultimately exhibit signs of mental disability, he will have failed to fulfill Finger's desire for repair and perfection and will thus signify a renewal of her own sense of having erred, of being a body gone wrong: "I will be even more of an oddity than I am now" (171). Finger draws a stark dichotomy between mother and son—the one physically impaired but intellectually acute, the other corporeally beautiful but at risk for cognitive problems—to confess her own privileging of consciousness over flesh and even her anxiety about whatever is "other," even if having a son who exactly replicated her would in itself constitute a form of failure. In this sense, Finger is not so much appropriating Max's narrative as revealing just how thoroughly her own reactions are determined by ableist criteria. "When I was growing up," she explains, "I was expected to live not in my body but in my mind. I was supposed to be smart and I was smart. . . . I was supposed to be outside the action, the observer, the one who explained. I was good at that role. Perhaps that is why I became a writer. Now I have a son who may be retarded. His body now is almost flawless. . . . But he may not be able to think the way that I can think. He may not be able to do the thing that I've built my life around" (171). Finger's worried comparisons drive home the point that identity is contextual: it is her "own obsession with intellect" (171), already a product of the internalized shame of her broken corporeal form, that establishes the hierarchy whereby Max is imagined to be "unsaddled by intellect" (184).

Again, issues of control get activated by the concern over whether, and in what precise way, Max will be disabled. Finger suggests that one of the most vexing lessons of Max's situation is her own sense of helplessness: "My son may be retarded and it doesn't matter what I do" (171). But while she may not be able to influence the immediate outcome of Max's birth experience—and certainly will not be able to predict what his condition will be in the years to come—she can nevertheless use the space of the text to turn "tragedy" into ironically elevated portraiture, transforming Max from the "inanimate object" (162), the distressed, possibly disabled newborn he was in the hospital. In a series of startling epithets, Finger calls Max "my lump of flesh"; "my little Still Life with Respirator" (148); "my outer space baby, my cartoon blimp-boy" (139); "my balloon baby" (142); "you bloated creature, you shit-stained baby boy, an old derelict with long, raggedy fingernails who they call my son" (143); and "my little baboon," "humanity's past" (175). The irreverent, caricaturing quality of these names stands in pointed contrast to more somber descriptions of Max surrounded by technical apparatus, "under the radiant warmer with the electrodes glued to his chest and the respirator taped across his mouth" (144).

This particular verbal register seems to evidence what Couser names the Gothic rhetoric of disability narrative, in which the disabled condition is represented as "grotesque" and described in a way that both reveals and provokes "revulsion" and shock. But Finger is also deploying what Couser asserts is "the Gothic's potential for political critique."[49] She takes what is most frightening about Max's circumstances—the indeterminate question of "whether or not [he] is going to be 'normal' " (147)—and effects a shift in meaning. By juxtaposing the endearing phrases of a mother ("my little," "my baby") with terms that figure Max as otherworldly, only "almost human" (146), Finger calls attention to the conflation of physical difference with ontological pathology that forms the basis of prevalent cultural attitudes toward disability. As Robert F. Murphy writes, because physical impairment "inundates all other claims to social standing," disability "is an identity," not merely one characteristic among many; more drastically, no less than the "full humanity" of a person with disabilities is "in doubt."[50] Max is alien and animal, an ironically literal "still life" and society's outcast, but somehow also a boy, someone's son. The point is not to deny, of course, Max's very real and life-threatening condition. Rather, Finger seems to use these arresting combinations to show what happens when parents confront the possibility of a disabled child, the ambivalent and awkward coincidence of love and horror.

But she is also taking possession of Max as her son in an importantly verbal way that resists the inscription of "abnormality" on disabled bodies. Revising her "dream of the perfect child" to accommodate the reality of Max's uncertain future entails accepting that she too is not "the perfect parent" (169); she had wished for "something perfect to come out of [her] body" (172) but receives instead the "purple scar" (180) of the C-section. In a description of seeing herself in a full-length mirror for the first time after Max's birth, Finger writes that "language has dug its way into [her] bones": "It used to be that the bad part of my body ended at the top of my legs.

Now, it's crept upward. . . . It's bad because it's ugly, . . . because the doctors have written on it. It's true, I don't experience my body as me. . . . It seems that it belongs to the medical world" (180). Her descriptions of Max as a lovable oddity, then, overtly contest the legacy of physical and emotional damage wreaked by Finger's surgeries. Max reactivates his mother's struggle with "self-hatred" and her youthful habit of "rejecting others who were disabled" (180–81), but *Past Due* chronicles Finger's reconciliation to both her body and her baby. This is, to quote Frank once again, "storytelling as repair work on the wreck."[51] Both mother's body and mother's baby are constructed for viewing in Finger's own words.

As if to imitate the interminable present tense of trauma, when outcomes and effects are still unknown, *Past Due* is written predominantly in the present tense. In this way, the motion of the narrative forestalls its own conclusion, even as Finger acknowledges a desperate longing for resolution. This narrative tactic highlights the text's investment in challenging an entrenched cultural investment in patterns of design, progression, and closure. Disability is a tangible reminder of the inevitable fact that things in life go not "wrong," but in multiple directions, many of which may be painful, arduous, and entirely unanticipated. To maintain the story in the present tense is to resist the linear logic of time that finds cause in past events and trusts to a future of resolution. Similarly, *Past Due* refuses to explain with any certainty "what happened," to attempt to locate a definitive cause, and perhaps most crucially, to assess blame. The text amasses possibilities; one doctor suggests that problems may have begun "on the way to the hospital," while another cites diabetes of pregnancy as a possible factor (123). Finger herself simply generates questions: "If I'd squatted during second stage would this not have happened? Could the herb tea that I'd drunk have caused this? . . . Was it that I hadn't pushed hard enough? Or was it that my pelvis was too narrow? . . . Could it have been lying on my back in the labor room that did it?" (125).

Although Finger indicates that she did consider the possibility of a lawsuit against her midwife ("Was it something that you did or didn't do, Laura? . . . If I sue . . ." [126]), *Past Due* refuses to adjudicate, leaving unresolved the matter of Max's birth. But while the open-endedness of the text's account of childbirth may accurately attest to the unpredictability of disability, there is also the troubling fact that this story of "failed home birth" (136) does have "a happy ending": Max ultimately proves to be " 'all right' " (199). The disturbing and paradoxical effect of this historical detail is to suggest that the display of distress at Max's potential cognitive impairment is possible because Finger writes from the safe position of knowing that her fears were not (or have not yet been) realized. Does Finger end up producing the very narrative closure she seems throughout the text to avoid? In turn, what is the effect of Finger's role as the organizing, clarifying "intellect" of the story, given those sections of the text that eschew the mind/body hierarchy in which she was inculcated as a young post-polio child? While *Past Due* does insist that there are "no easy lessons, no clean morals" (199), it nonetheless casts the preceding revelations of shame and ambivalence into a certain light that Max is, finally, "not disabled" (199).

5

a brief history of aging

The Journals of May Sarton

I have been suggesting throughout this book that the boundaries dividing "able" from "disabled" and "normal" from "dysfunctional" are tenuous in the extreme. As many have noted, the concept of normality is a fictional ideal, a putative ontology that exerts enormous social and ideological pressure despite the reality that no body exactly meets its standards. Embodiment and disability, as we have seen, take such a range of forms that even disability cannot coherently be deemed a category with consistent or inevitable attributes. But perhaps it is aging that most fully disproves the strict opposition of able and disabled. As Barbara Levy Simon notes, disability is a "given . . . for men and women who live past middle age," and Rosemarie Garland-Thomson has written similarly that "we will all become disabled if we live long enough."[1] In the course of aging, all bodies begin to change—slowing down, losing range of motion, and incurring unfamiliar systemic conditions—which may be felt, in a youth-oriented society, as shame-inducing diminishment. Like disabilities generally, the physical and cognitive shifts associated with aging become the unacknowledged, because feared, potential of human corporeal existence, at the same time giving the lie to the fetishized body of ableist culture. Disability and aging thus intersect in an exploration of how bodies become culturally meaningful, not so much because the elderly may indeed experience an increased rate of chronic illness or impairment, but rather because their juxtaposition emphasizes the point that bodies exist on a highly flexible, culturally specific corporeal continuum.

Given how American society has responded to aging, the older woman, not surprisingly, faces a set of incompatible stereotypes. She may seem frail and physically vulnerable but also to be the repository of aphoristic wisdom; she may be mythologized as a selfless nurturer who loves (and cooks) abundantly but also as a cranky complainer who drains her family's emotional and financial resources. The cultural types representing older women—grandmother, crone, spinster, and mother-in-law—perpetuate attitudes toward female identity as defined primarily through familial status and further split the aging woman's body into a kind of sweet/sour dichotomy, an idealized fleshiness associated with physical affection and food, and the smells and fluids of infirmity or death. To be sure, there is no single experience of aging for women any more than women generally, or people with disabilities, can be grouped together without obscuring significant differences of class, race, physical condition, sexual orientation, national region, and so on.[2] Yet current research by gerontologists and sociologists of aging suggests that despite the so-called graying of America, older women in particular continue to be "underrepresented, undervalued, and undersexed,"[3] a situation into which life writing by a woman like May Sarton—well into her seventies and eighties at the peak of her autobiographical production—usefully intervenes.

Broadly speaking, woman are invited not to accept aging, still less to appreciate or enjoy it, but rather to "defy" its visible signs, a concept used ubiquitously in women's cosmetics advertising. Susan Bordo has argued that the explosive popularity of cosmetic surgery in the United States encourages aging women to remake themselves, not even in the image of their own younger selves, but according to the characteristics of the prevailing feminine icon. Myra Dinnerstein and Rose Weitz go further, contending that women who "manage their aging bodies" through diet, strenuous exercise, or surgery often exploit stock feminist terms of strength, liberation, and self-control to justify capitulation to patriarchal gender norms.[4] Indeed, some have protested (in a manner that resonates with the complaints of many feminist disability scholars and activists) that mainstream American feminism sidelines the involvement of older women and represents its most prominent figures in ways that conceal rather than display the facts of aging. As Barbara Macdonald has written, in a heated call to leaders of the movement, "The message has gone out to those of us over sixty that your sisterhood does not include us. . . . You do not see us in our present lives, you do not identify with our issues, you exploit us, you patronize us, you stereotype us. Mainly you ignore us."[5]

The experience of aging may be further complicated when a woman chooses to conduct her life as a single, rather than married or partnered, individual. According to Jennifer Baumbusch, "Very little research has focused on the unique experiences of single women, particularly as they age." Baumbusch and others have contended that studies comparing older single women to women who are married, divorced, or widowed perpetuate marital status as the conceptual benchmark and sideline the unique psychosocial and medical issues pertinent to "lifelong singlehood" among women.[6] Just as gender oppression and dominant social attitudes toward sexual orientation and identity intersect with ableism in the lives of women with disabilities, ageism and sexism mutually inform a woman's experience of growing older in American society, and just as feminist disability scholars have called for disabled women to tell their stories, so too have feminist gerontologists recently begun to attend specifically to ever-single older women and their quality of life, focusing particularly on such concerns as chronic pain, caretaking networks, and work and retirement issues.[7] Given the still-prevalent stereotype of the "elderly spinster" as a "lonesome, egocentric, neurotic, irresponsible, or immoral deviant,"[8] the need for—and the counterdiscursive force of—more accurate accounts of older single women's lives seems obvious.

May Sarton's many diaristic works engage in complicated ways with these conventional notions about aging, particularly for a woman who lives alone, as a loss of a capability and social value. Sarton writes candidly about aging as a steady accumulation of losses and disappointments. Her texts make copious reference to friends recently dead, to new medications and appointments with demeaning physicians, and to the many things Sarton can no longer do alone, or even at all. Yet despite the morose tone and attitude of defeat she so often affects, Sarton is an unexpectedly optimistic diarist of growing old as a woman in the youth-, male-, and health-oriented environment of twentieth-century America. Alongside repeated claims that she is "miserable,"[9] "constantly frustrated" (79), "a failure" (140), and "unable to deal with [her] life,"[10] Sarton lingers with a kind of fierce determination over the rituals of her days, turning a quotidian chore into an opportunity to celebrate companionship, aesthetic pleasure, or the joys of a good meal or book. Detailed descriptions of her garden in bloom, her love of pets, the vagaries of Maine weather, and her trips to the post office and the beauty salon tell a story somewhat different from those passages devoted to depression and physical ailment. As she writes in *After the Stroke*, "I panted halfway up the stairs, but I also was able to sit and watch light change in the porch for an hour and be truly attentive to it, not plagued by what I 'ought' to be doing" (125).

One of the provocative tensions of Sarton's journals derives from how form tends to mitigate or counternarrate content: the fact of their dailiness offsets the despairing atmosphere produced by Sarton's frequent mention of anger, anxiety, and loneliness. More crucially, each new entry defers not only the end of autobiography but the literal end of life that the author admits to anticipating. Sarton thus embeds a hopeful open-endedness into her texts, in two important ways contesting reductive attitudes about elderly women: by opening up the story of aging, in its very real pain and prosaic annoyances, and by refusing to define herself entirely by the gendered or social parameters of that story. Each act of writing again, of recording another day, conveys a significant persistence and trust—in the validity of one's own story and in the fact of that story being heard or read. This is what led Carolyn Heilbrun, early in Sarton's journaling career, to deem Sarton's work "the watershed in women's autobiography"—its "great detail," its honest appraisal of a woman's experience alone, and its devotion to a writing life.[11] While the journals suggest that Sarton often felt emotionally drained by the effort of adjusting to the changes in her aging body, a different sort of cumulative effect is produced by the diary format, evidence that the author repeatedly made her way, halting as it may have been, upstairs to the space of writing.

Sarton refers to her journals as "long letters" (*Eighty-Two* 28) and remarks that "what makes a good journal so moving is not the big events but tea in the garden or its equivalent" (*Stroke* 76). The epistolary quality that Sarton ascribes to journaling suggests that she sought to align the performative nature of her work with the intimacy of a private communiqué (indeed, one often has the sense that the author's chief motivation is to unburden herself to a sympathetic audience).[12] But it is the record of "tea in the garden" that lends Sarton's journaling its peculiarly challenging aspect, insofar as the emphasis on domestic ritual—on small, daily tasks—seeks to validate an infrequently told life story. Sarton's stated purpose is to retrieve "the old" from the "place where they are simply a burden" and to "convey what is happening and make it seem real" (*Eighty-Two* 72). That project has its realization in her many acts of commemorating, across a dozen journals and nearly twenty years of steady writing, "the hundred little things" (171) that make up her life as an older woman alone. The goal, then, is to tell what happens in all its contradictory but self-generative detail: the longing for solitude and the dependence on others for caretaking and companionship, the pleasures of food and the inability to eat due to medication or illness, and the joys of gardening and the fatigue and unsteadiness that make it difficult to sustain.

In such journals as *Recovering* (1980), *At Seventy* (1984), *After the Stroke* (1988), *Encore* (1993), and *At Eighty-Two* (1996), written in the midst of aging and the immediate aftermath of various illnesses, Sarton displays her characteristic determination about keeping up her work, the self-work of daily writing. This need to be persistent exemplifies what is both clichéd and potentially revisionary about how Sarton narrates the conditions of her body. In *Recovering*, she is frustrated by any diminution of physical capacity understood as "holding [her] back,"[13] and she is prone to making uncritical evaluations of sickness as a symptom of unresolved emotional anguish, an enemy force that displaces the subject from her "real self" (*Stroke* 30). At the same time, and particularly in the later texts, corporeal change—the very unfamiliarity of a recovering or altering body—becomes for Sarton an opportunity to reformulate her own attitudes about sexuality, independence, and social value. Again, this can sometimes take a somewhat stereotypical form, as when Sarton writes that one of her postmastectomy "insights . . . is that physical disability rouses the will, so much so that extra power seems to be given in overcoming it" (*Recovering* 128). At her more subtle, however, Sarton records her multiple experiences with sickness and disability with forthright self-consideration, instigating thoughtful reassessments of the cultural situation of an aging woman.

In one of her earliest pieces of nonfiction, *Journal of a Solitude* (1973), Sarton asks, "Why go on living if one has ceased to grow?"[14] In the throes of a new love affair, she is prompted to address the scandal she represents: a fifty-nine-year-old woman, never married, involved with another woman. Speaking in generalized terms, Sarton ponders the fact that "for some reason Americans are terrified of the very idea of passionate love going on past middle age" (80), and she goes on to exclaim, "How unnatural the imposed view, imposed by a puritanical ethos, that passionate love belongs only to the young, that people are dead from the neck down by the time they are forty, and that any deep feeling, any passion after that age, is either ludicrous or revolting!" (90). If the sex lives of the aged incite the censure of youth- and health-obsessed America,[15] what may be even more provocative about Sarton's situation is the specter of the "middle-aged" (40) single woman living alone, "responsible only to her own soul" (40), fashioning an unconventional romantic life and writing. It "means something," Sarton avows in that same entry—as of course it would in late 1971—that a woman thus strives to determine her own choices and her identity.

These, then, are the preoccupations with which Sarton's autobiographical persona over twenty-five years repeatedly wrestles: issues of aging, the pleasures of relationality and solitude against the difficulties that both entail, and the drive to write. Each, in its own way, raises questions pertinent to a discussion of the lived and social experience of disability, and together they underscore the kinds of concerns that make Sarton's journals a fitting conclusion to this book. Her creative intentions here are obviously feminist and anti-ageist: as a writer she "can tell where she is" (40), both in her life of "chosen" solitude (134) and as an older woman with "wrinkles"

(80), a woman who now "know[s] so much more" (90) than when she was younger. She writes admiringly of older women friends living independently (whether married or not) and protests, after one friend's death, against a culture in which "people are shoveled away, as if that whole life of hard work, dignity, self-respect, could be discarded at the end like an old beer can" (23). Such comments invoke familiar goals of the disability community—to ensure that all lives can be carried out with dignity and that no bodies are discarded or shunted aside—and also suggest the ways in which self-narration can open out toward alternate stories, encouraging readers to re-examine received ideas about women and their aging bodies.[16]

Sarton's demand for solitude, however—the very penchant upon which this and subsequent autobiographical personae are fashioned, even as Sarton advances into her eighties—highlights the disagreement over autonomy that wrenches feminism from disability activism and separates disability theorists from scholars of autobiography. In a particularly poignant moment in *Journal of a Solitude*, Sarton complains that she has "done little . . . in this house but wait for people who do not or cannot come," and she then consoles herself by reporting her friend Heilbrun's opinion "that what I have done best—and what she thinks altogether new in my work—is to talk about solitude" (134). Here, with the endorsement of that most adamant critic of patriarchal power, is one of second-wave feminism's central tenets: to have the economic resources to live and work autonomously. Sarton presents two visions of herself: forlornly awaiting guests who cancel their dates and then deploying the journal as a working-through of feelings of loss and loneliness or, conversely, bemoaning friends' arrivals as an interruption of solitude that sends her into a "purgatory" (199) where she "feel[s] dispersed, scattered, in pieces," with no "time alone in which . . . to understand what has really happened" to her (195–96). Both models depend upon private space as a physical reality and a metaphor for self-actualization, and both figure the autobiographer as a lone individual holding sway over the "essence" (196) of experience.

But while a room of one's own, especially a room of one's own in which to write, may be a feminist aspiration, it does not necessarily accommodate a disabled or aged woman—or, to put this another way, such a space would signify very differently in the context of disabled or ailing existence, where "independent" does not inevitably mean that a person receives no financial or personal assistance. In this sense, Sarton's storied love of solitude may unwittingly recapitulate ableist constructions that promote a narrow definition of self-sufficiency, denigrate caretaking as "private" or women's work, and underwrite forms of life writing focused strictly on a solitary narrator. At the same time, however, one of the compelling features of Sarton's journaling process is that no assertion stays irreversibly fixed. This is not to say that Sarton is indecisive but, rather, that she does not seek to produce last words; she openly records the tug between opposing impulses and is prepared to reconsider and to revise herself directly on the page. And it is precisely this question of how to negotiate age—changes in her body, her increasing need for help at home, the shifting status of her relationships, and so on—that her journals willingly and increasingly take up. Though solitude remains one of the most cherished aspects of Sarton's lifestyle, deeply connected to her sense of herself as a woman and a writer, later journals recount the need to allow for, and also to appreciate, the sort of interdependence that comes with age.

In the summer of 1979, when she was sixty-seven, Sarton underwent a modified radical mastectomy of her left breast. Her journal of that year, *Recovering*, details a series of losses in which mastectomy seems almost the least traumatic: her thirty-five-year companionship with Judy Matlack ends, due to what Sarton calls Judy's "senility"; her novel *A Reckoning* (in which the terminally ill protagonist comes to terms with her love for another woman) is badly received by reviewers; and Sarton suffers a resurgence of depression, a condition that troubled her for much of her adult life. The entanglement of writing, illness and aging, and passionate love and solitude is once again the focal point of Sarton's self-construction.

As a text in which breast cancer is but one of several traumatic events (and, as I am suggesting, perhaps not even the most significant), *Recovering* cannot properly be deemed a breast cancer narrative—a veritable "subgenre" of autopathography, to use G. Thomas Couser's phrase, that emerged just at the time Sarton composed her journal, when breast cancer became "a publicly narratable personal crisis."[17] *Recovering* does not share many of the features of the self-writing that Couser examines: there are relatively few explicitly medical scenes, which Couser notes as "virtually obligatory" in the genre; Sarton downplays the issue of recurrence and makes no mention of whether she considered reconstructive surgery or wearing a prosthesis; and perhaps most importantly, rather than rejecting she often uncritically reiterates many of the negative tropes that attach to breast cancer. But despite what looks at times like surrender to the worst stereotypes about cancer and about women after mastectomy, Sarton's journal also records an intriguing indifference to the "loss of a breast" (119), as if to insist that her sense of self will not be diminished or defined by that event. Moreover, by virtue of embedding breast cancer into a narrative that precedes and then follows it, Sarton writes a life story in which cancer occurs, rather than constructing illness as the determinant of that story or that life.

The most obvious feature of this narrative approach is the fact that Sarton makes no reference to the situation—to mammograms, self-examination, or a lump—in the previous six months of the journal. The announcement comes unexpectedly, at the start of June: "Saw Dr. Dow yesterday, and, as I have suspected for some time, I shall be going into the York hospital on the seventeenth for a biopsy, followed at once, Dr. Dow believes, by a mastectomy of the left breast" (117). It may be that the abrupt quality of this revelation has something to do with Sarton's denial of what she "suspect[s]," and that reluctance to linger over a painful experience motivates the quick moves from a somewhat ponderous discussion of Eros and Agape on June 7 to news of the surgery on June 8 and then again to its aftermath on June 26. It may also be that what sustains her through this time is in fact turning her attention elsewhere, toward the life-sustaining small details evident in all of her journals: the "constant joy" of flowers, "the love of many, many friends," an oriole's song, her dog and cat, and so on (119); putting "a fresh dressing on [her] wound" has no more narrative weight than the need for "fresh towels," rain in the garden, or answering letters (121). Whatever the intent, the effect is one of textual closing-over: the familiar strains of Sarton's journaling technique return to move this health event along and to provide a kind of narrative resolution. There may be cancer, but there is also discovering one's own "resilience" (119) and "accepting dependence with grace" (121) and simply turning one's attention to other matters, to the business of getting on with a writing life.

Sarton offers a slightly different explanation when she claims that the news of the cancer "is no surprise, and in some ways a relief, for I know that the amount of suppressed rage I have suffered since last fall had to find some way out" (117). Here, in bald form, is what Susan Sontag calls the "cliché" that cancer "is caused by mismanaged emotions."[18] Sarton makes it explicit, adding that "I have always believed that my mother's cancer came from suppressed rage" and, of the mastectomy, that "I look on the operation as a kind of exorcism. Something had to give, as they say" (117–18).[19] "Exorcism" exaggerates the metaphor of cancer as the symptom of malevolent forces within, "no mere disease but a demonic enemy."[20] In this sense, the disclosure of illness without preamble may be connected to Sarton's focus, prior to June, on the emotional pains of depression, critical failure, and loneliness. But this points to an unexpected aspect of Sarton's narration of her illness, which, rather than following the step-by-step sequence of discovery, treatment, and recovery, instead introduces cancer in terms of concurrence. It simply coincides with other struggles—to feel "wholly myself" (113), to conquer the "killing poison" (115) of a love affair gone wrong, and to "[sort] myself out" (15). Though Sarton's etiology of cancer obviously plays into a problematic mind/body split, her narration of its occurrence in her life ends up depicting it not as a pernicious tide that overwhelms her sense of self but, rather, as isolable event that, once addressed, can be moved on from.

We are, nevertheless, still in the territory of illness or bodily affliction as a symptom of insidious emotion or bad character traits. It is curiously contradictory that Sarton can, on one hand, bemoan the "preconceived idea" that "to be in love at [her] age is ludicrous and somehow not proper" (205) and, on the other, comply so thoroughly with the kind of gendered stereotype that construes "breast cancer as a threat to womanliness."[21] Where is her critical self-awareness, for example, when she declares that "what the mastectomy does to each individual woman is, at least temporarily, to attack her womanhood at its most vulnerable, to devalue her in her own eyes as a woman" (131)? In the absence of any verifying evidence (Sarton does not cite, even anecdotally, any other women), one wonders if the representative "her," and the slightly neutral, detached tone in which she seems to deliver "facts" rather than subjective expressions of experience, reveals the presence more than the absence of shame and self-doubt. Indeed, by asserting a kind of omniscience into the workings of the body (the cancer was "no surprise"), Sarton seems invested in defying the imputation of loss of control; statements that deflect attention away from "the mutilated body" and toward the "phoenix"-like "spirit" (138) seem intended to counteract—but of course problematically reiterate—the belief that cancer patients are "culpable," that they have, in Sontag's words, "caused their disease" and even "deserv[e] it."[22] What is at work, I think, is a despair that long precedes cancer. This may be why the journal reports the mastectomy so swiftly and even so stereotypically; cancer is merely one instance of a deep-seated sense of worthlessness. *Recovering* is thus charged with a daunting task: to restore a sense of viable selfhood to one who "feel[s] devalued and abandoned at the center of [her] being," one who thinks she "should have been done away with at birth" (122).

I would nonetheless argue that Sarton manages something recuperative in this journal that addresses, on multiple fronts, the convergence of aging, illness, women's love for one another, and writing. Despite being read and (presumably and at least initially) written chronologically, *Recovering* shapes its episodes almost as if they happen simultaneously, an effect produced by the text's dual movements: while dates signal the advance of time, the entries themselves more often stall than achieve forward motion by repeatedly returning to the same problems and by implying psychological links between discrete events. Coincidental as they may in fact have been, critical rejection, being "starved for tenderness" (15), and breast cancer are staged as a kind of overlapping matrix from which a renewed and more self-aware individual ultimately emerges. It is work, finally—"keeping a journal again" (17)—that conducts Sarton back to a degree of resolution about solitude, her body, and herself. When the " 'bad thoughts' come creeping in," Sarton writes, "then it is time to get up, come up here to my study, and get to work. . . . So here I am" (26). That final phrase encapsulates the phenomenon of presence that *Recovering*, as all of Sarton's journals, seeks so deliberately to manufacture. The autobiographer inscribes her being; she is "here." In the aftermath of illness, the loss of love, or professional disappointment, that affirmation becomes powerfully meaningful.

So too in *After the Stroke*, begun in the spring of 1986 when Sarton was seventy-three, does Sarton present journaling as her mode of engagement with aging, embodiment, and gendered identity. One of the refrains of the text is the need to get back to a "real" self that has been silenced or suppressed by illness. Two months prior to her stroke, Sarton (already suffering the painful cramps of diverticulitis) is hospitalized for heart fibrillations and given medication that in turn produces intense nausea. These conditions persist after the stroke, and it is they, perhaps even more insistently than effects of the stroke itself, that define the self Sarton constructs in this journal. The combination of chronic discomfort, the disempowerment associated with being a patient, and a forced curtailing of activity (including writing, gardening, answering letters, and entertaining—the "work" of being May Sarton) leaves her feeling "disoriented, without an identity" (80). Illness is overtly construed as a displacement from authentic subjectivity: again and again she declares, "I am *not* my self [*sic*]" (18), "I'm not myself" (31), "I was not there" (42), "I am not myself" (47). Only the abating of symptoms marks a return to the genuine Sarton: "I am myself again. . . . I am putting on my life again like a dear old corduroy jacket, worn but comfortable" (108, 116).

In a similar move, Sarton pits the "passivity" of illness against the sense of daily accomplishment attached to being "well" (37, 87) and writing. Slowed down by and frequently hospitalized for her heart condition, Sarton describes herself as "simply ill, passively and hopelessly ill" (67), and claims that to "manage such a passive *waiting* life for so many months I have had to bury my real self" (78).

Sickness in such instances is not only experienced as a necessary (and temporary) readjustment of behavior but ethically condemned as meek obedience—compliance with the pill- and test-taking regimens of hospital life and a loss of self-determined action. This dichotomy is most properly understood in the context of Sarton's concept of work as what "matters most" (*Recovering* 46), an industriousness that comes from worrying about professional failure. Driven, in the face of critical indifference to her novels and poetry, to publish journals as her one predictably popular form of writing, Sarton reacts vehemently to what she perceives as the loss of self-actualizing activity. When friends encourage her to start a journal after the stroke, for instance, she reports answering, "I can't write a *line*! I'm not myself" (*Stroke* 31) and describes eventually starting the journal as "turning the corner at last" (28), a sign that "my real self was coming back" (30).

The paradox in all of this strict categorizing, however, is that Sarton actually *is* writing all the time, in sickness as in health; even as she protests not to be her true self, it is this "unreal" self—the supposedly submissive, disoriented, inactive one—who so often narrates and thus conducts the shape of the text. Though the very existence of the journal is implicitly attributed to being consistently well enough to write, the entries themselves record ongoing discomfort, fatigue, and anxiety about a return of heart fibrillations. What is the "ill" self, then, if not an actively writing, imaginatively self-constructing one? To what extent can it be securely opposed to the healthy self Sarton seems to idealize as essentially "her"? Journaling is heralded as the vehicle back, the mode of transportation from a false, dislocated self to an authentic one; moreover, its creation seems to depend on a healthy writer, one who is able to stay "on top of things and . . . 'at it' " (159). And yet the "I" of *After the Stroke* is, well beyond the "turn" toward wellness signaled by the inception of the manuscript, still an aging and infirm—if also creative, dynamic, and socially active—subject.

If Sarton can assert, then, that "youth . . . has to do with not being aware of one's body, whereas old age is often a matter of consciously *overcoming* some misery or other inside the body" (35; my emphasis), that notion of corporeality as a thing to be controlled by willpower is disproved by the "I" who comes to take possession of her "own aging self" (188). In a very different articulation of physical selfhood, Sarton strives to come to terms with the aging body's unpredictable needs. It is "odd," she remarks, "to feel and be so frail!" (162), but at the same time, "I felt rather proud to be myself and nearly seventy-five" (120). And if she is "sick and tired of feeling so ill," "sick of this old body," "a stupid sick animal" on May 3 (42), she had just weeks earlier paid tribute to the "courage it takes to grow old" (31), and by New Year's Day she can acknowledge all she has "learn[ed]" from "the poor old body and the heavy heart that somehow goes on beating" (235). The diary format of the text is at once a relatively inflexible temporal schema and an emotionally mobile form, its frame-by-frame movement allowing (even encouraging) a story of ever-shifting moods and variances of the body. The vacillations thus produced by Sarton's daily record suggest ongoing accommodation rather than either a confusion of attitude or identity or a neat trajectory of triumph over physical ailment.

This is especially significant, I would argue, given the cliché that "what it means to age wisely"[23] is to tolerate in silence the physical and emotional suffering that may come with aging, never complaining about one's hurts or objecting to how one is treated by doctors or other medical professionals. One of Sarton's more devoted readers lavishes praise on Sarton's "tactful" account of cancer in *After the Stroke*: "Sarton accepts the loss of her breast with quiet endurance . . . providing a model of quiet endurance that others can emulate" and "a model of endurance in the face of adversity."[24] The repetition in two short paragraphs of the paradigm of docile forbearance seems inadvertently to invoke the caricature of a crotchety old lady, and neither stereotype accurately depicts the lived experience of aging, in which both fortitude and outrage may coincide with the more temperate fluctuations of daily life. In her discussion of older women and chronic illness and disability, Barbara Levy Simon makes the more specific point that "never-married women in old age appear to incorporate such disruptions into their daily routines with relative ease and stoicism,"[25] but while this rightly acknowledges the self-reliant coping strategies that women may develop over the course of their single lives, the emphasis on stoical resolve implies the suppression of what might otherwise properly deserve articulation, protest, or repair.

From a different perspective, feminist gerontologists have begun to call for an increased archive of older women's personal narratives of how they address the physical, medical, and social aspects of aging. In their study of chronic pain management, for example, Karen A. Roberto and Sandra G. Reynolds found that because they fear "skepticism from others" in response to their pain, many aging women take on the role of "stoic bearers" of pain and try "not to verbalize complaints"; in the words of one of the study's participants, " 'We've become very good actors . . . who do not want to be seen as old and whining.' "[26] Such a remark suggests that when an ailing older woman is commended for her "stoicism" or her "quiet endurance," she may not just (or not at all) be serving as an example of how one might adjust in a self-determined way to the disabilities or illnesses of aging; to the contrary, she may be garnering praise for exemplifying passive acquiescence to—and thus perpetuating the hiddenness of—a life stage figured as "adversity." In this context, Sarton's journals are doing a vital piece of cultural work, putting forth stories of a woman who may occasionally grouse or whimper but does not in any sense slide gently into a submissive old age.

We find this in *After the Stroke* in those moments when Sarton registers dissatisfaction with the way she is treated by doctors or with the environment of hospitals, scenes that further complicate the putative split between inauthentic, ill self and hale, recovered one. Again, there is fluctuation. At times the hospital is a "safe cocoon" (45, 77) in which Sarton relishes the "complete passivity" (44) of being "taken care of" (43). Such statements may seem too easily to cede custody of the self to the institutional authority of the hospital, but they can also be read as concomitants of how Sarton constructs her life at home in Maine, where the constant stream of letters and solicitations from "unknowns" interrupts solitude and "silts [her] up"—though she is compelled to reply to it all—"till [she] feel[s] crazy with frustration" (262). In the hospital, at least, she can enjoy a respite from what she styles in each of her journals as a pressing need to respond to others' requests of her, whatever the emotional cost or inconvenience. The hospital, in this sense—and paradoxically, given that her presence there results from self-displacing illness, her worsening heart condition—is rendered a site of self-renewal beyond simple relief from her symptoms.

In another way, however, the hospital is also the target of critique about neglect and inattention. Over the course of several hospital stays, from May to August, related to heart fibrillations, Sarton complains most strenuously about being ignored—waiting for hours in an emergency room, getting no response from one doctor to "a written plea" (40) about diverticulitis pain, and having others dismiss her assertion that various medications don't work or make her feel worse. "The hardest thing psychologically to take," she writes of one physician, "is that he does *not* believe this drug makes me sick" (73). This is a familiar sentiment, one that all of the women discussed in this book have articulated: the frustration of being dependent upon and vulnerable to a health system that tends to disregard the whole individual and to minimize the significance of the patient's self-reporting (Arthur W. Frank describes the patient's experience in dialogue with a physician as one of "narrative surrender").[27] In Sarton's case, age is a further factor in her sense of being discounted by doctors who are younger and primarily male. Animal imagery makes the point. Twice, for instance, she refers to herself as a dog: in the emergency room, she is "a dog in a cage not knowing why it is there—hoping, waiting, punished she doesn't know why or what for" (102); later, she declares she will "not be put down permanently like a dying dog" (231). Both remarks encapsulate the power inequity inherent in the doctor/patient relationship and suggest that Sarton understands the hospital environment to require a kind of undignified obedience to the priority of youth, submission to the mastery of those in the know and in control.

When she writes that she has "become acclimatized to hospital life," then—adding that she no longer feels like "a trapped hedgehog with all its bristles erect" (103)—Sarton does not simply mean, in a positive sense, that she has relaxed her fearful or defensive guard.

The image of the cornered wild animal, even used, as it is here, in the negative, suggests the degree to which Sarton has relinquished something to her doctors; the image of the hedgehog raises, though it ostensibly seeks to dispel, the more insidious possibility that she has been tamed by the "deadly hospital atmosphere," "cold and inhuman" (103).[28] It seems significant that Sarton depicts herself as having behaved meekly with those doctors, like a child: "begg[ing]" them for relief, crying "storm[s] of tears" (73), and only "murmuring" rather than self-assuredly stating her concerns about a relapse (105). Whatever her affect had actually been, Sarton emphasizes the disparity between her ailing self and the hospital staff by means of an age and emotional disjunction that invokes stereotypical tropes of the elderly patient as overly emotional, helpless, and uncontrolled. At the same time, however, and to entirely different effect, Sarton produces here, in the pages of her journal, a stinging critique (a form of what Chon Noriega has coined an "oughtabiography"); though in the moment, we are left to assume, she had deferred to their authority, *here* she can characterize those same physicians and nurses as "irritated" (105), imperious, and even "sadistic" (102).

After the Stroke is uncertainly probing on the subject of aging's disabilities. Sarton can stalwartly defend against the sense of diminishment that comes both from one's personal experience of loss after a stroke or heart failure and from the framework of the health care system, with its bureaucratic and hierarchical habits. But she capitulates to some old stereotypes, just as she does in *Recovering*. Illness is often discussed as a struggle that must be "surmount[ed]" (*Stroke* 31); self-worth seems at times to have more to do with some metaphysical "inside" than with outward signs of aging ("wrinkles that write a lifetime into a face" [125], for example) that can be bracketed as irrelevant to what Sarton elsewhere refers to as "essence" (*Recovering* 109). These are untheoretical claims, to be sure, and they intimate a certain conventionality in Sarton's way of thinking about the relationship between body and identity. Still, she does arrive at the possibility that illness can open up new avenues of experience and understanding—that parts of the self associated with a certain level of physical activity, for instance, can be "*gladly* given up" (*Stroke*

125)—and she does articulate the crucial point that the body cannot be transcended by will or effort. As a record of a woman coming finally to terms with "old age" (279) and with "the body [as] part of our identity" (125), *After the Stroke* seems to offer the lesson that corporeality is constitutive of, and not merely a hindrance to or depletion of, identity. "I can recover and go on creating" (231), Sarton announces optimistically at the end of this journal. "There is much I still hope to do. And I rejoice in the life I have recaptured and in all that still lies ahead" (280).

If this "I" seems to claim a kind of transparent self-awareness, if it purports to be restored to itself after the dislocations of illness and to be now fully known to itself, that effect is both a trick of the autobiographical enterprise and a fiction that Sarton understands she is creating. In a documentary film produced in 1979, for example, Sarton refers to journaling as a form of mythmaking that seeks to understand and perhaps also to quell the "monster" that is the emotional, embodied, gendered, sexual, and aging self: "We have to make myths of our lives or we wouldn't be able to stand them."[29] Journaling transforms experiences (even apparently insignificant ones, such as weeding a garden) by giving them narrative shape and position; of her own process, Sarton explains that "when I write [an event] into the journal, it sort of becomes something else," something meaningful. Sarton openly acknowledges here that her journals, with their celebration of solitude and their open discussion of aging, have made her "a kind of symbol of the woman living alone," that the very "self-exposure" that makes her work appealing to readers is also a function of textual crafting. She is a symbol, a text, a creation; "she" is a transformation produced by writing it down. So who really knows her? Does she know herself? Who controls this story?

It is writing, as I have suggested, that keeps Sarton going. I mean this in two ways. As she emphasizes in each of her journals, the process of writing provides a "framework" that helps to organize the sense of chaos that follows illness and physical change (see *Eighty-Two* 15, 78, 149). Writing wards off depression and self-doubt, and completed journals serve as "long letters" (28) that attach her to others and reward her by providing comfort to some of those readers. At the same time, the journals literally keep "Sarton" going, perpetuating the autobiographical persona (one that, somewhat ironically, the narrating subject often bemoans: "I create the illusion of caring out of compassion and out of guilt," she admits in *Journal of a Solitude* [201], and she complains in *After the Stroke*, "I wish sometimes I had never written all those books that attract people like deer to a salt lick. I am almost licked to death" [243]). But however much she may bristle at the demands of accessibility created by her own self-revelatory openness, Sarton nevertheless returns year after year to journal writing as a mode of analysis and self-discovery. It is as if Sarton would not know how to *be* herself otherwise; as James Olney has said of Augustine: "To live a life is not enough; it must be narrated, even compulsively, obsessively narrated."[30] In Sarton's own words, "This business of being May Sarton will never be sorted out" (*Eighty-Two* 82).

Such a statement makes obvious the gap between the autobiographer Sarton and the Sarton she produces as a textual effect, but it is unclear to what extent she intends to insist on this distinction. As if to defend herself against the intrusions of "people who know [her] from my journals but whom [she does] not know" (*Eighty-Two* 70), Sarton frequently contrasts the apparent interiority and truth-effect of the journals with what she reveals not only in letters but also in novels. "Although I seem to give away a great deal in the journals," she writes, "I also have kept a great deal private" (157), and she states, somewhat coyly, that "there are things I have never put into the journals" (84). Yet if she can deplore the way in which readers assume intimate knowledge of and access to some "real" May Sarton, the "I" who speaks from the pages of these texts invites that very expectation of familiarity through her own narrative style, one that trades on being "natural and open" (297). As with any autobiography, of course, there is the question of staging a self: Sarton watches Sarton become Sarton by being written and then read. Autobiography makes private public, and it is Sarton's peculiar resentment that people assume a level of intimacy she has not anticipated or intended. This seems both to evacuate and to consolidate her sense of herself and explains, I think, the constantly reiterated ambivalence about correspondence and visitors. The attention of others validates her sense of self-worth, but it also provokes resentment about the obligation to attend to the needs of those same others.

If all of this suggests a troubling narcissism (Sarton solicits attention but blames her fans for wanting her to notice them, too), it also, and perhaps more to the autobiographical point, bespeaks the complications attendant upon the impulse to narrate a self—that is, sorting out the business of being someone entails making sense of one's relationships with others. We can think of this quality of Sarton's work in the context of what Susanna Egan has called "interactive autobiography," a tendency in contemporary life writing to proceed "by means of dialogic or mirroring encounters" in which the autobiographical self is secured by the reflective regard of others.[31] These same others, however, may be significant to life writing precisely "for their *mis*readings" of the author, which the autobiographical "I" is then "eager to correct."[32] As I have been exploring throughout this book, life writing has just this revisionary potential in defiance of negative cultural stereotypes of disability. Each of the authors examined thus far has capitalized on autobiography's discursive capacity to fashion new stories of identity that directly confront the intrusion of ableism into even the most private of relationships.

If, then, sentences such as the ones that close *After the Stroke* seem to make too fixed a link between artistic viability and recovery, between "life" and health, or between "I" and a sense of independence, Sarton's final journal, *At Eighty-Two*, complicates any such easy connections. The interweaving of two predominant themes in this text—Sarton's struggle to regain a sense of physical and emotional equilibrium, and the shifting state of her relationships with others—suggests how thoroughly her narrative persona has had to adjust to a self made unfamiliar by aging. Here, in the journal she dubs *kairos* ("a Greek word referring to . . . an opportunity for change" [27]), Sarton attempts to recast the narrative of aging from inevitable "decline" (86) to "a unique time in a person's life" in which she might seize the invitation "to be alive to challenge and to possibility" (27). But this does not come easily. Again and again, she articulates how consciously and deliberately she must make the effort to accept becoming strange to herself. If breast cancer had been "no surprise" in 1972, by 1992 the physical and cognitive losses associated with strokes and with Sarton's ongoing heart and digestive conditions seem *continually* to surprise her; the embodied self, no longer fully known to itself, steadily and painfully requires alterations in routine that destabilize Sarton's mythic solitude and self-determination. "The whole business of how to handle my life here," Sarton writes in a muted remark that encapsulates what this journal undertakes, "is quite troubling" (172).

Far more than in any of Sarton's earlier journals, the narrator in *At Eighty-Two* seems acutely distressed that she can no longer claim fully or transparently to know who she is. Watching a video of herself at a poetry reading taped in 1985 prior to her first stroke, she observes "a person I no longer am and can never be again because I no longer have that vitality, that actual physical strength, the breath that I had then. So . . . here it is. I am old" (88). (As John Updike once wrote of aging, we "leave behind this litter of dead, unrecoverable selves.")[33] Depression and subsequent strokes make her feel "all the time not like myself. . . . It is so strange; I do not feel real" (198). Bewildered in the absence of recognizable identity, she writes, "I do not know whether my problem right now is old age, the stroke, or the drug I am taking, Prozac, which alters the mind" (313), and she can provide no definitive answer to her own question, "Where is my self?" (262). Often too tired to engage in the activities that "keep at bay" (78) depression and weakness or to enjoy the moments that sustain her authorial identity (such as the arrival of a new book of edited letters), Sarton succumbs to a pressing, reiterated sensation of "not being real." Who, then, is narrating the text? Is there a real Sarton to whom the ailing woman might return, and if so, where does she reside—in the younger body of the 1985 poetry reading, in the woman who wrote her now-collected letters, or in the narrator of previous journals?

One response to this problematic in *At Eighty-Two* emerges in a discussion of psychological testing, prompted by a reading of Betty Friedan's *The Fountain of Age*. Sarton writes of such exams that "the questions are not right" and argues that tasks "based on the tests of young people" ignore the fact that "in some good way we have changed from the person at twenty-five who might have gotten high marks" (72). In effect, *At Eighty-Two* responds to a different set of questions, one that takes seriously an older person's "well of experience and wisdom" (72) and in this way construes the project of making real "a very old lady" (73) as shifting the kinds of paradigms that limit even as they elicit subject position. But this is not to say that Sarton presents a stereotypically oracular older voice or that she perpetuates the fiction of a self-assured autobiographical persona. To the contrary, her customary position here, troubled by self-doubt, physical discomfort, and fear, asserts only paradoxically that the old are wise. What is known, she implies, is precisely the truth that nothing about the body or self can be guaranteed; everything is subject to change and loss. Through writing, however—the daily exercise of giving depth and shape to "what is happening"—comes a version of self-discovery that can counteract the sense of unreality, of not being "my real self" (112), produced by illness and its attendant depressions.[34]

A further cause of autobiographical dislocation in *At Eighty-Two* is the fact that Sarton can no longer live completely on her own. While each of Sarton's journals, as I have discussed, wrestles with the question of how to balance solitude and relationality, that tension takes on a particular urgency as she begins to acknowledge that she cannot manage the tasks of daily living without increased personal assistance. The particular fear that impels such remarks as "I am in the perennial panic of not knowing how to handle my life. . . . I feel weak and unable to cope" (83) is of helplessness, while the steadily encroaching weakness that makes "small things like trying to button my shirt" a source of "continual frustration" (27) also signifies a loss of Sarton's career solitude. The recognition that her interactions with others must modulate from friendships or mentoring relationships to a form of interdependence that involves caretaking requires that Sarton relinquish her hold on a self-image based on the perceived empowerment of autonomy. To "get more help" is not just "to have to change [her] way of life" (172), as Sarton concedes; it is also to alter the very foundation of the myth she has created of herself, the myth of the solitary woman. But as relationships shift, so too does the autobiographical self. Speaking of Susan Sherman, a schoolteacher she befriends, Sarton admits, "I have been feeling frightened by my dependency on Susan when she is here in the summer," and then she asks of herself, "Let me accept that I am very dependent on her when she is here and that it is a good thing, a part of our relationship as it is" (159). This is what Egan describes as the autobiographer "adjust[ing] self-definition" in response to the changing demands of intersubjectivity. As Sarton becomes more resolved about having to give up "the way [she is] living now" (172), so too does her written sense of identity construct itself around adaptation to unaccustomed types of intimate interaction.

A further problem is the widening disjunction between Sarton's textual and corporeal selves, between her public identity as a serial diarist and her private experience as a woman dealing with the increasing impairments of age. Writing that "people simply do not realize, I think do not add up, how old I am," she tries to collapse the distinction. But in so doing she insists on the gap as inherent in the autobiographical project: "Of course, the journals suggest somebody who is still very much alive as I am, but lately I have felt I cannot handle it and do not know how to manage" (143). One can imagine a reader puzzling over the ambiguity of such a statement: the author confesses despair at not feeling competent or in control, and yet she is very much the competent author in control of her narrative. In some sense, Sarton has throughout all of her journals attempted to use autobiography to "adjust self-definition"[35] in response to how others relate to her—to needy fans, uncomprehending critics, and the friends on whom she progressively more honestly depends for assistance through cancer, stroke, abdominal pain, forgetfulness, and fatigue. Though she had once called herself "a solitary" as if with quasi-religious significance (*Recovering* 81), in *At Eighty-Two* she understands the need to communicate to readers a different identity, one that realigns itself with unfamiliar interdependence.

This returns us to the ways in which life writing can serve as a mode of reevaluation that conducts both autobiographer and reader toward alternative ways of imagining older embodiment and identity. Sarton is no longer the emphatic and fully stable center of this narrative, however much "May Sarton" seems to act as its organizing consciousness, its controlling presence. She returns once again to the scene of making a self, attempting to ground herself in the regularity of journaling, but physical impairment and psychological or cognitive disorientation make the journey to her desk both literally more difficult and conceptually less guaranteed. The routine mechanism of daily recording[36] may stall an emotional chain reaction sparked by the recognition of "real old age" (*Eighty-Two* 27)—feeling "stupidly frail" (160), "a stupid old woman" (196), "frustrated by [her] impotence and weakness" (222), "too ill to go anywhere" (249), and worried that "something serious is wrong which [she] cannot control" or understand (295). The committed diarist surmounts her impulse to "give up" by forcing herself to "climb the stairs, those two flights of stairs, and do a little, a very little" (306); she can still (unlike the memoirist who narrates at a distance) attend to the immediacy of being in the moment.

Yet the journal that captures that labor is charged with a peculiarly difficult responsibility. It can resist a narrative trajectory of decline by demonstrating that the aged, ailing writer has kept to her work, day after day. But maintaining a level of honesty about the travails of that mission—to record, day after day, how arduous the task is and how close to ending it the writer at every moment feels herself to be—threatens to derail the project, along with the self it is in the process of constructing. The narrator's continuity becomes especially unstable in *At Eighty-Two* because we know it was Sarton's last journal. The writer, too (although she does not actually "know"), confirms more directly than in her previous works how the self-observations of daily recording can make textually and psychologically real the self approaching death but also, in so doing, effectively distance that same self. "I have entered a new phase and am approaching my death," Sarton says. "If I can accept this, not as a struggle to keep going at my former pace but as a time of meditation when I need ask nothing of myself, will nothing except to live as well as possible as aware as possible, then I could feel I am preparing for a last great adventure as happily as I can" (252).

This is what Couser would refer to as the comic plot employed by many writers of illness, in which the happy ending of recovery affords, often prematurely, narrative closure. Sarton's journal extends beyond this moment, however; three months later, for example, she writes, "It is an extraordinary life I am leading because it is all the time impossible. The effort is staggering. The wish to die is staggering. To give up. Not to have to make the effort any longer" (306). Reading such words, we know that Sarton did, indeed, "make the effort"; the words on the page—and three months' worth of subsequent entries—mark the author's presence, as well as that of the autobiographical persona who begets herself by carrying on. The open-endedness of a diary structure, in addition to the very fact of all those previous journals with their provisionally terminal last entries, forestalls the end of the written self even as she may declare, "I am going to die after all" (193).

One obvious hope for the journals is that they will speak for Sarton—that they will *be* Sarton—after her death. In the entry describing the taped poetry reading in *At Eighty-Two*, she comments that the video will outlive her as a "record which will be there forever and people can hear it after I am dead" (88–89). So too is the journal itself such a record, which people will read or hear after Sarton's death. Here autopathography has become autothanatography, a writing forward from the dying self to the readers who will bring her into being in the future. Identity refracts, a palimpsest of personae: the recording Sarton describes an infirm self looking backward at a former, healthier self reading poetry to an appreciative audience, then imagines herself being read and remade by readers in the future. We might think of this as what Egan calls the "virtual performance" of autobiographical self-representation, which, for all that it resides in textuality and multiply splits the subject, "need not therefore be invalidated."[37] Through the vision of future interaction, of readers and listeners acknowledging and thus creating for the narrating—dying—self some future recorded persona, Sarton at once establishes a continuity of being denied by the closure of death and acknowledges the perpetual fracture of self instigated by autobiography and aging alike. "I am not myself" (288), Sarton records just months before the end of her final utterance, evoking the plaintive chorus of so many of her journals of aging and illness, but the statement never gets revised or corrected here. The autobiographical "I" seems to have absorbed, at last, the otherness of its own death.

Like Nancy Mairs, Sarton returned again and again to the process of writing out a life; like Mairs, Sarton used life writing to conduct a conversation with herself, to "[think] hard things out" (*At Seventy* 105) and, importantly, to gain an audience. While Mairs makes far more subtle use of feminist theory, and though her autobiographical self is defined in more contingent and provisional terms than Sarton's, both writers fashion an "I" who strives toward self-awareness while recognizing the limits of that endeavor. Paradoxically, given Mairs's post-structuralist leanings (but perhaps because Sarton ultimately trusts more fully than Mairs that the self can become known), Sarton often seems befuddled by the elusive quality of her own identity: she fails to understand why she behaves in certain ways; she struggles with both cause and effect of her emotional outbursts; she feels betrayed by the promise of a stable, loving relationship and of professional success; and she copes daily with the pains and losses of aging, which often make her a stranger to herself. But it is her frankness about those confusions, and her daily, yearly inquiry into the puzzling mystery that is the aging, embodied self, that lends Sarton's journals their uniquely contestatory character. She rejects the autobiographical tradition of summing up a life, as if it could be made to fit the neat perimeter of a retrospective narrative; instead she lurches—formally, physically, emotionally—through "the day-to-day struggle" (*Eighty-Two* 109).

Perhaps this narrative perseverance does not sufficiently attack entrenched practices in American culture that delimit women's capacity to manage the impairments of aging. The argument could be made, as it has been made about first-person disability narratives generally, that Sarton's highly individualized journals do not go far enough toward addressing the serious issues pertinent to older women aging in America. There is, I think, an undeniably individualized quality to Sarton's work in the negative sense—her emphasis on solitary selfhood, for instance, which isolates the narrative voice and seems to bracket political and social issues except in the most cursory of ways. The predominant focus on flowers, pets, meals, friends, and complaints (rather than ideologically informed arguments) about the body may seem stylistically precious or philosophically narrow. Still, the totality of Sarton's work asks us to reconsider the notion of what is ideologically efficacious in autobiographical writing. Is a story being told enough? In the documentary film *World of Light*, Sarton states that "the old feel like pariahs . . . they feel unwanted." Writing openly and often that aging is neither a burden nor a source of shame, her journals tell an alternative story about what an older woman's life might look like. There is something provocative, finally, in making ordinary aging simply ordinary.

The small details are thus precisely the point, however insignificant they may seem to a reader looking for the broad strokes of a more public or conventionally retrospective life story; they prove that Sarton made good on her belief in the importance of maintaining, even in "old age," "the curiosity, the intense interest in everything from a bird to a book to a dog" (*At Seventy* 76). Sarton's journals do not pursue the kinds of patterns that Anne Hunsaker Hawkins has discovered in many narratives of illness; stories neither of triumph nor compensation, the journals textualize "intense interest" as a way of countering a social narrative of diminishing capability and value. It is true that Sarton often frets over a sense that, in age and illness, she is not sufficiently "useful," equating viable identity with action and with work.[38] Such a relationship has problematic implications for people with chronic illness or disability, if to "be" something meaningful is bound up with a notion of use value or if episodes of sickness and impairment become tolerable only when construed as having some psychological, spiritual, or even literary usefulness. At the same time, Sarton's stated pleasure in "be[ing] *used*" (*Recovering* 161)—by which she means being sought out and respected for her ideas—makes the point that an aging woman writer has cultural capital. To be "used" in this way is to be granted that elusive existential quality Sarton so often bemoaned the lack of, to be made "real."

For all that the journals may seem, then (as they certainly have to some readers and reviewers over the long span of the author's career), unfocused and tedious at best, petulant and self-indulgent at worst, Sarton's life writing nevertheless mounts an indisputable grievance against what she calls in the documentary the "youth ethos" of American culture. The prevalent attitude toward age reads it as a "catastrophe" that must be defended against by the young; more to the point, an aging woman may seem to the young (or her readers) to be "trapped [in] an alien and alienating body."[39] It is to address the sensation and the position of social irrelevance that Sarton writes, year after year, the story of her agedness. That story may be sometimes repetitive, often uncomfortably revealing; but it is not one we are accustomed to hearing, and that gives it point. For as Sarton herself remarks, "To be absolutely open and transparent . . . makes you very vulnerable, and few people dare. It's too dangerous."

epilogue

Autobiography scholars have long recognized the important cultural work performed by life stories told from the margins, alternative stories that resist dominant patterns of subject formation. Women's autobiography, memoirs of exile, autoethnography, survivor narrative, relational autobiography, autobiographics, biomythography—these are stories of identity that foreground their ideological and rhetorical transgressions, raising questions about whose lives "count" and writing against the conventions that restrict our choices for making and narrating selves. To this list we can add disability narrative. In the ten years since Nancy Mairs described G. Thomas Couser's *Recovering Bodies* as a "brave beginning" in the study of life writing about illness and disability, scholars and creative writers alike have stressed the counterdiscursive possibilities of what Mairs names (with signature irony) "the literature of personal disaster" and "the memoir of mischance."[1] The narratives I consider in this book, composed with the stated intent of contesting social prejudice against anomalous corporeality, have such transformative and liberationist goals.

My aim in this book has also been to show the ways in which women writers have responded to a particular sense of exclusion from both feminist and disability communities. Calls for more direct articulation of women's perspectives about disability have come from a number of quarters—including feminist sociologists and philosophers, activists and cultural theorists, and artists and scholars—and many recent compilations of women's stories respond to that desire for more nuanced examinations of how gender and disability intersect in women's lives. A more sharply theorized feminist disability studies has emerged in the last decade as mainstream feminism has confronted not simply its inattention to the way in which disability complicates and even overturns central feminist assumptions but, in fact, an actively (if unacknowledged or unconscious) ableist position on such matters as abortion rights or sexual objectification. At the same time, feminist disability activists have pushed the movement to take up matters of access to health care and personal care, job availability and workplace accommodation, and child care and education, as these affect women, and also to draw attention to the politics of representation and the (in)flexibility of normative sexual behavior and gender roles as they pertain to disabled women. Again, the authors studied here interweave these several threads in various ways into their narratives, writing from their embodied perspectives to expand the parameters of what matters to disability and feminist theories.

Book-length literary life writing constitutes a unique form of praxis in the context of disability and feminism. In *Recovering Bodies*, Couser differentiates between "illness narrative" as work that focuses on a specific episode of illness and "full-life narrative" as "a comprehensive account" in which illness is but one of the many events of a life.[2] I would suggest that the texts included in *Unruly Bodies* fit into neither category precisely or, rather, that they exhibit characteristics of both, incorporating disability or illness into the life story as its defining but not delimiting feature. These are body stories that suggest how thoroughly impairment, loss of function, or unusual bodily contours matter to a person's sense of self, but not in the ways an ableist and patriarchal society might understand that interconnection or assign meaning to those physical particulars. By narrating identity in terms of a body that is gendered (if ambiguously) and disabled, scarred, or ill, the writers I have studied here represent significant interventions into modes of thinking about embodiment that collude in neglecting the full range of human physical variation and unpredictability. They address the simultaneous fact of the flesh and scriptedness of subjectivity, and they do so in a keenly literary way, not simply voicing experience but shaping and crafting embodied selves through the revisionary properties of language.[3]

These writers thus directly answer the questions posed by Linda J.

Roberts and Beth Blue Swadener in the introduction to their edited collection *Semiotics and Dis/Ability: Interrogating Categories of Difference*: "What happens to the person whose physical body or intellectual or perceptual world is quite different from the normative features of a cultural fabula[?] . . . What about the experiences and events of a person outside the typical stories of growing up, achieving maturity, being successful or not successful, reaching resolution, collecting the expected markers of a life?"[4] The obvious presumption behind these queries is that such a person disappears from the cultural landscape; to be "different from" or "outside of" is to be unrecognized by, or unintelligible within, a culture's prevailing stories about selfhood. But to respond slightly differently, what also happens—as each of the eight writers examined here uniquely shows—is that the very nature of perception shifts; indeed, the very nature of what we understand to be "real" undergoes dramatic refiguring. What happens, if we attend to these atypical stories of growing up and into disabled identities, is an altogether altered understanding of how to mark a life.

Recent scholarship argues that autobiographies do not exist in a one-to-one relation with the historical people who write them. The writing of the text brings into being the self it names, rather than simply mirroring that self. And the shape of the text is determined not simply by the life events it describes but, more fundamentally, by the kinds of life plots and subject positions a cultural and historical moment makes available. We read autobiography not as the transparent product of a preexistent and singular individual but, rather, as a process of shared creation, text and self mutually informing each other, even as both text and self are mediated by the kinds of stories our cultural milieu presents to us as viable, legitimate models of identity. If, as Paul John Eakin has said of the autobiographical enterprise, we become who we are by narrating ourselves not just retrospectively but in every present moment of experience, and if those acts of narration are themselves influenced by prevalent patterns of storytelling, then a greater circulation of life writing about disability has significant consequences for how we live and what we know ourselves to be.

It is important, in this regard, that the authors I focus on resist conventional tropes that represent disability as hindrance to be defeated by willpower or gracefully borne by fortitude. The idea that disability is a source of pride rather than shame, a subject position from which one speaks or signs or performs rather than apologizes or explains, is far from a broadly held conviction—so that the task of writing, of *righting*, an unruly body entails articulating and stimulating a disability consciousness even for those who may be resistant to the notion. One of the significant characteristics of the texts I study here is their engagement of nondisabled readers in a kind of cooptation that makes "disabled" the universal bodily state and that unsettles able-bodied trust in the security and longevity of so-called normalcy. Robert McRuer writes that the dominant model of multiculturalism understands difference as "a good thing that should be (at best) celebrated or (at worst) tolerated," a view that merely "takes note of difference" without any disruption of the structures that hold social inequities in place.[5] A benevolent tolerance of disability that congratulates itself for accepting others but fails to challenge the hierarchies of privilege is not truly liberatory (as one of my students once said, people in wheelchairs aren't bad, but he certainly wouldn't want to be one), just as a life writer who validates herself while capitulating to stereotypes about disability perpetuates rather than dismantles oppression. Mairs reminds readers in *Waist-High in the World* that disability exists only in relation to its (privileged) other, a formulation she employs to shift the norm to a state of difference. But even more forcefully, she and the other writers I have discussed in this book also construe disability not as a binary term at all, even a recuperated one. It is, in their texts, simply human embodiment: *the* human condition.

The point has been made by several scholars that representations of disabled figures in literature, visual art, theater, and film are hardly rare; to the contrary, as many have remarked, disability images are "ubiquitous."[6] Disability narratives in the form of both creative personal essays and sociological reportage are also quite numerous, as evidenced by such recent collections as *Points of Contact: Disability, Art, and Culture* and *Working against Odds: Stories of Disabled Women's Work*

Lives. At issue is whether or not those representations manifest a disability rights consciousness, whether or not they participate in what Rosemarie Garland-Thomson refers to as a "routinization of disability imagery" that facilitates the process of imagining oneself "as a part of the ordinary world."[7]

"Ordinary": it is a word that occurs often in conversations about disability that seek to redress the alienating legacy of the freak show and the schoolyard, the doctor's office and the operating theater, the charity campaign and the telethon, and the averted looks or the false camaraderie of the nondisabled. It is the very word Mairs uses to title an early collection, *Ordinary Time*, in which the "endless dragging around of an increasingly crippled body"[8] is simply one other ordinary, daily task, no worse or more extraordinary than writing, teaching, or parenting. Not just more representations of disability, then, but better stories—"bold, brash stories," to reprise Eli Clare, about "changing the world"—and a greater circulation of tales that yield new knowledge about the entanglements of gender, sex, impairment, age, motherhood, discourse, family, work, and memory. It has been my purpose in this book—as it is also, I think, the hope of the writers whose work I explore—to introduce several vital and vibrant life stories into the conversation, so that many more of us might say, with Anne Finger, "Here I was at last among people who understood."[9]

notes

Introduction

1 See Oliver, *Politics of Disablement* and *Understanding Disability*. A clear description of the social model is provided by Shelley Tremain in the introduction to her edited collection *Foucault and the Government of Disability*, 9; see also her article "On the Subject of Impairment." For a discussion of early disability activism in the United States, see Longmore and Goldberger, "League of the Physically Handicapped."

2 Hughes and Paterson, "Social Model of Disability," 326.

3 Ibid., 329.

4 Shakespeare, "Response to Liz Crow," 40.

5 See Hughes and Paterson, "Social Model of Disability," in addition to Snyder and Mitchell, "Re-engaging the Body." See also Linton, *Claiming Disability*. For discussions of phenomenology and disability studies, see Diedrich, "Breaking Down," and Iwakuma, "Body as Embodiment."

6 Siebers, "Disability in Theory," 750. In "Compulsory Bodies," Kafer details the ableist assumptions behind such classic feminist texts as Adrienne Rich's "Compulsory Heterosexuality and Lesbian Experience."

7 Siebers, "Disability in Theory," 747.

8 Ibid.

9 For discussions of the complex relationship between disability studies and feminist theory, see Deegan and Brooks, *Women and Disability*; Fine and Asch, *Women with Disabilities*; Hillyer, *Feminism and Disability*; Wendell, *Rejected Body*; Keith, "Encounters with Strangers"; Thomson, *Extraordinary Bodies*; Linton, *Claiming Disability*; Meekosha, "Body Battles"; Shildrick and Price, "Breaking the Boundaries"; Frank, *Venus on Wheels*; and Herndl, "Reconstructing the Posthuman Feminist Body."

10 Lloyd, "Politics of Disability and Feminism," 716. See also O'Toole, "Sexist Inheritance of the Disability Movement."

11 Morris, *Encounters with Strangers*, 5, 8.

12 Thomas, *Female Forms*, 99, 68.

13 Wendell, *Rejected Body*, 93; Bonnie Sherr Klein, "'We Are Who You Are': Feminism and Disability," *Ms.*, November–December 1992, 72, qtd. in ibid.

14 Among her many discussions of the integration of feminist and disability theory, see Thomson, "Integrating Disability," along with the essays included in that special issue of *NWSA Journal*.

15 See Kent, "In Search of a Heroine," 93.

16 Lloyd, "Politics of Disability and Feminism," 723.

17 There are many excellent summaries of both conventional autobiography theory and feminist divergences both theoretical and creative. See, for instance, Shumaker, *English Autobiography*; Morris, *Versions of the Self*; Delany, *British Autobiography*; Olney, *Autobiography* and *Studies in Autobiography*; Spengemann, *Forms of Autobiography*; Jelinek, *Women's Autobiography*; Gunn, *Autobiography*; Benstock, *Private Self*; and Smith, *Poetics*. See also Neuman's article "Autobiography and the Construction of the Feminine Body," the first sentence of which proclaims, "Bodies rarely figure in autobiography" (293).

18 Mitchell, "Body Solitaire," 311. Mitchell makes a similar point with coeditor Snyder in the introduction to *The Body and Physical Difference*, where they write that while personal narrative can effectively correct the "preeminent social invisibility" of people with disabilities, the "confessional mode" of autobiographical writing tends to place "physical and cognitive limitation and difference on display to be consumed," while "the parading of personal misfortune inevitably assures the reader/viewer of his or her comparative good fortunes or assuages a shared societal sense of guilt and insensitivity" (11, 10).

19 Mitchell, "Body Solitaire," 312.

20 Davis, *Enforcing Normalcy*, 3–4.

21 Meekosha, "Body Battles," 175; Wendell, "Toward a Feminist Theory of Disability," 266.

22 Couser, *Recovering Bodies*, 291.

23 Couser, *Vulnerable Subjects*, 164. See also Couser's groundbreaking *Recovering Bodies*.

24 Couser, *Recovering Bodies*, 182. See also Couser's earlier article "Embodied Self," 4.

25 Couser, introduction to "Empire of the 'Normal,' " 305.

26 Snyder and Mitchell, "Re-engaging the Body," 386.

27 Frank, *Wounded Storyteller*, 2–3.

28 Corker and Shakespeare, *Disability/Postmodernity*, 15.

29 Subsequent references to Hathaway's memoir will appear parenthetically in text and notes.

30 Mairs quotes an anonymous foreword to the jointly published journals and memoir (242).

31 Many scholars have addressed the particular issue of mothers in women's autobiography; see, e.g., Malin, *Voice of the Mother*; Siegel, *Women's Autobiographies*; and Miller, "Mothers, Daughters, and Autobiography."

32 It is worth noting that Hathaway falls into some conventional gender traps, seeming to fault her mother while protecting her father and brother, describing the latter two in highly sexualized, even overtly incestuous terms. For instance, she writes that she and her father "were conscious of each other, almost as lovers are," and that in comparison to her "interesting and

essential" father, her mother was "clumsy," awkward, and "dull" (37). In a later extended section recounting her brother Warren, Hathaway lingers over a strange scene in which Warren intimates to her that he is attracted to her, and she blames herself for not hearing this as a testament to her potential attractiveness to other men as well. See 47–58.

33 Couser, *Vulnerable Subjects*, 151.

34 See Fine and Asch, *Women with Disabilities*, 3.

35 Mairs, *Plaintext*, 16.

36 Eiesland, *Disabled God*, 90, 98.

Chapter 1

1 Mairs, *Waist-High in the World*, 8. Subsequent references to *Waist-High* will appear parenthetically in the text.

2 Mairs, *Carnal Acts*, 96. Subsequent references to *Carnal Acts* will appear parenthetically in the text.

3 In *Phenomenology of Perception*, Merleau-Ponty claims that he *is* his body, rather than having one.

4 Smith, *Subjectivity*, 184.

5 Mairs, *Plaintext*, 113. Subsequent references to *Plaintext* will appear parenthetically in the text.

6 Mairs, *Voice Lessons*, 113. Subsequent references to *Voice Lessons* will appear parenthetically in the text.

7 Siebers, "Disability in Theory," 746.

8 Cixous, "Laugh of the Medusa," 251.

9 Lennard J. Davis argued several years ago that ableist assumptions are written into contemporary body theory: "The body is seen as a site of *jouissance*," he contends, "a native ground of pleasure" that "takes dominant culture and its rigid, power-laden vision of the body to task." The "nightmare" doppelganger of this body is "deformed, maimed, mutilated, broken, diseased" —so horrifying, Davis suggests, that critics recoil from its real presence and take refuge in "the fluids of sexuality" or "the glossary of the body as text" rather than "contemplat[e] the paraplegic, the disfigured, the mutilated, the deaf, [or] the blind" (*Enforcing Normalcy*, 11).

10 Thomson, *Extraordinary Bodies*, 24 (my emphasis).

11 Lindgren, "Bodies in Trouble," 147.

12 Ibid., 146, 160.

13 The exception to this is *Remembering the Bone-House*, a more standard chronological autobiography. Even in *Bone-House*, however, Mairs deliberately disrupts a forwardly linear motion by looping backward in memory, hinting at future events whose full significance becomes evident only in view of the past, revisiting events from different perspectives, and focusing as much on the interior life of the mind as on external temporal markers.

14 Mitchell and Snyder, *The Body and Physical Difference*, 10–11.

15 Ibid., 10 (my emphasis).

16 See my article "Dear (Embodied) Reader."

17 Thomson, *Extraordinary Bodies*, 22.

18 Lindgren, "Bodies in Trouble," 148, 160.

19 Davis, *Bending Over Backwards*, 31–32.

20 Couser, *Recovering Bodies*, 293.

21 But see Hillyer's discussion in *Feminism and Disability*, particularly the third chapter, "Language and Biography," of the delicate ideological issues surrounding the semantics of naming. See also Linton's sections on "nice words" and "nasty words" in *Claiming Disability*.

22 Published in 1986, *Plaintext* predates the Kate Moss era of emaciated supermodels.

23 The landmark study of the "freak" is Fiedler's *Freaks*. See also Bogdan's book *Freak Show* and Thomson's anthology, *Freakery*.

24 Thomson, *Extraordinary Bodies*, 7.

25 Thomson writes, "The normative female body . . . occupies a dual and paradoxical cultural role: it is the negative term opposing the male body, but it is also simultaneously the privileged term opposing the abnormalized female body" (ibid., 28).

26 Gunn, *Autobiography*, 20–21.

27 Hevey, "Enfreakment of Photography," 332. But see Thomson, "Politics of Staring," 66, which suggests that advertisers have begun to tap the 54-million-person "disability market."

28 Smith, *Subjectivity*, 162.

29 Ibid., 157.

30 See Gunn, who writes, "Autobiography completes no pictures. Instead, it rejects wholeness or harmony . . . as a false unity which serves as no more than a defense against the self's deeper knowledge of its finitude" (*Autobiography*, 25).

31 Smith, *Poetics*, 58.

32 See Benstock's "Authorizing the Autobiographical" and Nussbaum's "Eighteenth-Century Women's Autobiographical Commonplaces," in Benstock's anthology *The Private Self*.

33 For a fuller discussion of these narrative trends, see my "Ordinary Vessels."

34 Miner, " 'Making Up the Stories,' " 285–86.

35 On the notion that the body of the "freak," which seems to "represent the absolutely 'Other' (thus reassuring us who come to gape that we are 'normal')," is in fact "a revelation of what in our deepest psyches we recognize as the Secret Self," see Fiedler, *Tyranny of the Normal*, 152.

36 Compare Asch and Fine's claim that "our culture views being female and

disabled as 'redundant,' whereas being male and disabled is a contradiction," in "Nurturance, Sexuality, and Women with Disabilities," 249.

37 Siebers, "Tender Organs," 53.

38 Mairs, "Sex and Death and the Crippled Body," 163.

39 Thomson, *Extraordinary Bodies*, 14–15.

40 See Hillyer, who writes that "the complexity of our scrupulously individual statements can begin to form women's movement. To repeat each woman's story is essential, of course, but the next and crucial task is to attend to the 'connecting exchange' between them. Thereby we weave a more complex, colorful, significant web, composed of many women's stories, of many women's words" (*Feminism and Disability*, 46).

41 Lindgren, "Bodies in Trouble," 152. Lindgren contrasts Mairs's narratives with those of Drew Leder, Robert Murphy, and Susan Wendell, which foreground disembodiment, transcendence, and body/self splitting in accommodating to illness or impairment. See also 149–53.

42 Gilmore, *Limits of Autobiography*, 96, 103.

43 On Mairs's work as exemplifying an ethic of caring for others, see Frank, *Wounded Storyteller*, and Diedrich, "Breaking Down."

Chapter 2

1 Mulvey, "Visual Pleasure and Narrative Cinema."

2 Stacey, *Star Gazing*, 129. In Mary Ann Doane's words, "The woman's sexuality, as spectator, must undergo a constant process of transformation. She must look, as if she were a man with the phallic power of the gaze, at a woman who would attract that gaze, in order to be that woman" (qtd. in ibid., 121).

3 Gamman and Marshment, 16. For a discussion of "a black female gaze," see Roach and Felix, "Black Looks." It is also possible to reformulate the meaning of the gaze from within psychoanalytic theory itself (I am thinking particularly of Jessica Benjamin's theory of recognition). Describing the network of gazes that animates *Wuthering Heights*, for example, Newman, " 'Situation of the Looker-On,' " 461, argues that the novel destabilizes the control associated with looking, contesting the "power of the gazes" that lie behind storytelling.

4 Thomson, "Politics of Staring," 57, and *Extraordinary Bodies*, 26.

5 Bogdan, *Freak Show*. See also Thomson's edited volume *Freakery*.

6 Thomson, "Staring Back," 335. See also Keith, *"What Happened to You?"*

7 In addition to Thomson's discussion of disabled performance artist Mary Duffy in "Staring Back," see also Alexa Wright's description of her photographic self-portraits in " 'I' "; the performance pieces included in Snyder and Mitchell, *Vital Signs*; Sandahl and Auslander, *Bodies in Commotion*; and Lewis, *Beyond Victims and Villains*.

8 See Smith and Watson's discussion of multilayered autobiographical "I" in *Reading Autobiography*, 58–65. See also Gilmore's discussion of autobiographical surveillance in *Limits of Autobiography*, 20.

9 Seventeenth-century English writers Anna Trapnel and Margaret Cavendish are particularly good examples of this tendency in women's self-representational work.

10 Grealy, *Autobiography of a Face*, 124. Subsequent references to *Autobiography of a Face* will appear parenthetically in the text.

11 Smith and Watson, *Reading Autobiography*, 45.

12 Frank, *Wounded Storyteller*, 69.

13 Goffman, *Stigma*, 3.

14 Wendell, *Rejected Body*, 44. As Wendell suggests, if we believe the body to be totally "created" by discourse, then Grealy's facial "disability" should disappear in a culture that does not reject difference.

15 Grosz, *Volatile Bodies*, 18.

16 Jeffreys, "Visible Cripple," 33, 35.

17 Hampl, *Romantic Education*, quotes on pp. 127, 106, 133. Iris Marion Young's classic essay "Throwing Like a Girl" also describes women's experience of their bodies as an "encumbrance" (34).

18 Frank writes that the "disciplined body experiences its gravest crisis in loss of control" and seeks to "compensate for contingencies it cannot accept" through "actions of *self-regimentation*." "Such single-minded pursuit of regimens transforms the body into 'it' to be treated; the self becomes *dissociated* from this 'it' " (*Wounded Storyteller*, 41). Grealy clearly experiences such dissociation and responds to the unruliness of her face in part through excessive exercise—control of her body.

19 In this, Grealy seems studiously to defy the inherent relationality of both identity formation and autobiography. See Eakin's chapter "Relational Selves, Relational Lives" in *How Our Lives Become Stories*.

20 Wendell, *Rejected Body*, 125, 128.

21 Hawkins, *Reconstructing Illness*, 78.

22 In her essay "Medical Identity," Cook also describes "invasive" medical tests as introducing her to "a material selfhood heretofore invisible." "These continuous reminders of the materiality and interiority of my body challenge the ways that I have been used to thinking about my 'self' as a fairly disembodied subject" (65).

23 Grealy records a progression from "detaching myself from my desires" (179) to the "major step forward" of "begin[ning] to own my desires" (205).

24 Thomson, *Extraordinary Bodies*, 11.

25 A. G. Gowman, *The War Blind in American Social Structure* (New York: American Foundation for the Blind, 1957), quoted in Goffman, *Stigma*, 6.

26 Woolf, "Professions for Women," 288.

27 Gilmore, *Autobiographics*, 239.

28 Smith, *Subjectivity*, 157.

29 Gilmore, *Autobiographics*, 239.

30 Grosz, *Volatile Bodies*, 23.

31 This scene has always provoked disagreement among my students. Some declare it as proof of Grealy's liberation from self-punitive evaluations of her face and self; others see it as further demonstration of her need for male approval. To add to the controversy, in the final paragraph of the book Grealy describes wanting to tell her companion about a "revelation" she's just had about the meaning of image and self, "but he was involved in his own thoughts and I did not want to interrupt him" (223). Student interpretations fall into the same divided camps: those who claim that Grealy doesn't need to tell the man anything to legitimize her discovery and others who find her capitulating to the man's priority in the conversation.

Grealy's death in 2002 sparked a flurry of commentary on *Autobiography of a Face*, some of which suggested that suicide problematized the hopeful ending of the memoir. For a trenchant account of the debate, see Couser, "Obituary of a Face."

32 Thomson, *Extraordinary Bodies*, 11; Couser, *Recovering Bodies*, 182.

33 This is akin to Grealy's surprise at discovering that what she had was "cancer." Kleege, *Sight Unseen*, 206–7. Subsequent references to *Sight Unseen* will appear parenthetically in text and notes.

34 Frank, *Wounded Storyteller*, 61.

35 See Wendell, *Rejected Body*, chap. 3.

36 Young's study of female bodily comportment, "Throwing Like a Girl," claims that what characterizes women's typical motion is that they "tend not to put their whole bodies into engagement with a physical task" and that "the space available to our movement is a constricted space" (33). Women move with an "inhibited intentionality" (38) and "react to motions, even our own motions, as though we are the object of a motion . . . rather than taking ourselves as the subject of motion" (41). While Kleege's style of looking may seem to constrict her physical range, even beyond what Young describes, because she must move slowly before objects and narrow her distance from them, I would argue that *Sight Unseen* expands looking physically as much as conceptually. Kleege activates her whole body in a way that a sighted person misses and looks with a kind of intentionality that seeks to discover rather than master.

37 The masculine pronoun here is revealing. Kleege's text, though pointedly "disableist" and also keen to the specific representations of disabled women, does at times seem to minimize the genderedness of the dynamics she describes.

38 Price and Shildrick, "Bodies Together," 69. See also Shildrick's "Relational Economy of Touch."

39 Chinn, "Power of Touch," 187.

40 In defense of listening to books on tape, for example, Kleege writes that "reading this way almost always feels like a shared experience. I feel myself not merely a passive audience but engaged in a kind of exchange. Readers are not reading to me; we are reading together. I have a sense of a continuous back-and-forth commentary. . . . This is precisely what confounds the sighted reader who thinks of reading as a private and intensely personal act, a solo flight" (181). Kleege claims that reading aloud to someone is an "act of generosity" (191).

41 I will follow Kleege here in using the lowercase "braille" for the system of raised dots and uppercase "Braille" for the inventor of that system. Kleege's imaginative identification with Braille has its counterpart in *Blind Rage: Letters to Helen Keller*. This epistolary deconstruction of the mythic Helen Keller as an impossible model for blind people offers a more realistic, and ultimately admiring, portrait of Keller.

42 Eakin, *How Our Lives Become Stories*, 86.

Chapter 3

1 Butler, introduction to *Bodies That Matter*, 368.

2 McRuer, "As Good As It Gets," 79.

3 Ibid., 82.

4 Kafer, "Compulsory Bodies," 82.

5 Ibid.

6 Wilkerson, "Disability, Sex Radicalism, and Political Agency," 43.

7 Brownworth, introduction to *Restricted Access*, xii.

8 Subsequent references to Panzarino, *Me in the Mirror*, and Clare, *Exile and Pride*, will appear parenthetically in text and notes.

9 See my "Dear (Embodied) Reader."

10 Clare, "Flirting with You," 134, and "Stolen Bodies," 364.

11 Gilmore, *Limits of Autobiography*, 100–101.

12 Mitchell and Snyder, *Narrative Prosthesis*, 6.

13 Couser, *Recovering Bodies*, 203.

14 Murphy, *Body Silent*, 107.

15 The word is from Harris and Wideman, "Construction of Gender and Disability," 126.

16 Ibid.

17 Murphy, *Body Silent*, 204.

18 Harris and Wideman, "Construction of Gender and Disability," 117.

19 On the impact of authoritarian figures on self-narration, see Gilmore's *Limits of Autobiography*, particularly the introduction.

20 Mitchell, "Narrative Prosthesis and the Materiality of Metaphor," 20.

21 Judy Rohrer writes that "women with severe disabilities cannot keep bodily issues private, because they cannot keep their bodies private," and quotes Cheryl Marie Wade: "We have no place in our bodies (other than our imaginations) that is private. And yes, this makes us different from you who have privacy of body" (Rohrer, "Toward a Full-Inclusion Feminism," 52).

22 Harris and Wideman, "Construction of Gender and Disability," 133.

23 Thomas, *Female Forms*, 78.

24 Wendell, *Rejected Body*, 63.

25 Tremain, *Pushing the Limits*, 21, 16, 17.

26 Ibid., 16, 17, 21.

27 Morris, *Encounters with Strangers*, 11.

28 Shildrick and Price, "Breaking the Boundaries," 443.

29 Price and Shildrick, "Bodies Together," 68.

30 Thomas, *Female Forms*, 99.

31 Kafer, "Compulsory Bodies," 85.

32 Egan, *Mirror Talk*, 228.

33 Frank, *Wounded Storyteller*, 27.

34 Martha Vicinus examines the definitional problems pertinent to lesbian identity ("Put bluntly, we lack any general agreement about what constitutes a lesbian"), and she quotes Jackie Stacey: "We cannot assume any coherent or unified collective identity when we recognize the diversity of definitions and experiences of lesbians" (" 'They Wonder to Which Sex I Belong,' " 433). Clare is neither a "woman-identified woman" nor a radical separatist feminist, and the historical typologies—romantic friendships, Boston marriages, butch-femme, and so on—fall short of accounting for the complexity of her situation, experience, fantasy, memory, desire. Like the French painter Rosa Bonheur, whom Vicinus describes at the start of her essay, "they wonder to which sex I belong" (ibid., 432).

Furthermore, the question of how to utilize gender pronouns in Clare's case is ambiguous in the extreme. As *Exile and Pride* makes clear, Clare rejects the confinement of strictly gendered terms, self-identifying as androgynous or "not-boy-not-girl." Clare is referred to by scholars and book reviewers alternately as "she" and "he," with emphasis on the former. I have followed that typical practice in this chapter in part because *Exile and Pride* is the story of an individual who grew up known as a girl, was treated (and abused) as such as a child, and became involved early on with lesbian and dyke communities, and because the articulation of disability identity in the text is bound up with the pressure to abide by—if also the resistance to—normative female behaviors and bodily movements.

35 Like Lucy Grealy's closing image in the café (see Chapter 2) or like Georgina Kleege moving us to an "interior" that is simultaneously an explosion of

what we think "blindness" or disability is, Clare's conclusion is radically open-ended.

36 In the *Gay Times* of May 1992, Keith Alcorn declared, " 'Queer' is a volcanic eruption equivalent to gay liberation. If queer is angry, contradictory, irreverent, iconoclastic, volatile, millenarian, sexually and racially diverse, questioning every sacred cow of the last twenty years, then surely it epitomizes the 1990s?" In that same issue, Alan Sinfield claimed, "Queer is not just a change in language, it's a change in mood. We've had twenty year[s] of Gay, and it has only got us so far."

37 Watson, "Unspeakable Differences," 399.

38 Gilmore, *Limits of Autobiography*, 131.

39 Compare Lucy Grealy, who writes, "Looking at myself in the mirror, I was in little danger of having to think of myself as a 'real' girl doing real girl things. I'd been trying for an androgynous effect, and with my slight figure shrouded in baggy clothes, I was often mistaken for a boy. I felt very safe dressed this way. As I watched my friends dress up, I felt very far away from my own femininity" (*Autobiography of a Face*, 202–3). "Shrouded" seems an especially pointed usage here: the inability to achieve the look of "normal" femaleness is deadening for Grealy, while for Clare it becomes a space of liberation.

40 Cf. Butler, introduction to *Bodies That Matter*. Clare also asks, "How natural are the rigid, mutually exclusive definitions of male and female if they have to be defended by genital surgery performed on intersexed people?" (128).

41 In *Epistemology of the Closet*, Eve Sedgwick compares the trope of "inversion" (a man's soul trapped in a woman's body, and vice versa) and gender separatism, whereby people of the same gender bond together, rather than crossing gender boundaries. In the former, identification and desire are distinct, but in the latter, they are "reassimilate[d]" (58). Clare exemplifies neither of these.

42 Biddy Martin, quoting Teresa de Lauretis's *Technologies of Gender*, in "Lesbian Identity and Autobiographical Difference(s)."

43 Sedgwick, *Epistemology of the Closet*, 53–54.

44 Entering the urban gay scene as a young woman, for instance, Clare confronts both city/rural and class distinctions: while the city provides the organized community and activism that enables her to "com[e] into [her] queer identity" (37), her blue jeans, chamois shirt, and work boots are also more than just "a fashion statement" (135) and thus mark her difference from other women. Such disjunctions are frequently described in the text.

45 Fraser, "Language of Nature," 170.

46 Daniel, "Impoverishment of Sightseeing."

47 Johnson, "Defective Fetuses and Us." Johnson, founder of *Disability Rag* and *Ragged Edge* magazines, pursues the point in *Make Them Go Away* that such

"quest[s] for cure" as Christopher Reeve's—"the most famous disabled person since Roosevelt"—actively militate *against* disability rights. See also Wendell, who mentions "the widely held belief that life with a disability is not worth living" (*Rejected Body*, 154).

48 Wendell, *Rejected Body*, 156. See Longmore's trenchant analysis of telethons in "Conspicuous Contribution."

49 Snyder and Mitchell, "Re-engaging the Body," 370, 373.

50 Clare points out that in some instances in the freak show arena, the disabled "have taken advantage of white people's and nondisabled people's urge to gawk" (95). Bogdan corroborates:

> To some the word "freak" is offensive. It was the preferred term in the amusement industry, even among the exhibits themselves, at least through the 1930s. . . . Human exhibits were not offended by the term because they did not take the nouns people used to refer to them seriously. Their main concern was to make money. Any designation that facilitated profit was acceptable. As freaks sat on the platform, most looked down on the audience with contempt—not because they felt angry at being gawked at or at being called freaks, but simply because the amusement world looked down on "rubes" in general. Their contempt was that of insiders toward the uninitiated. ("Social Construction of Freaks," 35)

See also Gerber, " 'Careers' of People Exhibited in Freak Shows."

51 Gilmore, *Limits of Autobiography*, 128–29.

52 Sedgwick, *Epistemology of the Closet*, 52.

53 Rapp and Ginsburg, "Enabling Disability," 552 (emphasis in original).

54 Wilkerson, "Disability, Sex Radicalism, and Political Agency," 51.

Chapter 4

1 Bordo, *Unbearable Weight*, 81, 72, 79, 83.

2 Haraway, *Simians, Cyborgs, and Women*, 180, 150–51.

3 Ibid., 155.

4 Following Merleau-Ponty, Iwakuma writes that an object such as a cane or a wheelchair is more than a mere accoutrement; it becomes literally embodied as "part of the identity of the person to whom it belongs" ("Body as Embodiment," 76–87, 79).

5 Herndl, "Reconstructing the Posthuman Feminist Body," 152, 154.

6 Haraway, *Simians, Cyborgs, and Women*, 180.

7 Davis, *Bending Over Backwards*, 30.

8 Finger, *Past Due*, 180. Subsequent references to *Past Due* will appear parenthetically in text and notes. My interest in this chapter is Finger's depiction of disability in the context of motherhood, but I would also call readers' atten-

tion to her book *Elegy for a Disease*, a more comprehensive personal account of Finger's childhood experience with polio, as well as a social history of the disease.

9 Bordo, *Unbearable Weight*, 95. This fear also seems to resonate with hesitation in the disability community to focus on the physical details of impairment.

10 Ibid. (my emphasis).

11 Jacobson, *Question of David*, 89. Subsequent references to *Question of David* will appear parenthetically in text and notes.

12 Harbour, "A Few Thoughts about Children," 19, and Wates, "Are You Sure You Can Cope?," 95.

13 Frank, *Wounded Storyteller*, 132.

14 Morris, *Encounters with Strangers*, 10.

15 It is important to note here that Jacobson presents this incident as proof of David's ability to think abstractly and solve problems, rather than as a demonstration of his taking care of her. See Keith and Morris on the "children as carers" debate in "Easy Targets."

16 The baby literally takes over the space of the independent writer ("I could no longer go into the office and focus on my work, centering on my desire to be a writer" [73]). But here, in the memoir, the writing supersedes mothering; mothering becomes equivalent to language, writing, textual creation.

17 Wendell, *Rejected Body*, 88–89.

18 Keith, "Encounters with Strangers," 71.

19 Ibid.

20 Wates, "Are You Sure You Can Cope?," 96.

21 In interviews with disabled mothers conducted in Washington state in 1980, Susan Shaul, Pamela J. Dowling, and Bernice F. Laden asked participants whether they felt there were advantages to having disabilities. According to the authors, "Most stressed that their children had an increased sense of independence because the child knew that some things wouldn't be done for him/her" ("Like Other Women," 139).

22 He covers a different territory, but David is really no different from other children in this sense. Kids whose parents walk obviously "know" their parents can come to get them; it is a way of testing the limits based on what they've come to depend on in their parents—a kind of modified *fort-da*. Earlier in the book, Jacobson thinks to herself, watching an eleven-month-old crawling around the floor, "*Perhaps David would be disabled just enough to slow him down so I'd be able to catch him*" (32). The comment seems ironic but also opens onto ways of conceiving of disability as an advantage.

23 Keith, "Encounters with Strangers," 84.

24 Rapp and Ginsburg, "Enabling Disability," 540, and Lloyd, "Politics of Disability and Feminism," 724, 723 (emphasis in original). By contrast, Daniel Engster has argued for limiting the definition of care to "basic capabilities,"

that which is "necessary for basic functioning," rather than the fostering of such things as artistic expression, religious belief, athletic capability, or sexual freedom. By this definition, problematically, a disabled woman who requires assistance in attending to the "basic functioning" of her child would seem to be prevented from fulfilling a caring function; see "Rethinking Care Theory," 53.

25 Does Jacobson also reveal a desire for a certain kind of constructed femininity here? A longing to be more "mysterious," more "feminine," less visible or obvious than her CP renders her? This may coincide with her description of her emotions: a reappropriation of a certain kind of femininity or womanliness—a culturally defined and also disapproved-of kind, but "female emotion" nonetheless. At the same time, does the reference to the womb show how arbitrary it is as a site or sign of maternity? Neither womb nor penis is involved in the Jacobsons' parenting of David, which thus also reminds us of the uterus's superfluity, made inactive by both CP and adoption. Importantly, Chavallah is also described hysterically: "spewing" and "rav[ing]," "crouch[ing] and lung[ing] around the kitchen": animalistic, out of control.

26 On the prevalence of this narrative trope in pathographies, see Hawkins, *Reconstructing Illness*, chap. 3, "Myths of Battle and Journey." See also Wendell's discussion of the common belief that "recovery from illness and disability can be accomplished with the right attitude" (*Rejected Body*, 102).

27 Sontag, *Illness as Metaphor*, 57.

28 The dedication to *The Question of David* reads, "In memory of my loving mother, Lillian Blauschild Sherer, who always knew." Putting on the socks is like an inverted birth scene, where Lillian "guide[s]" Jacobson's feet "into her lap" and "slip[s] on each cotton sock" (48). The mother pulls the daughter back into her lap, and the scene is dark and womblike; Denise is half-asleep and in bed, the room twice described as dark. It is a moment of intimacy that overtly excludes the father and the sister and establishes an explicit contrast to the father, who wakes Jacobson up with "impatience" and shouts at her to put on her own socks. "You've gotta help me out here!" (49).

29 "In my everyday encounters with the world," Keith continues, "the first thing others look at is my wheelchair." "Just as in our society babies are not quite considered to be 'whole' people, especially in public places . . . people in wheelchairs are considered to be not quite whole either" ("Encounters with Strangers," 71, 79).

30 Bieler, "Right to Maternity," 37.

31 Keith and Morris, "Easy Targets," 94.

32 One wonders, of course, what Georgina Kleege might have to say about Jacobson's insistence on eye contact not just to demonstrate the immediacy of her connection to David but also as the proof of the essential *rightness* of the adoption.

33 Brakman and Scholz, "Adoption," 59.
34 Linton, *Claiming Disability* 5 (emphasis in original).
35 Cf. Rapp and Ginsburg, "Enabling Disability," 552.
36 Ibid., 544.
37 See also Asch and Fine, "Shared Dreams," 298.
38 Ibid., 304.
39 Ibid., 303.
40 Two recent studies addressing these questions are Parens and Asch, *Prenatal Testing*, and Rapp, *Testing Women*.
41 Rapp and Ginsburg, "Enabling Disability," 539.
42 See Michele Wates's "Are You Sure You can Cope?" on the issue of exceptionality.
43 Cf. Michie's "Confinements."
44 Frank, *Wounded Storyteller*, 71.
45 See also Wendell's discussion of alternative medicine and myths of control, *Rejected Body*, 97–98.
46 Rapp and Ginsburg, "Enabling Disability," 540.
47 Couser, *Vulnerable Subjects*, 57.
48 Rapp and Ginsburg, "Enabling Disability," 547.
49 Couser, "Conflicting Paradigms," 80, 84.
50 Murphy, *Body Silent*, 90, 131.
51 Frank, *Wounded Storyteller*, 54.

Chapter 5

1 Simon, "Never-Married Old Women and Disability," 218, and Thomson, *Extraordinary Bodies*, 13–14.
2 On this point, see Haber, "Witches, Widows, Wives, and Workers."
3 George Gerbner, "Women and Minorities on Television: A Study in Casting and Fate" (1993), qtd. in Sherman, "Images of Middle-aged and Older Women," 19.
4 Dinnerstein and Weitz, "Jane Fonda, Barbara Bush, and Other Aging Bodies," 189, and Bordo, *Unbearable Weight*, 25–26.
5 Macdonald, "Outside the Sisterhood," 6. See also Troll, who writes that "full-page pictures of Gloria Steinem and other feminist icons . . . attest to their not showing any of the signs of shame: no dry skin, no sagging muscles, no sallow coloring, no wrinkles" ("Issues in the Study of Older Women," 20).
6 Baumbusch, "Unclaimed Treasures," 106. While Baumbusch rightly objects to the "labels of 'never-married,' 'unmarried' and 'unattached' " (106) as terms that "reinforce negative stereotypes of singles" (107), her use of "ever-single" and "lifelong singlehood," though perhaps more positive in tone, do

not exactly eschew reference to marital status. See also Newtson and Keith, "Single Women in Later Life."

7 See, for instance, Roberto and Reynolds, "Older Women's Experiences with Chronic Pain," 6.

8 Aiken, *Aging*, 217, qtd. in Newtson and Keith, "Single Women in Later Life," 386.

9 Sarton, *At Eighty-Two*, 333. Subsequent references to *Eighty-Two* will appear parenthetically in text and notes.

10 Sarton, *After the Stroke*, 227. Subsequent references to *Stroke* will appear parenthetically in text and notes.

11 Heilbrun, "Women's Autobiographical Writings," 21, 24.

12 Much has been written about the diary as an authentic record of experience, particularly women's experience, as well as a legitimate form for critical study by scholars of autobiography. Because Sarton's journals are obviously intended for publication, they cannot be read strictly as private diaries; they have been shaped and edited for readers' consumption (a fact Sarton makes explicit in many of her texts, either by overtly suppressing information or by acknowledging that she has added or corrected material after the fact). Nonetheless, the notion that a diary sustains its writer, and readers, in "real-life perpetual motion" is key to Sarton's use of journaling as a way to counter the narrative decline of aging. See Lensink, "Expanding the Boundaries of Criticism," 161. For a discussion of Anaïs Nin's multivolume diary, by which Sarton was clearly influenced, see Bloom and Holder, "Anaïs Nin's *Diary* in Context."

13 Sarton, *Recovering*, 24. Subsequent references to *Recovering* will appear parenthetically in text and notes.

14 Sarton, *Journal of a Solitude*, 80. Subsequent references to *Journal* will appear parenthetically in text and notes.

15 Sherman writes that "the sexuality of older women has been a problematic theme" in Western cultures for centuries. While "sexuality for older people of both genders [has been] considered inappropriate, immoral, disgusting, unhealthy, and perverse," the stereotypes that attach to sexual older women take on a more insidious charge, thematically represented in literature, art, and prevalent stereotyping as "evil, controlling, deceiving, seductive, sinister, predatory, and witchlike." See "Images of Middle-aged and Older Women," 17.

16 In *Women with Disabilities Aging Well*, researchers Walsh and LeRoy concur that storytelling has beneficial and empowering effects for women rarely invited to talk about their life experiences.

17 Couser, *Recovering Bodies*, 39.

18 Sontag, *Illness as Metaphor*, 71.

19 Several months prior to the revelation of her own cancer, Sarton quotes a letter she receives in response to *A Reckoning* in which the writer describes terminal cancer as "a psychosomatic disease having to do with a fairly specific personality complex and certain life experiences—most of all a sense of despair about not having lived one's own life." Sarton later cites this letter as support for her own belief that cancer is at least partially a result of unresolved emotional and identity conflict. See also *At Eighty-Two*, where Sarton repeats this assessment of her mother's death: "I am convinced that she died of cancer from buried anger and that this perhaps happens more often than we know" (299). By implication, *A Reckoning*'s Laura falls ill because of buried emotions, specifically her unarticulated love for women.

20 Sontag, *Illness as Metaphor*, 57.

21 Couser, *Recovering Bodies*, 46.

22 Sontag, *Illness as Metaphor*, 57.

23 Fulk, *Understanding May Sarton*, 132.

24 Ibid., 131–32.

25 Simon, "Never-Married Old Women and Disability," 221.

26 Roberto and Reynolds, "Older Women's Experiences with Chronic Pain," 18.

27 Frank, *Wounded Storyteller*, 6.

28 A recent piece by Allison Arieff in the *New York Times* advocates wholesale redesign of hospital architecture and interior space to promote an atmosphere of calm and wellness rather than coldness, anonymity, and inhumanity.

29 Simpson and Wheelock, *World of Light*.

30 Olney, *Memory and Narrative*, 10.

31 Egan, *Mirror Talk*, 10–11.

32 Ibid., 60 (my emphasis).

33 Updike, *Self-Consciousness*, 226. In *Reading Autobiography*, 61, Smith and Watson refer to the "palimpsest" of "old selves" visible in autobiography.

34 Woodward argues that "wisdom in the old is a stereotype that does not carry real meaning" and that "we need to change what has been called an affect script for older people in our culture" by "telling stories." Stories, Woodward contends, can "relay forms of feeling" that counter suppression of "unbecoming" emotions in the elderly, such as anger. See "Against Wisdom," 205–6, 194.

35 Egan, "Encounters in Camera," 597.

36 It should be noted that Sarton is now literally recording her daily entries on a tape recorder and then reading over the transcription to make edits. A written journal creates the impression of proximity with its narrating subject by virtue of logging what has apparently been written down in the moment of its occurrence. Sarton produces a different sense of intimacy in *At Eighty-Two* by initially recording, rather than writing, her narrative, a process she began during the composition of *Endgame* in 1991. The technique is made

explicit, as when Sarton remarks that she is "recording this in [her] bedroom" (*Eighty-Two* 238), deepening the effect of immediacy by emphasizing a currently speaking voice and by situating that utterance within the most private interior space of Sarton's house. It hardly needs pointing out, of course, that the impression of sharing the moment with Sarton results from eliding the recollected subject and from autobiography's collapse of writing and speaking "I"s. Nonetheless, proclaiming that "the past is obsessive" and that she "want[s] to live in the present" (193), Sarton does sustain her readers in a space of present-tense continuity that deliberately opposes the reflective summing-up of traditional autobiography. Such a structure is not so much formally as conceptually innovative, in that it represents the aging woman in terms of a vital ongoingness. At the same time, Sarton makes it very clear in each of her journals that an unguarded spontaneity is only part of the representational goal. At the most material level, she transcribes her tapes after the fact; a comment like "long gap on tape" (193) reminds us that we are not really "hearing" May Sarton.

37 Egan, *Mirror Talk*, 212–13.

38 See Newtson and Keith, who argue that ever-single women "derive greater fulfillment" and "more of their social validity from work than their married peers" and have "a stronger work orientation than the previously married" ("Single Women in Later Life," 393–94).

39 George, "Women Poets on Aging," 141.

Epilogue

1 Nancy Mairs, foreword to Couser, *Recovering Bodies*, xii, x.

2 Couser, *Recovering Bodies*, 6.

3 Both Couser and Hawkins acknowledge that many of the autopathographies they examine would not be considered "literature in the traditional sense" (ibid., 292).

4 Roberts and Swadener, *Semiotics and Dis/Ability*, 5.

5 McRuer, "As Good As It Gets," 97.

6 Fox and Lipkin, "Res(Crip)ting Feminist Theater," 78.

7 Thomson, "Politics of Staring," 72.

8 Mairs, *Ordinary Time*, 23.

9 Finger, *Past Due*, 16.

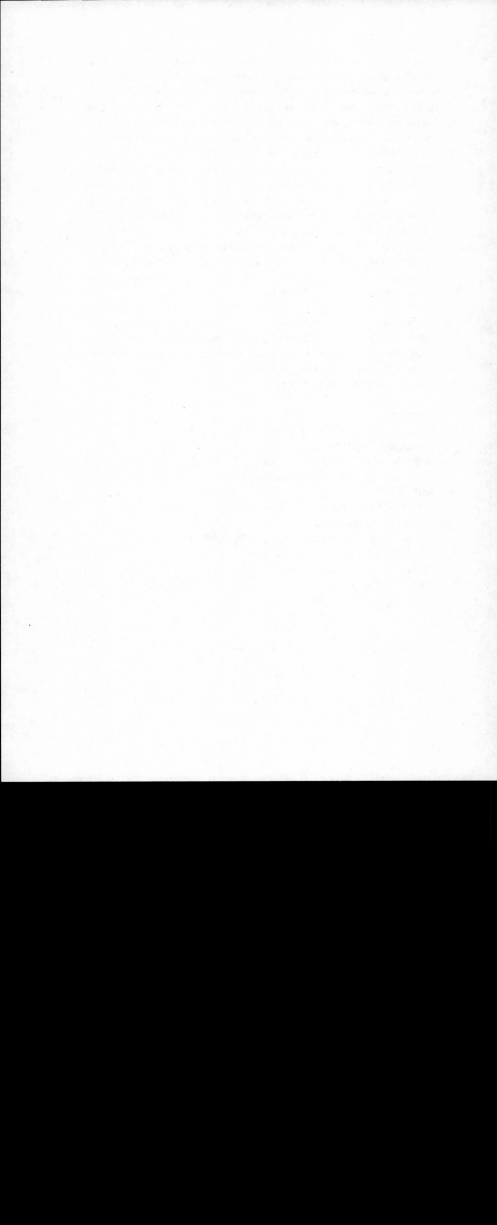

bibliography

Aiken, Lewis. *Aging*. Thousand Oaks, Calif.: Sage, 1995.

Alcorn, Keith. *Gay Times*. May 1992.

Arieff, Allison. "What Healthcare Should Look Like." *New York Times*. September 28, 2006.

Asch, Adrienne, and Michelle Fine. "Nurturance, Sexuality, and Women with Disabilities." In *The Disability Studies Reader*, edited by Lennard J. Davis, 241–59. New York: Routledge, 1997.

——. "Shared Dreams: A Left Perspective on Disability Rights and Reproductive Rights." In *Women with Disabilities: Essays in Psychology, Culture, and Politics*, edited by Michelle Fine and Adrienne Asch, 297–305. Philadelphia: Temple University Press, 1988.

Baumbusch, Jennifer L. "Unclaimed Treasures: Older Women's Reflections on Lifelong Singlehood." *Journal of Women and Aging* 16, no. 1/2 (2004): 105–21.

Benstock, Shari, ed. *The Private Self: Theory and Practice of Women's Autobiographical Writings*. Chapel Hill: University of North Carolina Press, 1988.

Bieler, Rosangela Berman. "The Right to Maternity." In *Bigger Than the Sky: Disabled Women on Parenting*, edited by Michele Wates and Rowen Jade, 35–38. London: Women's Press, 1999.

Bloom, Lynn Z., and Orlee Holder. "Anaïs Nin's *Diary* in Context." In *Women's Autobiography: Essays in Criticism*, edited by Estelle C. Jelinek, 206–20. Bloomington: Indiana University Press, 1980.

Bogdan, Robert. *Freak Show: Presenting Human Oddities for Amusement and Profit*. Chicago: University of Chicago Press, 1988.

——. "The Social Construction of Freaks." In *Freakery: Cultural Spectacles of the Extraordinary Body*, edited by Rosemarie Garland Thomson, 23–37. New York: NYU Press, 1996.

Bordo, Susan. *Unbearable Weight: Feminism, Western Culture, and the Body*. Berkeley: University of California Press, 1993.

Brakman, Sarah-Vaughan, and Sally J. Scholz. "Adoption, ART, and a Re-Conception of the Maternal Body: Toward Embodied Maternity." *Hypatia* 21, no. 1 (Winter 2006): 54–73.

Brownworth, Victoria A. Introduction to *Restricted Access: Lesbians on Disability*, edited by Victoria A. Brownworth and Susan Raffo. Seattle: Seal Press, 1999.

Butler, Judith. Introduction to *Bodies That Matter*. Reprinted in *Women, Autobiography, Theory: A Reader*, edited by Sidonie Smith and Julia Watson, 367–79. Madison: University of Wisconsin Press, 1998.

Chinn, Sarah E. "Audre Lorde and the Power of Touch." *GLQ* 9, no. 1–2 (2003):

181–204. Special issue, "Desiring Disability: Queer Theory Meets Disability Studies," edited by Robert McRuer and Abby L. Wilkerson.

Cixous, Hélène. "The Laugh of the Medusa." In *New French Feminisms*, edited by Elaine Marks and Isabelle de Courtivron, 245–64. New York: Schocken, 1980.

Clare, Eli. *Exile and Pride: Disability, Queerness, and Liberation*. Cambridge, Mass.: South End Press, 1999.

——. "Flirting with You: Some Notes on Isolation and Connection." In *Restricted Access: Lesbians on Disability*, edited by Victoria A. Brownworth and Susan Raffo, 127–35. Seattle: Seal Press, 1999.

——. "Stolen Bodies, Reclaimed Bodies: Disability and Queerness." *Public Culture* 13, no. 3 (Fall 2001): 359–65. Special issue, "The Critical Limits of Embodiment: Reflections on Disability Criticism," edited by Carol A. Breckenridge and Candace Vogler.

Cook, Kay K. "Medical Identity: My DNA/Myself." In *Getting a Life: Everyday Uses of Autobiography*, edited by Sidonie Smith and Julia Watson, 63–85. Minneapolis: University of Minnesota Press, 1996.

Corker, Mairian, and Tom Shakespeare, eds. *Disability/Postmodernity: Embodying Disability Theory*. London: Continuum, 2002.

Couser, G. Thomas. "Conflicting Paradigms: The Rhetorics of Disability Memoir." In *Embodied Rhetorics: Disability in Language and Culture*, edited by James C. Wilson and Cynthia Lewiecki-Wilson, 78–91. Carbondale: Southern Illinois University Press, 2001.

——. "The Embodied Self." *a/b: Auto/Biography Studies* 6, no. 1 (Spring 1991): 1–7.

——. Introduction to "The Empire of the 'Normal': A Forum on Disability and Self-Representation." Special issue of *American Quarterly* 52, no. 2 (June 2000): 305–10.

——. "The Obituary of a Face: Lucy Grealy, Death Writing, and Posthumous Harm." *a/b: Auto/Biography Studies* 12, no. 1 (April 2004): 1–15.

——. *Recovering Bodies: Illness, Disability, and Life Writing*. Madison: University of Wisconsin Press, 1997.

——. *Vulnerable Subjects: Ethics and Life Writing*. Ithaca, N.Y.: Cornell University Press, 2004.

Crutchfield, Susan, and Marcy Epstein, eds. *Points of Contact: Disability, Art, and Culture*. Ann Arbor: University of Michigan Press, 2000.

Daniel, John. "The Impoverishment of Sightseeing." In *Being in the World*, edited by Scott H. Slovic and Terrell F. Dixon, 592–600. New York: Macmillan, 1993.

Davis, Lennard J. *Bending Over Backwards: Disability, Dismodernism, and Other Difficult Positions*. New York: NYU Press, 2002.

——. *Enforcing Normalcy: Disability, Deafness, and the Body*. London: Verso, 1995.

——, ed. *The Disability Studies Reader*. New York: Routledge, 1997.

Deegan, Mary Jo, and Nancy A. Brooks, eds. *Women and Disability: The Double Handicap*. New Brunswick, N.J.: Transaction Books, 1985.

Delany, Paul. *British Autobiography in the Seventeenth Century*. New York: Columbia University Press, 1969.

Diedrich, Lisa. "Breaking Down: A Phenomenology of Disability." *Literature and Medicine* 20, no. 2 (2001): 209–30.

Dinnerstein, Myra, and Rose Weitz. "Jane Fonda, Barbara Bush, and Other Aging Bodies: Femininity and the Limits of Resistance." In *The Politics of Women's Bodies: Sexuality, Appearance, and Behavior*, edited by Rose Weitz, 189–203. New York: Oxford University Press, 1998.

Dubus, Andre. *Meditations from a Movable Chair*. New York: Vintage, 1998.

Eakin, Paul John. *How Our Lives Become Stories: Making Selves*. Ithaca, N.Y.: Cornell University Press, 1999.

Egan, Susanna. "Encounters in Camera: Autobiography as Interaction." *Modern Fiction Studies* 40, no. 3 (February 1995): 593–618.

——. *Mirror Talk: Genres of Crisis in Contemporary Autobiography*. Chapel Hill: University of North Carolina Press, 1999.

Eiesland, Nancy. *The Disabled God: Toward a Liberatory Theology of Disability*. Nashville: Abingdon Press, 1994.

Engster, Daniel. "Rethinking Care Theory: The Practice of Caring and the Obligation to Care." *Hypatia* 20, no. 3 (Summer 2005): 50–74.

Felski, Rita. "On Confession." In *Women, Autobiography, Theory: A Reader*, edited by Sidonie Smith and Julia Watson, 83–95. Madison: University of Wisconsin Press, 1998.

Fiedler, Leslie. *Freaks: Myths and Images of the Secret Self*. New York: Simon and Schuster, 1978.

——. *Tyranny of the Normal: Essays on Bioethics, Theology, and Myth*. Boston: Godine, 1996.

Fine, Michelle, and Adrienne Asch, eds. *Women with Disabilities: Essays in Psychology, Culture, and Politics*. Philadelphia: Temple University Press, 1988.

Finger, Anne. *Elegy for a Disease: A Personal and Cultural History of Polio*. New York: St. Martin's Press, 2006.

——. *Past Due: A Story of Disability, Pregnancy, and Birth*. Seattle: Seal Press, 1990.

Fox, Ann M., and Joan Lipkin. "Res(Crip)ting Feminist Theater through Disability Theater: Selections from the DisAbility Project." *NWSA Journal* 14, no. 3 (Fall 2002): 77–98. Special issue, "Feminist Disability Studies," edited by Kim Q. Hall.

Frank, Arthur W. *The Wounded Storyteller*. Chicago: University of Chicago Press, 1995.

Frank, Gelya. *Venus on Wheels: Two Decades of Dialogue on Disability, Biography, and Being Female in America*. Berkeley: University of California Press, 2000.

Fraser, Gregory. "The Language of Nature, the Nature of Language: Richard

Hugo's Eco-Poetics." *ISLE: Interdisciplinary Studies in Literature and Environment* 9, no. 2 (Summer 2002): 155–71.

Fulk, Mark K. *Understanding May Sarton*. Columbia: University of South Carolina Press, 2001.

Gamman, Lorraine, and Margaret Marshment, eds. *The Female Gaze: Women as Viewers of Popular Culture*. 1989. Reprint, Seattle: Real Comet Press, 1991.

George, Diana Hume. " 'Who Is the Double Ghost Whose Head Is Smoke?' Women Poets on Aging." In *Memory and Desire: Aging, Literature, Psychoanalysis*, edited by Kathleen Woodward and Murray M. Schwartz, 134–53. Bloomington: Indiana University Press, 1986.

Gerber, David A. "The 'Careers' of People Exhibited in Freak Shows: The Problem of Volition and Valorization." In *Freakery: Cultural Spectacles of the Extraordinary Body*, edited by Rosemarie Garland Thomson, 38–54. New York: NYU Press, 1996.

Gilmore, Leigh. *Autobiographics: A Feminist Theory of Women's Self-Representation*. Ithaca, N.Y.: Cornell University Press, 1994.

——. *The Limits of Autobiography: Trauma and Testimony*. Ithaca, N.Y.: Cornell University Press, 2001.

Goffman, Erving. *Stigma*. New York: Penguin, 1963.

Goldstein, Melissa Anne. *Travels with the Wolf: A Story of Chronic Illness*. Columbus: Ohio State University Press, 2000.

Grealy, Lucy. *Autobiography of a Face*. Boston: Houghton Mifflin, 1994.

Grosz, Elizabeth. *Volatile Bodies: Toward a Corporeal Feminism*. Bloomington: Indiana University Press, 1994.

Gunn, Janet Varner. *Autobiography: Toward a Poetics of Experience*. Philadelphia: University of Pennsylvania Press, 1982.

Gutkind, Lee. "Style and Substance." *Creative Nonfiction* 10 (1998): 1–4.

Haber, Carole. "Witches, Widows, Wives, and Workers: The Historiography of Elderly Women in America." In *Handbook on Women and Aging*, edited by Jean M. Coyle, 29–40. Westport, Conn.: Greenwood Press, 1997.

Hampl, Patricia. *A Romantic Education*. Boston: Houghton Mifflin, 1992.

Haraway, Donna J. *Simians, Cyborgs, and Women: The Reinvention of Nature*. New York: Routledge, 1991.

Harbour, Wendy S. "A Few Thoughts about Children." In *Bigger Than the Sky: Disabled Women on Parenting*, edited by Michele Wates and Rowen Jade, 18–22. London: Women's Press, 1999.

Harris, Adrienne, and Dana Wideman. "Construction of Gender and Disability in Early Attachment." In *Women with Disabilities: Essays in Psychology, Culture, and Politics*, edited by Michelle Fine and Adrienne Asch, 115–38. Philadelphia: Temple University Press, 1988.

Hathaway, Katherine Butler. *The Little Locksmith: A Memoir*. 1942. Reprint, New York: Feminist Press, 2000.

Hawkins, Anne Hunsaker. *Reconstructing Illness: Studies in Pathography*. West Lafayette, Ind.: Purdue University Press, 1993.

Heilbrun, Carolyn. "Women's Autobiographical Writings: New Forms." *Prose Studies* 8 (1985): 14–28.

Herndl, Diane Price. "Reconstructing the Posthuman Feminist Body Twenty Years after Audre Lorde's *Cancer Journals*." In *Disability Studies: Enabling the Humanities*, edited by Sharon L. Snyder, Brenda Jo Brueggemann, and Rosemarie Garland Thomson, 144–55. New York: Modern Language Association of America, 2002.

Hevey, David. "The Enfreakment of Photography." In *The Disability Studies Reader*, edited by Lennard J. Davis, 332–47. New York: Routledge, 1997.

Hillyer, Barbara. *Feminism and Disability*. Norman: University of Oklahoma Press, 1993.

Hughes, Bill, and Kevin Paterson. "The Social Model of Disability and the Disappearing Body: Towards a Sociology of Impairment." *Disability and Society* 12, no. 3 (1997): 325–40.

Iwakuma, Miho. "The Body as Embodiment: An Investigation of the Body by Merleau-Ponty." In *Disability/Postmodernity: Embodying Disability Theory*, edited by Mairian Corker and Tom Shakespeare, 76–87. London: Continuum, 2002.

Jacobson, Denise Sherer. *The Question of David: A Disabled Mother's Journey through Adoption, Family, and Life*. Berkeley: Creative Arts Book Co., 1999.

Jeffreys, Mark. "The Visible Cripple (Scars and Other Disfiguring Displays Included)." In *Disability Studies: Enabling the Humanities*, ed. Sharon L. Snyder, Brenda Jo Brueggemann, and Rosemarie Garland Thomson, 31–39. New York: Modern Language Association of America, 2002.

Jelinek, Estelle C. *Women's Autobiography: Essays in Criticism*. Bloomington: Indiana University Press, 1980.

Johnson, Mary. "Defective Fetuses and Us." *Disability Rag*, March/April 1990, 34.

——. *Make Them Go Away: Clint Eastwood, Christopher Reeve, and the Case against Disability Rights*. Louisville, Ky.: Avocado Press, 2003.

Kafer, Alison. "Compulsory Bodies: Reflections on Heterosexuality and Able-bodiedness." *Journal of Women's History* 15, no. 3 (2003): 77–89.

Keith, Lois. "Encounters with Strangers: The Public's Response to Disabled Women and How This Affects Our Sense of Self." In *Encounters with Strangers: Feminism and Disability*, edited by Jenny Morris, 69–88. London: Women's Press, 1996.

——, ed. *"What Happened to You?" Writing by Disabled Women*. London: Women's Press, 1996.

Keith, Lois, and Jenny Morris. "Easy Targets: A Disability Rights Perspective on the 'Children as Carers' Debate." In *Encounters with Strangers: Feminism and Disability*, edited by Jenny Morris, 89–115. London: Women's Press, 1996.

Kent, Deborah. "In Search of a Heroine: Images of Women with Disabilities in

Fiction and Drama." In *Women with Disabilities: Essays in Psychology, Culture, and Politics*, edited by Michelle Fine and Adrienne Asch, 90–110. Philadelphia: Temple University Press, 1988.

Kleege, Georgina. *Blind Rage: Letters to Helen Keller*. Washington, D.C.: Gallaudet University Press, 2006.

——. *Sight Unseen*. New Haven: Yale University Press, 1999.

Lane, Harlan. "Constructions of Deafness." In *The Disability Studies Reader*, edited by Lennard J. Davis, 153–71. New York: Routledge, 1997.

Lensink, Judy Nolte. "Expanding the Boundaries of Criticism: The Diary as Female Autobiography." In *Women and Autobiography*, edited by Martine Watson Brownley and Allison B. Kimmich, 151–62. Wilmington, Del.: SR Books, 1999.

Lewis, Victoria Ann, ed. *Beyond Victims and Villains: Contemporary Plays by Disabled Playwrights*. St. Paul, Minn.: Theatre Communications Group, 2006.

Lindgren, Kristin. "Bodies in Trouble: Identity, Embodiment, and Disability." In *Gendering Disability*, edited by Bonnie G. Smith and Beth Hutchison, 145–65. New Brunswick, N.J.: Rutgers University Press, 2004.

Linton, Simi. *Claiming Disability: Knowledge and Identity*. New York: NYU Press, 1998.

Lloyd, Margaret. "The Politics of Disability and Feminism: Discord or Synthesis?" *Sociology* 35, no. 3 (2001): 715–28.

Longmore, Paul K. "Conspicuous Contribution and American Cultural Dilemmas: Telethon Rituals of Cleansing and Renewal." In *The Body and Physical Difference: Discourses of Disability in the Humanities*, edited by David T. Mitchell and Sharon L. Snyder, 134–58. Ann Arbor: University of Michigan Press, 1997.

Longmore, Paul K., and David Goldberger. "The League of the Physically Handicapped and the Great Depression: A Case Study in the New Disability History." *Journal of American History* 87, no. 3 (December 2000): 888–922.

Longmore, Paul K., and Lauri Umansky, eds. *The New Disability History: American Perspectives*. New York: NYU Press, 2001.

Macdonald, Barbara. "Outside the Sisterhood: Ageism in Women's Studies." *Women's Studies Quarterly* 17, no. 1/2 (1989): 6–11.

Mairs, Nancy. *Carnal Acts*. 1990. Reprint, Boston: Beacon, 1996.

——. *Ordinary Time: Cycles in Marriage, Faith, and Renewal*. Boston: Beacon, 1993.

——. *Plaintext*. Tucson: University of Arizona Press, 1986.

——. *Remembering the Bone-House: An Erotics of Space*. New York: Harper, 1989.

——. "Sex and Death and the Crippled Body: A Meditation." In *Disability Studies: Enabling the Humanities*, edited by Sharon L. Snyder, Brenda Jo Brueggemann, and Rosemarie Garland Thomson, 156–70. New York: Modern Language Association of America, 2002.

——. *Voice Lessons: On Becoming a Woman Writer*. Boston: Beacon, 1994.

——. *Waist-High in the World: A Life among the Nondisabled*. Boston: Beacon, 1997.

Malin, Jo. *The Voice of the Mother: Embedded Maternal Narratives in Twentieth-Century Women's Autobiographies*. Carbondale: Southern Illinois University Press, 2000.

Martin, Biddy. "Lesbian Identity and Autobiographical Difference(s)." In *The Lesbian and Gay Studies Reader*, edited by Henry Abelove, Michèle Aina Barale, and David M. Halperin, 274–93. New York: Routledge, 1993.

Mason, Mary Grimley. *Working against Odds: Stories of Disabled Women's Work Lives*. Boston: Northeastern University Press, 2004.

Mattingly, Cheryl, and Linda Garro, eds. *Narrative and the Cultural Construction of Illness and Healing*. Berkeley: University of California Press, 2000.

McRuer, Robert. "As Good As It Gets: Queer Theory and Critical Disability." *GLQ* 9, no. 1–2 (2003): 79–105. Special issue, "Desiring Disability: Queer Theory Meets Disability Studies," edited by Robert McRuer and Abby L. Wilkerson.

Meekosha, Helen. "Body Battles: Bodies, Gender, and Disability." In *The Disability Reader: Social Science Perspectives*, edited by Tom Shakespeare, 163–80. London: Cassell, 1998.

Merleau-Ponty, Maurice. *Phenomenology of Perception*. New York: Routledge, 1962.

Michie, Helena. "Confinements: The Domestic in the Discourses of Upper-Middle-Class Pregnancy." In *Making Worlds: Gender, Metaphor, Materiality*, edited by Susan Aiken, Ann Brigham, Sallie A. Marston, and Penny Waterstone, 258–73. Tucson: University of Arizona Press, 1998.

Miller, Nancy K. "Mothers, Daughters, and Autobiography." In *Mothers in Law*, edited by Martha Fineman and Isabel Karpin, 3–26. New York: Columbia University Press, 1995.

Miner, Madonne. " 'Making Up the Stories as We Go Along': Men, Women, and Narratives of Disability." In *The Body and Physical Difference: Discourses of Disability in the Humanities*, edited by David T. Mitchell and Sharon L. Snyder, 283–95. Ann Arbor: University of Michigan Press, 1997.

Mintz, Susannah B. "Dear (Embodied) Reader: Life-Writing and Disability." *Prose Studies* 26, no. 1–2 (April–August 2003; pub. 2004): 131–52. Reprinted in *Women's Life Writing and Imagined Communities*, edited by Cynthia Huff. New York: Routledge, 2004.

——. "Ordinary Vessels: Disability Narrative and Representations of Faith." *DSQ* 26, no. 3 (summer 2006). Online edition, special issue on religion and spirituality, edited by Gerry E. Hendershot and Nancy L. Eiesland.

Mitchell, David T. "Body Solitaire: The Singular Subject of Disability Autobiography." *American Quarterly* 52, no. 2 (June 2000): 311–15.

——. "Narrative Prosthesis and the Materiality of Metaphor." In *Disability Studies: Enabling the Humanities*, edited by Sharon L. Snyder, Brenda Jo Brueggemann, and Rosemarie Garland Thomson, 15–30. New York: Modern Language Association of America, 2002.

Mitchell, David T., and Sharon L. Snyder. *Narrative Prosthesis: Disability and the Dependencies of Discourse*. Ann Arbor: University of Michigan Press, 2000.

——, eds. *The Body and Physical Difference: Discourses of Disability in the Humanities*. Ann Arbor: University of Michigan Press, 1997.

Morris, Jenny, ed. *Encounters with Strangers: Feminism and Disability*. London: Women's Press, 1996.

Morris, John N. *Versions of the Self*. New York: Basic Books, 1966.

Mulvey, Laura. "Visual Pleasure and Narrative Cinema." In *Visual and Other Pleasures*. Bloomington: Indiana University Press, 1989.

Murphy, Robert Francis. *The Body Silent: The Different World of the Disabled*. 1987. Reprint, New York: Norton, 2001.

Neuman, Shirley. " 'An Appearance Walking in a Forest the Sexes Burn': Autobiography and the Construction of the Feminine Body." In *Autobiography and Postmodernism*, edited by Kathleen Ashley, Leigh Gilmore, and Gerald Peters, 293–315. Amherst: University of Massachusetts Press, 1994.

Newman, Beth. " 'The Situation of the Looker-On': Gender, Narration, and Gaze in *Wuthering Heights*." In *Feminisms: An Anthology of Literary Theory and Criticism*, edited by Robyn R. Warhol and Diane Price Herndl, 449–66. Rev. ed., New Brunswick, N.J.: Rutgers University Press, 1997.

Newtson, Richard L., and Pat M. Keith. "Single Women in Later Life." In *Handbook on Women and Aging*, edited by Jean M. Coyle, 385–99. Westport, Conn.: Greenwood Press, 1997.

Nussbaum, Felicity. "Eighteenth-Century Women's Autobiographical Commonplaces." In *The Private Self: Theory and Practice of Women's Autobiographical Writings*, edited by Shari Benstock, 147–71. Chapel Hill: University of North Carolina Press, 1988.

Oliver, Michael. *The Politics of Disablement*. London: Macmillan, 1990.

——. *Understanding Disability: From Theory to Practice*. London: Macmillan, 1996.

Olney, James, *Memory and Narrative: The Weave of Life-Writing*. Chicago: University of Chicago Press, 2000.

——, ed. *Autobiography: Essays Theoretical and Critical*. Princeton: Princeton University Press, 1980.

——. *Studies in Autobiography*. New York: Oxford University Press, 1988.

O'Toole, Corbett Joan. "The Sexist Inheritance of the Disability Movement." In *Gendering Disability*, edited by Bonnie G. Smith and Beth Hutchison, 294–300. New Brunswick, N.J.: Rutgers University Press, 2004.

Panzarino, Connie. *The Me in the Mirror*. Seattle: Seal Press, 1994.

Parens, Erik, and Adrienne Asch, eds. *Prenatal Testing: A Review of Prenatal Testing and Disability Rights*. Washington, D.C.: Georgetown University Press, 2000.

Pollitt, Katha. "Solipsisters." *New York Times Book Review*, April 18, 1999, 35.

Price, Janet, and Margrit Shildrick. "Bodies Together: Touch, Ethics, and

Disability." In *Disability/Postmodernity: Embodying Disability Theory*, edited by Mairian Corker and Tom Shakespeare, 62–75. London: Continuum, 2002.

Price, Reynolds. *A Whole New Life: An Illness and a Healing*. New York: Penguin, 1995.

Rapp, Rayna. *Testing Women, Testing the Fetus: The Social Impact of Amniocentesis in America*. New York: Routledge, 2000.

Rapp, Rayna, and Faye Ginsburg. "Enabling Disability: Rewriting Kinship, Reimagining Citizenship." *Public Culture* 13, no. 3 (Fall 2001): 533–56. Special issue, "The Critical Limits of Embodiment: Reflections on Disability Criticism," edited by Carol A. Breckenridge and Candace Vogler.

Roach, Jackie, and Petal Felix. "Black Looks." In *The Female Gaze: Women as Viewers of Popular Culture*, edited by Lorraine Gamman and Margaret Marshment. 1989. Reprint, Seattle: Real Comet Press, 1991.

Roberto, Karen A., and Sandra G. Reynolds. "Older Women's Experiences with Chronic Pain: Daily Challenges and Self-Care Practices." *Journal of Women and Aging* 14, no. 3/4 (2002): 5–23.

Roberts, Linda J., and Beth Blue Swadener, eds. *Semiotics and Dis/Ability: Interrogating Categories of Difference*. Albany: State University of New York Press, 2001.

Rohrer, Judy. "Toward a Full-Inclusion Feminism: A Feminist Deployment of Disability Analysis." *Feminist Studies* 31, no. 1 (Spring 2005): 34–63.

Sandahl, Carrie, and Philip Auslander, eds. *Bodies in Commotion: Disability and Performance*. Ann Arbor: University of Michigan Press, 2005.

Sarton, May. *After the Stroke: A Journal*. 1988. Reprint, New York: Norton, 1990.

——. *At Eighty-Two: A Journal*. New York: Norton, 1996.

——. *Journal of a Solitude*. 1973. Reprint, New York: Norton, 1992.

——. *Recovering: A Journal*. 1980. Reprint, New York: Norton, 1997.

Saxton, Marsha, and Florence Howe, eds. *With Wings: An Anthology of Literature by and about Women with Disabilities*. New York: Feminist Press, 1993.

Sedgwick, Eve Kosofsky. *Epistemology of the Closet*. Berkeley: University of California Press, 1990.

Shakespeare, Tom. "A Response to Liz Crow." *Coalition*, September 1992, 40–42.

——, ed. *The Disability Reader: Social Science Perspectives*. London: Cassell, 1998.

Shaul, Susan, Pamela J. Dowling, and Bernice F. Laden. "Like Other Women: Perspectives of Mothers with Physical Disabilities." In *Women and Disability: The Double Handicap*, edited by Mary Jo Deegan and Nancy A. Brooks, 133–42. New Brunswick, N.J.: Transaction Books, 1985.

Sherman, Susan R. "Images of Middle-aged and Older Women: Historical, Cultural, and Personal." In *Handbook on Women and Aging*, edited by Jean M. Coyle, 14–28. Westport, Conn.: Greenwood Press, 1997.

Shildrick, Margrit. "The Relational Economy of Touch." In *Embodying the Monster: Encounters with the Vulnerable Self*, 103–19. London: Sage, 2002.

Shildrick, Margrit, and Janet Price. "Breaking the Boundaries of the Broken Body." In *Feminist Theory and the Body*, edited by Janet Price and Margrit Shildrick, 432–44. New York: Routledge, 1999.

Shumaker, Wayne. *English Autobiography: Its Emergence, Materials, and Form*. Berkeley: University of California Press, 1954.

Siebers, Tobin. "Disability in Theory: From Social Constructionism to the New Realism of the Body." *American Literary History* 13, no. 4 (2001): 737–54.

——. "Tender Organs, Narcissism, and Identity Politics." In *Disability Studies: Enabling the Humanities*, edited by Sharon L. Snyder, Brenda Jo Brueggemann, and Rosemarie Garland Thomson, 40–55. New York: Modern Language Association of America, 2002.

Siegel, Kristi. *Women's Autobiographies, Culture, Feminism*. New York: Peter Lang, 1999.

Simon, Barbara Levy. "Never-Married Old Women and Disability: A Majority Experience." In *Women with Disabilities: Essays in Psychology, Culture, and Politics*, edited by Michelle Fine and Adrienne Asch, 215–25. Philadelphia: Temple University Press, 1988.

Simpson, Marita, and Martha Wheelock, dirs. *World of Light: A Portrait of May Sarton*. Documentary film. New York: Ishtar Films, 1979.

Smith, Sidonie. *A Poetics of Women's Autobiography: Marginality and the Fictions of Self-Representation*. Bloomington: Indiana University Press, 1987.

——. *Subjectivity, Identity, and the Body: Women's Autobiographical Practices in the Twentieth Century*. Bloomington: Indiana University Press, 1993.

Smith, Sidonie, and Julia Watson. *Reading Autobiography*. Minneapolis: University of Minnesota Press, 2001.

Snyder, Sharon L., and David T. Mitchell. "Re-engaging the Body: Disability Studies and the Resistance to Embodiment." *Public Culture* 13, no. 3 (Fall 2001): 367–89. Special issue, "The Critical Limits of Embodiment: Reflections on Disability Criticism," edited by Carol A. Breckenridge and Candace Vogler.

——, dirs. *Vital Signs: Crip Culture Talks Back*. Chicago: Brace Yourself Productions, 1997.

Snyder, Sharon L., Brenda Jo Brueggemann, and Rosemarie Garland Thomson, eds. *Disability Studies: Enabling the Humanities*. New York: Modern Language Association of America, 2002.

Sontag, Susan. *Illness as Metaphor and AIDS and Its Metaphors*. New York: Picador USA, 2001.

Spengemann, William C. *The Forms of Autobiography: Episodes in the History of a Literary Genre*. New Haven: Yale University Press, 1980.

Stacey, Jackie. *Star Gazing: Hollywood Cinema and Female Spectatorship*. New York: Routledge, 1994.

Stiker, Henri-Jacques. *A History of Disability*. Ann Arbor: University of Michigan Press, 1999.

Thomas, Carol. *Female Forms: Experiencing and Understanding Disability*. Buckingham, England: Open University Press, 1992.

Thomson, Rosemarie Garland. *Extraordinary Bodies: Figuring Physical Disability in American Culture and Literature*. New York: Columbia University Press, 1997.

——. "Integrating Disability, Transforming Feminist Theory." *NWSA Journal* 14, no. 3 (Fall 2002): 1–32. Special issue, "Feminist Disability Studies," edited by Kim Q. Hall.

——. "The Politics of Staring: Visual Rhetorics of Disability in Popular Photography." In *Disability Studies: Enabling the Humanities*, ed. Sharon L. Snyder, Brenda Jo Brueggemann, and Rosemarie Garland Thomson, 56–75. New York: Modern Language Association of America, 2002.

——. "Staring Back: Self-Representations of Disabled Performance Artists." *American Quarterly* 52, no. 2 (June 2000): 334–38.

——, ed. *Freakery: Cultural Spectacles of the Extraordinary Body*. New York: NYU Press, 1996.

Tremain, Shelley. Introduction to *Foucault and the Government of Disability*, edited by Shelley Tremain. Ann Arbor: University of Michigan Press, 2005.

——. "On the Subject of Impairment." In *Disability/Postmodernity: Embodying Disability Theory*, edited by Mairian Corker and Tom Shakespeare, 32–47. London: Continuum, 2002.

——, ed. *Pushing the Limits: Disabled Dykes Produce Culture*. Toronto: Women's Press, 1996.

Troll, Lillian. "Issues in the Study of Older Women: 1970 to 1985." In *Health and Economic Status of Older Women*, edited by A. Regula Herzog, Karen C. Holden, and Mildred M. Seltzer, 17–23. Amityville, N.Y.: Baywood, 1989.

Updike, John. *Self-Consciousness: Memoirs*. New York: Knopf, 1989.

Vicinus, Martha. " 'They Wonder to Which Sex I Belong': The Historical Roots of the Modern Lesbian Identity." In *The Lesbian and Gay Studies Reader*, edited by Henry Abelove, Michèle Aina Barale, and David M. Halperin, 432–53. New York: Routledge, 1993.

Walsh, Patricia Noonan, and Barbara LeRoy. *Women with Disabilities Aging Well*. Baltimore, Md.: Paul H. Brookes Publishing, 2004.

Wates, Michele. "Are You Sure You Can Cope?" In *Bigger Than the Sky: Disabled Women on Parenting*, edited by Michele Wates and Rowen Jade, 94–97. London: Women's Press, 1999.

Wates, Michele, and Rowen Jade, eds. *Bigger Than the Sky: Disabled Women on Parenting*. London: Women's Press, 1999.

Watson, Julia. "Unspeakable Differences: The Politics of Gender in Lesbian and Heterosexual Women's Autobiographies." In *De/Colonizing the Subject: The*

Politics of Gender in Women's Autobiography, edited by Sidonie Smith and Julia Watson. Minneapolis: University of Minnesota Press, 1992.

Wendell, Susan. *The Rejected Body: Feminist Philosophical Reflections on Disability*. Routledge, 1996.

——. "Toward a Feminist Theory of Disability." In *The Disability Studies Reader*, edited by Lennard J. Davis, 260–78. New York: Routledge, 1997.

Wilkerson, Abby L. "Disability, Sex Radicalism, and Political Agency." *NWSA Journal* 14, no. 3 (Fall 2002): 33–57. Special issue, "Feminist Disability Studies," edited by Kim Q. Hall.

Wolff, Tobias. *This Boy's Life: A Memoir*. New York: Harperperennial, 1990.

Woodward, Kathleen. "Against Wisdom: The Social Politics of Anger and Aging." *Cultural Critique* 51 (2002): 186–218.

Woolf, Virginia. "Professions for Women." In *Collected Essays*, 2:284–89. New York: Harcourt, Brace and World, 1967.

Wright, Alexa. " 'I.' " *Public Culture* 13, no. 3 (Fall 2001): 506–10. Special issue, "The Critical Limits of Embodiment: Reflections on Disability Criticism," edited by Carol A. Breckenridge and Candace Vogler.

Young, Iris Marion. "Throwing Like a Girl: A Phenomenology of Feminine Body Comportment, Motility, and Spatiality." In *On Female Body Experience: "Throwing Like a Girl" and Other Essays*, 27–45. Oxford: Oxford University Press, 2005.

index